TIME FOR JUDGEMENT

God's judgement and ours in times of crisis

PAUL YEULETT

DayOne

Biblical wisdom is the ability to discern the times according to the fear of God. In his book, Time For Judgement, *Paul Yeulett provides this very thing with a penetrating look at various crises in our current times through a biblical lens. He examines the Covid Pandemic (pestilence), the Russia/Ukraine war (sword) and the Cost-of-Living Crisis (famine) as judgements from God that teach his people how to judge what is right and true. This book is a must read.*

Gavin Peacock, Pastor at Calvary Grace Church, Canada, and former professional footballer in the English Premier League

In his book, Time For Judgement, *Paul Yeulett sets before us a way of looking at the events of this world which was common only a few generations ago. Sadly, that perspective has seemingly been lost, even in the Church! Using Jeremiah 15:1–2, Paul gives us a basis for thinking about the Covid-19 pandemic, the war in Ukraine, and the economic downturn in the West. The biblical argument is that these are not isolated events, or even coincidental calamities, but rather a judgement from the hand of God. This judgement serves variously to chastise, warn, and ultimately to call God's people to a right understanding of the meaning of life and biblical repentance.*

It is at one and the same time a biblical apologetic exposition, and an encouraging call to see that our God is able to do far more abundantly than all that we ask or think, according to the power at work within us.

Jeff Kingswood, Senior Pastor, Grace Presbyterian (Associate Reformed Presbyterian) Church, Woodstock, ON, Canada

Paul Yeulett is uncompromisingly biblical in the way he brings the whole counsel of God to bear upon a broad range of key issues in the public discourse – the pandemic, Russian aggression in Ukraine, climate change activism, among many others – but he does so with personal warmth and insight, particularly on the most controversial points, of which there are many. Among the growing number of post-pandemic Christian reflections of the early 2020s, this is one of the best.

Rev. Dr Thomas Brand, EFCC (Evangelical Fellowship of Congregational Churches) Ministry Director and Affinity Chairman

Unless otherwise indicated, Scripture quotations are from The Holy Bible, English Standard Version (ESV), copyright © 2001 by Crossway Bibles, a division of Good News Publishers. Used by permission. All rights reserved.

© Day One Publications 2024

First published in Great Britain in 2024

All rights reserved. No part of this publication may be reproduced, stored in a retrieval system or transmitted in any form or by any means, electronic, mechanical, photocopying, recording or otherwise, without the prior permission of the publisher or the Copyright Licensing Agency.

British Library Cataloguing in Publication Data
A record for this book is available from the British Library

ISBN: 978-1-84625-765-0

Cover design by Kathryn Chedgzoy

Printed by 4edge

DayOne, Ryelands Road, Leominster, HR6 8NZ
Email: sales@dayone.co.uk
Website: www.DayOne.co.uk

Dedication
This book is dedicated to all Millennials and
Generation Zs across the worldwide church,
that they might know, fear and love the
God of judgement, mercy and salvation.

Let all the earth fear the Lord;
let all the inhabitants of the world stand in awe of him!
(Ps. 33:8)

Acknowledgements

This book has been a highly collaborative effort, and the advice and constructive criticism of many valued friends has been invaluable. Long discussions on the phone, on email and face-to-face, have contributed greatly towards the publication of this book as you now have it. I would like to express my deep and sincere gratitude to Sharon James, Peter Sanlon, Gavin Peacock, Jeff Kingswood, Ian Hamilton, and especially to Tom Brand, Oliver Gross and Jonathan Winch, who offered very specific and detailed observations, which certainly did not go to waste. I am greatly indebted to Helen Clark at Day One Publications, whose astonishingly minute scrutiny of every sentence and every word of the manuscript has undoubtedly enhanced the quality of the whole work.

I am grateful to God for the warm, united, prayerfully supportive folk at Grove Chapel, Camberwell, whom it is a privilege to serve.

And above all, I thank the Lord for my wife, Ruth, and for our children, Rebecca, Matthew and Daniel, all of whom have borne with a very busy and distracted husband and father for a great deal of the time. In addition, they have been full of advice in relation to this book, not least the cover design—an area of expertise in which I am singularly lacking!

Contents

Foreword	9
Introduction	11
Chapter 1: Thursday, 24 February 2022	17
PART ONE: GOD, THE BIBLE, AND JUDGEMENT	35
Chapter 2: Jeremiah and judgement	37
Chapter 3: The God of judgement	49
Chapter 4: Why is God judging the church?	65
PART TWO: PESTILENCE	77
Chapter 5: Disease and death	79
Chapter 6: Life or liberty?	97
Chapter 7: Connection and communion	115
PART THREE: SWORD	137
Chapter 8: Sunlit uplands?	139
Chapter 9: Blood and soil	157
Chapter 10: Rough and tumble	181
PART FOUR: FAMINE	203
Chapter 11: Where have all the Avos gone?	205
Chapter 12: Vows of prosperity	223
Chapter 13: The January test	247
PART FIVE: CAPTIVITY	269
Chapter 14: Take me to your captives.	271

Chapter 15: A captive audience	289
Chapter 16: The grownups in the room	307
PART SIX: SUMMING UP	**331**
Conclusion: Human judgement	333
Conclusion: Divine judgement	351
Afterword: Israelites, Israelis and Israel	381
Appendix 1	397
Bibliography	399
Endnotes	405

Foreword

'Judgement' is a word that many Christians avoid, most often out of fear: 'Will my friends and family think I am a religious extremist? Will my colleagues at work look at me with a mixture of puzzlement and pity, before avoiding me?' In *Time For Judgement*, Paul Yeulett has refused to be intimidated by what the world, or the church, thinks about the subject of judgement. In this book, Paul has provided for thinking people a *robust, honest, courageous and comprehensive biblical worldview* of life as it is.

From beginning to end, he looks at the world through the clarifying lens of Scripture, enabling us to exercise a thoughtful analysis of the myriad of cataclysms and catastrophes that have wreaked havoc in our world during the past few decades, and indeed throughout history. The aim of *Time For Judgement*, however, is not simply analytical. Alongside the penetrating analysis, the chapters provoke us to ask questions and to search for answers. In his Introduction, Paul highlights the audience he had in mind as he wrote *Time For Judgement*: 'I am writing for anyone who, living through all this, has stopped to ask the question, "What does all this mean? What should we make of it, and what should we do about it, if indeed we can do anything?"'

Analysing a problem, trying to understand its nature,

Foreword

is most often both necessary and helpful. But problems are there not just to be analysed, but to be solved. As a trained mathematician, as well as the pastor of a church, Paul understands the importance of problem-solving. From the perspective of a committed Christian, who believes the Bible is the living Word of the living God, Paul introduces us to the Bible's wisdom, which is nothing less than the trans-generational wisdom of the God who eternally is; who created all things; upholds all things; and sovereignly, if often bewilderingly to us, directs all things. *Time For Judgement* is a timely, relevant, engaging, thoughtful, passionate plea from a 'Watchman' (see Ezekiel 3:17) for Christians, and non-Christians, to take God seriously. The book is filled with penetrating insight into the Bible's teaching on judgement. It harnesses thoughtful words from thoughtful writers outside the Bible to further provoke the reader to think.

Paul Yeulett has provided us with a fresh, engaging comment on why our world is the way it is and why we should embrace the Bible's wisdom to help us navigate our way through the sadnesses and tragedies that afflict our world in every age. You may not always agree with Paul's robust convictions or conclusions, but he will challenge you to think, and hopefully to take seriously the God who is, and who has always been.

Ian Hamilton
President of Westminster Seminary UK
Dec 2023

INTRODUCTION

> *Frodo: I wish the Ring had never come to me. I wish none of this had happened.*
> *Gandalf: So do all who live to see such times, but that is not for them to decide. All we have to decide is what to do with the time that is given to us.*[1]
>
> J. R. R. Tolkien, *The Lord of the Rings*

The title of this book, *Time For Judgement*, contains a quite deliberate double meaning. It is about God's judgement, but it is also about human judgement. *This is the key to understanding everything that follows.*

The words of the title are taken from the first part of 1 Peter 4:17: 'For it is time for judgment to begin at the household of God.' Here the word, 'judgement', is meant in the first of the two senses, that of divine judgement. This verse clearly refers to the 'judgements' which God brings upon the world and upon the Church. This leads to the second meaning of 'judgement', which is that God's people are called to exercise their faculty of judging what is right and true at times such as this. Indeed, my case is that God 'judges', and has recently been 'judging' in very specific ways, precisely in order that his people should themselves know how to 'judge'.

It needs to be added straightaway that the meanings

Introduction

of the verb, 'to judge', in God's case and in ours, are not identical:

- God judges the lives of *people*, determines what he will do with them in time and in eternity, and he does so as the Sovereign Lord and Ruler of the whole universe, before whom every knee will bow, to whom we must all give account.
- God's people, on the other hand, must judge their *response* to certain circumstances, with the understanding and wisdom God gives them by his Word and Spirit.

The motivation behind this book, and the heart of its substance, is the consideration of three events which have dominated the news headlines and affected our lives since the beginning of 2020; these are the Covid-19 Pandemic, the Russia-Ukraine War and the Cost-of-Living Crisis.[2] For reasons which I will explain at the beginning of Chapter 1, I have classified these under the headings of 'pestilence', 'sword' and 'famine', respectively.

In order to anticipate all that follows, I here submit my own definition of a 'divine judgement', which guides my thinking throughout all the chapters and pages that follow:

> A divine judgement is a providence of God in this world that significantly affects one or many human lives, intended to cause people to acknowledge

INTRODUCTION

God, putting them in mind of the final judgement and their eternal state.

Section One examines the biblical basis for divine judgement. The need for people 'to acknowledge God', however, links to the second use of 'judgement'; it is the God of the Bible who needs to be acknowledged, whose revelation and character need to be studied and applied. In dealing with Covid-19, Ukraine and the Cost-of-Living Crisis—which are addressed in Sections Two, Three and Four respectively—the underlying question throughout is this: what responses are consistent with a biblical, Christian worldview? Have Christians fallen in too readily with the thinking and the assumptions of the world around them as they have wrestled with these challenges?

In Section Five, on the theme of 'captivity', I seek to pull together the various strands from earlier in the book and draw out lessons which are increasingly urgent and necessary as we look to the future. I will demonstrate the nature of the 'captivity' that Christian people must acknowledge, and from which they must flee as far as possible. This is then followed by Section Six, which consists of theological conclusions in relation to the two types of judgement that have been considered.

As should already have become abundantly clear, I am writing as a Christian and, probably for the most part, I am writing for Christians. This book is full of God, Jesus Christ,

Introduction

and the Bible. I write in this way because it expresses the all-encompassing conviction which controls how I think, speak, and write. As I often say to the congregation I serve at Grove Chapel in Camberwell, South London, the main reason I believe the Christian message is that it is the only way I can make sense of the world, including myself and everyone else in it. Every other system of thought will ultimately prove to be riddled with dead ends as well as loose ends and will eventually crumble under the weight of its own contradictions. As the apostle Paul told the Corinthians, 'No one can lay a foundation other than that which is laid, which is Jesus Christ' (1 Cor. 3:11). Heaven and earth will pass away, but the words of Jesus Christ, indeed the whole counsel of God, as revealed in the Bible, will never pass away (Matt. 24:35).

A word of explanation may be needed at this early stage: because this work has been completed in 'dribs and drabs' over a two-year period, and because the themes it covers are so diverse, various gearshifts do take place from chapter to chapter, and even from paragraph to paragraph. Sometimes—especially in Chapter 1 and then in Sections Two, Three and Four—the text is anecdotal, even at times semi-autobiographical; elsewhere, in Sections One, Five and Six, it reflects a somewhat more academic biblical-theological or historical-topical approach, although I have tried to keep footnotes to a minimum. While reviewing this work, it occurred to me that I might level out some of these contours to produce a more uniform style, but I concluded that this would be to the detriment of the final product. Readers, of course, are free to disagree.

Who should read this book? The short answer is that *you* should, and having started you should continue! But, as family and friends often press me on this question, the answer is that this book should be read by anyone who has a genuine concern about their lives, the lives of their loved ones, their churches, their communities, their past, present and future, indeed the whole world. I hope that children and teenagers will read this book, and I hope their grandparents will do the same. I am writing for anyone who has been watching the world since the beginning of this present decade of the 2020s, which has thrown up troubling and largely unpredicted events that have already significantly affected our lives and will go on shaping the lives of our children and our children's children in the years and decades to come. I am writing for anyone who, living through all this, has stopped to ask the question, 'What does all this mean? What should we make of it, and what should we do about it, if indeed we can do anything?'

We do not know what lies ahead in the rest of the 2020s and beyond—this is one key area, of course, where God's judgement diverges so widely from ours. Like Frodo, we may wish that none of these present events had ever happened to us; but it is God's judgement, not ours, that

Introduction

has resulted in our current situation. Our part is not to murmur or complain but, following wise old Gandalf's counsel, determine what we should do and above all how we should *think* in the years ahead. May God himself equip us with such a mind; and in his judgement may he remember mercy.

1 Thursday, 24 February 2022

My theme is memory, that winged host that soared about me one grey morning of war-time. These memories, which are my life—for we possess nothing certainly except the past—were always with me.[1]

Evelyn Waugh

For much of the last thirty years I have kept a journal—not always evenly, not always consistently, and sometimes I have put the whole thing away for a year or two. These days I tend to jot something down on a Monday, which is generally a quiet day after a busy Sunday as a pastor.

But this day happened to be a Thursday, 24 February 2022. It was a day that demanded that I write something. The headline news that morning was that the Russian army, which had evidently been massing on the northern and eastern borders of Ukraine for several months, had begun its predicted invasion. By the time I sat down to write, buildings had already been shelled and a vast column of tanks was rolling ominously towards Kyiv, while a mass westward exodus of people and cars from the Ukrainian capital was taking place. Clearly this was a momentous day in history.

Chapter 1

But 24 February 2022 had long been anticipated, here in England at any rate, for quite a different reason. Nearly two years had passed since Boris Johnson, the Prime Minister, had addressed the nation on television with those memorable words, 'From this evening I must give the British people a very simple instruction: you must stay at home.' This Thursday was the day when all legally binding Covid-19 restrictions would at last be lifted, including the requirement to self-isolate following a positive Covid test.

It just so happened that these two days coincided.

In addition, it 'just so happened' that my Old Testament reading for the day was from the Book of Jeremiah, Chapter 15. I read the first two verses, then blinked, drew a sharp intake of breath, and read them again. I quote them here:

> Then the LORD said to me, 'Though Moses and Samuel stood before me, yet my heart would not turn toward this people. Send them out of my sight, and let them go! And when they ask you, "Where shall we go?" you shall say to them, "Thus says the LORD:
>
> > 'Those who are for *pestilence*, to *pestilence*,
> > and those who are for the *sword*, to the *sword*;
> > those who are for *famine*, to *famine*,
> > and those who are for *captivity*, to ca*ptivity*'"'
> >
> > (Jer. 15:1, 2).

Thursday, 24 February 2022

The words 'pestilence' and 'sword' in verse 2 hit me forcibly. What a coincidence that these two words should come so close together, on this day of all days! A day on which, at least from my perspective, 'pestilence' was on the way out, but the Russian 'sword' was being mercilessly unsheathed.

This set me thinking rapidly. What about the other two disasters listed in verse 2: 'famine' and 'captivity'? There was already looming talk of a 'Cost-of-Living Crisis' in the UK, as well as widespread concerns about global economic downturn, on the back of Covid-19. It was already clear that a war in Europe could only make matters worse. But could we call this 'famine'? And then, looking to the end of Jeremiah 15:2, what kind of 'captivity' might possibly lie ahead?

Life went on

Whatever might lie ahead, it looked as though big changes were afoot. Since March 2020, life had certainly felt different to everything that had gone before. And now that season of change looked set to continue.

Prior to Covid-19, it had seemed for the most part that life had gone on without any great disturbance or upheaval. Even when events of national or global significance were reported, the resulting impact on relatively sheltered lives like mine never amounted to much. I am too young to remember the three-day weeks

Chapter 1

of 1973 and 1974 in the UK, but the Winter of Discontent in 1978–79 meant schools closing for a few icy days due to a lack of fuel deliveries, though not for long enough to create a genuine crisis. What crisis?

I was twelve years old when the Argentine junta ordered the invasion of the Falkland Islands in 1982. I recall the mounting sense of concern: the BBC initially reporting it as the 'Falklands Crisis', then the 'Falklands Conflict', and finally the 'Falklands War'. I remember the lad who tore into our classroom on a thundery day in May, announcing to everyone present with beaming excitement, 'The Task Force has landed!' Our headmaster, remembering World War Two, spoke with Churchillian gravitas about Britain going to war, and how the names of servicemen who laid down their lives for Queen and Country would appear in the newspapers as they had forty years earlier. We wondered, as schoolboys used to wonder in those days, whether the nuclear-armed Soviet Union would intervene on the Argentinian side—at that time there was much animated talk about red buttons, four-minute warnings, underground shelters, wholesale destruction and similarly intriguing prospects—but for pretty much everyone, in mainland Britain at any rate, life went on just as before.

Jumping forward a couple of decades, when I heard that two aeroplanes had struck the Twin Towers of the World Trade Center and that they had both collapsed, my response was one of acute personal shock. I recalled how, six years earlier, I had stood on the summit of the South Tower, surveying the whole of Manhattan a vertical quarter mile beneath me, and sensing the sheer immensity of the mighty structure that was holding us up. Knowing that these towers had now crumbled into dust produced an intensely visceral reaction in me, almost as if I had come crashing down with the buildings. The images broadcast around the world transfixed billions of people, and the closer they were to New York, the more devastating the consequences. Of course, the 9-11 attacks were followed by the declaration of the 'War on Terror' and wholesale upheaval for millions of people in Afghanistan, Iraq and other countries. But, on Wednesday 12 September 2001, and for the days, months and years which followed, many if not most people carried on as they had before. No sweeping changes to daily routines took place because of what had happened in New York and Washington.

Then followed the financial crisis of 2008. I do not regard myself as anything remotely resembling an economist, but I could tell, following the initial collapse of the Northern Rock Building Society in the UK, then the far weightier demise of Lehman Brothers in the USA, that events of seismic magnitude were taking place. In time, there were economic and political consequences which no one could overlook: central government intervention with bailouts of the banking sector on an astronomic scale; and

Chapter 1

a Coalition Government in the UK which pursued a policy of 'austerity', with significant cuts to public services and a sweeping overhaul of the financial sector.

Two distinct impressions began to form in my mind around that time, one quite comforting and the other most unsettling. My first response was that this crisis was, for most of us, nothing like the 'austerity' that our grandparents of the immediate post-war generation in Britain had endured. But I also sensed a gnawing unease: that this country, and indeed the whole Western World, may have just passed a critical tipping point.

Without being able to articulate exactly why, I began saying around that time, 'In fifty years Britain will be a third-world country.' When I did so, people looked at me askance. But that uncomfortable impression steadily gained strength in the years which followed.

A giant control panel

No such descent into ruin seemed about to strike at any time during the second decade of the twenty-first century. If anything, life seemed to become ever more comfortable.

You could still travel widely and inexpensively. These were the halcyon years of budget airlines. You could order your books and your takeaways online. The tributaries of online retailers extended beyond books, conveying pretty much everything to our front doors. Smartphones and other mobile devices became more

Thursday, 24 February 2022

plentiful, more powerful, more fun, and more addictive. These were the heady days of the accelerating digital revolution. Facebook and Twitter (recently renamed 'X') were already established but they, and more recent social media platforms, such as YouTube, Instagram, Tik Tok and Snapchat, were migrating to smaller and smaller screens. CDs, so new and exciting in the distant 1980s, gave way to music streaming services, and DVDs became almost redundant as online video streaming services took centre stage. E-reader software had begun to replace books, although physical books seemed, and still seem, unwilling to beat such a hasty path to extinction. Catch-up TV meant that you did not have to watch your favourite programme at a certain time, or even bother to record it.

Whether or not money was plentiful—perhaps more and more of us never gave this much thought—it seemed more remote, which meant that people spent it with less forethought. Handling physical cash was becoming more of a rarity, so that the tangible value of money in the pocket or the purse seemed a thing of the past. Online banking, like online purchasing, was now largely carried out using mobile devices. Printed bank statements gave way to digital files which you could choose to view or to ignore. And we began to hear about strange new digital currencies, which left many of us baffled.

The whole of life seemed to feel more and more like a *giant control panel*. Whatever you wanted, you could

Chapter 1

probably get hold of it by a few clicks here and there. You could gain a sense of personal mastery over so much of your environment. The evolution of successive technology standards for networks—3G, 4G and 5G—promised ever more extensive and integrated connection, and control, or, if you preferred, the relinquishing of control. Driverless cars, which formerly would have sounded like an oxymoron, became a serious possibility.

From time to time, we would hear about health scares, some that seemed to present a global threat, but they never amounted to much more than a talking point. It all sounded rather frightening back in the 1980s when the AIDS epidemic began to surface—haunting adverts with icebergs and warnings of millions of fatalities. Later we heard about Bird Flu and Swine Flu, but the only lasting effect of these was the replacement of bars of soap with plastic bottles of hand wash. Reports of Severe Acute Respiratory Syndrome (SARS) in East Asia, and of Ebola in sub-Saharan Africa, came to our attention, but this was largely news from foreign fields. The 2011 film, *Contagion*, portrayed a world in which a flu-like illness, first appearing in Hong Kong, would quickly morph into a global pandemic. And there was scary talk of the evolution of bacteria that would increasingly dodge the antibiotics that our doctors were becoming more reluctant to prescribe.

But most of these were minor irritations at worst—for

many of us in the West, anyway. The year 2016 was by all accounts a critical year, with political earthquakes on both sides of the Atlantic: Brexit in the UK and the election of Donald Trump in the US. Viewpoints and discussions became more polarized, but very little of this got in the way of *life*. We were in Control.

Acts of God?

'Heaven is a Place on Earth' sang Belinda Carlisle way back in 1987.[2] For the last thirty-six years, many of us have tried to prove that she was right. We could make whatever we wanted of our lives, our opportunities, our resources, our whole world. The insurance industry was there to safeguard us against the encroachment of significant risks to our vehicles, our properties, our businesses, our bodies, and our lives. Crises and disasters took place, of course, affecting individuals, families, corporations, and nations, but the driving ambition of the Western World was not seriously undermined: we could make this present world a paradise for ourselves, pushing back against anything and everything that might threaten.

However, every now and then, specific events took place which should have caused this uneasy resolve to wobble, even literally.

On 7 December 1988, a massive earthquake struck the region just north of the city of Spitak in Armenia, then still part of the Soviet Union. The loss of life was estimated as

Chapter 1

anything up to 50,000, and another 130,000 people were injured.[3] Exactly two weeks later, another disaster took place much closer to home: the terrorist detonation of a bomb on Pan Am Flight 103, which crashed in Lockerbie, in the south of Scotland, with 270 deaths. 'Lockerbie' became a household byword for tragedy, as Hillsborough would become a few months later, as Aberfan had become back in 1966, and as Dunblane would become in 1996.[4]

That Christmas, in the immediate aftermath of both these events, I was speaking with a family member about these disasters. We spoke about Lockerbie for a few minutes, lamenting not only the loss of life but the evil of the attack. Then I mentioned the Armenian earthquake. 'But that's so different; that's an act of God', she said.

That phrase, 'act of God', stuck with me. At the time, I had not yet become a Christian. I did not know then that the term, 'act of God', while not being rooted in any specific religious belief, has legal currency in the world of business and insurance; that it describes an event that lies beyond human activity or control, in which an insurance company's liability for damages is either limited or indeed wholly removed.

If such 'acts of God' take place in this present world from time to time, then to say that 'Heaven is a Place on Earth' is, at the very least, a questionable claim. Perhaps there are little corners of the world where 'acts of God', of this kind, never imperil anyone. Perhaps, for many people, the illusion that we can go on trying to create our own paradise continues to persist. But the events which began to unfold in 2020 should really have blown away any such assumptions once and for all.

The hour to think, speak and act.

Back to 'pestilence', 'sword', 'famine' and 'captivity'. If these things have hit us, are hitting us, and are about to hit us, then we should sit up and take notice. If they are indeed 'acts of God', then we need to pay more than passing attention to them. Covid-19, though it now occupies our rear-view mirrors, has resulted in sweeping changes to our lives which have been impossible to ignore. To go through a litany of them all now would be as tedious for you as it is for me.

But the great issue at stake is this: have these things made us stop and think, and ask the big, important and deep questions about what we should learn? If, after all the upheavals of the past four years, there is nothing other than a determination to pick up exactly where we left off, and simply hope that nothing similar rears its ugly head at any time in the future, then we have made no progress.

As a Christian who is persuaded of the authority, the accuracy and the abiding relevance of the whole Bible, Old and New Testaments, my cast-iron conviction is that nothing other than a robust, honest, courageous and comprehensive biblical worldview—to look at the world

Chapter 1

through the clarifying lens of Scripture—will help us at a time like this. This will be a painstaking and, at times, a deeply painful activity. But now is the hour to think, speak and act in this way.

In the three chapters which follow, I intend to lay a clear and secure biblical foundation for the first central thesis of this book: that through acts of this kind—'pestilence', 'sword', 'famine' and 'captivity'—the Sovereign God of the universe works in judgement.[5] I will explore the basis for God's judgement, and how that judgement is differentiated between the Church, as the visible people of God, and the world outside the Church. I will consider how Christians should respond to acts of judgement in the light of God's central purposes in human history. Then, in the next three sections, I will look at the first three categories in turn, trying to ascertain the specific lessons that Christians need to learn; that is, how we should exercise the type of 'judgement' which is appropriate to us as creatures made by God and accountable to him. This will involve a certain amount of reflection and analysis of the way that Christian believers have reacted to recent events, as well as how they relate to one another, to the world around them, and to God himself. In the final major section, on 'captivity', I will undertake a careful analysis of what this theme meant in Bible times, as well as what it may mean today, before coming to what I believe are relevant and necessary applications for the Church today and into the future.

I now need to outline a most important caveat before concluding this first chapter.

Impartiality impossible

For several days in March 2023, the British news was dominated by the controversy surrounding Gary Lineker, one-time star striker for the England football team and now the long-established presenter of BBC's *Match of the Day*. Following comments that he posted on Twitter (renamed 'X') in relation to the immigration policy pursued by the British Government—comparing it in some senses to that pursued by Germany in the 1930s—Lineker was suspended from presenting *Match of the Day* for a single weekend. The reason cited for his suspension was that he had breached BBC guidelines on 'impartiality'. This provoked a media (and social media) storm, with a number of Lineker's colleagues in the BBC boycotting scheduled broadcasts in sympathy with him. Lineker was promptly, if not hastily, reinstated, and the debate concerning 'impartiality' died down, but it is still very far from being resolved.

This is because, in the final analysis, impartiality is impossible.

Was Lineker right? Was he wise? Was he sensitive? I would maintain that on this occasion he was none of

Chapter 1

these, and that someone who *could* be described by these three adjectives would not have posted in the way he did. But the fact remains that he held, and presumably still holds, to these views. Lineker cannot be genuinely 'impartial' without being dishonest; he believes that the Government's immigration policy is wrong. He has a clear opinion on the matter. He does not claim indifference or neutrality on the issue.

All of us have views on various issues, some trivial and some serious. We may prefer butter to margarine or Manchester City to Manchester United; we may have definite opinions on issues such as drug legalization and abortion, as well as immigration, and with respect to these latter subjects we would be irresponsible *not* to hold robust and well-reasoned views. How we express these views and where we express them—on social media or wherever—is a matter for our discretion. But, if no one expressed any views or preferences on social media, no one would bother using it. And even if we do not use social media, all of the everyday conversations of any interest or substance would quickly evaporate if we held to a line of, 'I always observe strict impartiality'.

This matters a great deal, because when the Bible talks about impartiality it always has to do with the just and equable treatment of *people*, not of statements or beliefs.[6] The Greek word for 'partiality' carries the idea of 'regarding the face', the gist of it being that, if I like your

Thursday, 24 February 2022

face, I will act more favourably towards you. We—not only the law courts but all of us—should treat people as equals regardless of such things as physical appearance, wealth, age, sex, ability, ethnicity and other circumstances to do with the people themselves.

But impartiality is impossible when it comes to statements or beliefs. We must not pretend that we can be neutral or indifferent regarding these, unless we remain absolutely silent. Christians know that statements about the goodness of God, the authority of the Bible, the sanctity of life, the rightness of biblical marriage, the sinfulness of sin, and the uniqueness of Jesus Christ, for example, are matters where studied 'impartiality' would be sheer disobedience, inevitably with a large measure of cowardice thrown in.

In 1 Corinthians 15:3-4, the apostle Paul announces that it is a matter of 'first importance ... that Christ died for our sins in accordance with the Scriptures, that he was buried, that he was raised on the third day in accordance with the Scriptures'. Paul could not be 'impartial' on this issue, however hard he tried, because 'impartiality' is simply the wrong category to apply to such truth-claims, indeed the weightiest truth-claims of all. To put it more boldly still, Paul could not be 'impartial' in relation to such matters for the simple reason that God himself is not 'impartial'. In the Bible, God has revealed a testimony about himself which emphasizes that he is anything but

Chapter 1

'neutral'; he is concerned for righteousness, for holiness, for truth, for the spiritual well-being of his people; for the praise of his own glory. Conversely, God is set against sin, idolatry, injustice, adultery and every false way.

So, I must state at the outset this vitally important disclaimer: I disavow any attempt to be 'impartial' in what is written in this book. Those who claim to speak for the God of the Bible are constrained above all others to communicate in this fashion. I seek, throughout, to build on the solid foundation of what God has revealed in the Bible, and in line with the wisest minds in long centuries of Christian tradition. That is not to say that everyone who reads will agree with me; it is certainly not to say that what I have written cannot be contested! But it *is* to say that God is a God of truth, and as long as we are humbly seeking to discern his mind on any and every issue, we are heading in the best direction.

Political minus the parties

Nevertheless, this book is not intended to be *party* political. I use that word 'party' very carefully. Our English words, 'political' and 'politics', trace their ancestry to the Greek *polis*, a city—a word which in turn gives rise to *politēs*, meaning a citizen. I write as a citizen—in my specific case of the United Kingdom—because I can write, at least write informatively, from no other context. Where there are people, there is necessarily politics, and only a

Thursday, 24 February 2022

hermit could write in a strictly non-political vein. It would be vain to attempt to conceal all my political leanings from my readership, but I would robustly maintain that any serious Christian should ensure that his/her political views, on any and every subject, are solidly grounded in a biblical Christian worldview.

I will, however, try as far as possible to avoid *party* political points, which would run the risk of prejudicing any number of readers. To be 'conservative' is not the same as to be 'Conservative'. You can be an advocate of democracy without being a 'Democrat'. It is possible to say, hand on heart, as I do, 'black lives matter', without being constrained to capitalize the initial letters of those three words and shove a hashtag at the front.

Maintaining a stretch of clear blue water—or water of any colour!—between Christianity and party politics is not a practice that has been universally followed. In the late nineteenth century, the Church of England was widely seen as 'the Tory Party at prayer', while non-Conformists were regarded as 'the Liberal Party at prayer'. The Baptist minister of London's Metropolitan Tabernacle, C. H. Spurgeon (1834–92), did not exactly hide his admiration for the Liberal Prime Minister W. E. Gladstone (1809–98).[7] This problem is not confined to the past: in present-day America it is becoming increasingly difficult to disentangle political issues—indeed moral and spiritual

Chapter 1

issues—from a form of party politics which is becoming ever more polarized and tribal.

In some respects, this is not surprising because, as we will see shortly, today we are facing a set of circumstances that the greatest of statesmen, in their own spheres and times, could scarcely have imagined.

Part one: God, the Bible and Judgement

2 Jeremiah and Judgement

Where there is no judge on earth, the appeal lies to God in heaven.[1]

John Locke

Pestilence, Sword, Famine and Captivity. Although Jeremiah 15:2 is the only verse in the Bible where all four of these words are found together, each of them makes frequent appearances in the Scriptures and especially in the Book of Jeremiah.

Leaving aside Jeremiah 15:2, the first three of these words—*pestilence, sword* and *famine*—appear together a further twenty-six times in the Bible: of these, sixteen are in Jeremiah, seven are in Ezekiel, with the other three being found in the two Books of Chronicles and in Revelation 6:8. Another permutation of three—*pestilence, sword* and *captivity*—appear together in Jeremiah 43:11.

Similar exercises can be repeated with two out of the four words: *pestilence* and *sword, pestilence* and *famine,* and so on. They reveal a common pattern, which is that the first three judgements in particular—*pestilence, sword* and *famine*—are found together rather often, and that the Book of Jeremiah, especially, abounds with such references.[2]

CHAPTER 2

This suggests that we need to spend some time thinking about Jeremiah, his life and times, and the message he was bringing from the God of Judgement.

The Weeping Prophet

Jeremiah has received the nickname, 'The Weeping Prophet', and as you read through the fifty-two chapters of his prophecy—the longest book in the Bible by word count—it is not hard to see why. In less common usage today, a 'jeremiah' is someone habitually given to pessimism, and a 'jeremiad' is a work of prose that gives expression to such a spirit.

The Book of Jeremiah itself is not a *jeremiad*, pure and simple. There are wonderful and beautiful exceptions to the general pattern, above all Chapters 30 to 33—sometimes referred to as Jeremiah's 'Book of Consolation'—which scale the highest peaks in 31:31–34 with the glorious prophecy of the New Covenant. But there certainly is a good deal of weeping in Jeremiah, often the weeping of the prophet himself, as in 9:1:

> Oh that my head were waters,
> and my eyes a fountain of tears,
> that I might weep day and night
> for the slain of the daughter of my people!

Why did Jeremiah weep? Because he was, above all, a prophet called to announce God's judgement against the people of Judah in the latter years of that kingdom. Chosen and appointed by God to be a prophet before his birth, even before his conception (1:5), and born in the middle of the seventh century BC—we cannot be certain about his date of birth, but it was probably in the 640s BC—Jeremiah was called by God while he was 'only a youth' (1:6). The Lord told him that he was appointed:

> over nations and over kingdoms,
> to pluck up and to break down,
> to destroy and to overthrow,
> to build and to plant.
> (Jer. 1:10)

While Jeremiah's prophetic ministry extended to other 'nations' and 'kingdoms', and Chapters 46 to 51 contain those prophecies, the vast bulk of his material was directed towards the nation of Judah. Jeremiah was active during the reigns of five kings: Josiah (640–609 BC), Jehoahaz (609 BC), Jehoiakim (609–598 BC), Jehoiachin (598 BC) and Zedekiah (598–587 BC).

Josiah was an exceptionally godly king, of whom we read in 2 Kings 23:25, 'Before him there was no king like him, who turned to the Lord with all his heart and with all his soul and with all his might, according to all the Law of Moses, nor did any like him arise after him.'[3] The trouble was that Josiah stood out, not so much like a sore thumb but like a very healthy thumb surrounded by lots

Chapter 2

of extremely diseased fingers. The reforming work of his reign seems to have gone to waste. His three sons and one grandson (Jehoiachin, not Zedekiah) who succeeded him were all ungodly men. During the twenty-two years that followed his death, the menacing shadow of Babylon, ruled by King Nebuchadnezzar, encroached ever further upon Judah. In three distinct waves, in the years 605, 597 and 587-86 BC, Nebuchadnezzar made significant incursions into Jerusalem, looting and plundering, and deporting the population into his ever-expanding Babylonian Empire. The prophet Daniel was exiled in the first of these waves, the prophet Ezekiel in the second, and the third of them witnessed the wholesale destruction of the temple and the subjugation of the whole land.

Why did all this happen? The final chapter of Jeremiah, Chapter 52, contains a summary of these climactic and catastrophic events. There in verse 3 we read:

> For because of the anger of the LORD it came to the point in Jerusalem and Judah that he cast them out from his presence.
>
> (Jer. 52:3)

We need to know where this 'anger of the LORD' came from.

Tingling ears and upside-down dishes

Not only did Josiah have wicked and ungodly offspring,

his immediate forebears were no better; if anything they were considerably worse. Most significant in this regard was his grandfather Manasseh (697–643 BC). The sordid account of his reign can be read in 2 Kings 21:1–18.[4]

The defining characteristic of Manasseh's reign was its blatant and extreme idolatry, which accelerated the decline of Judah towards exile in Babylon. It was as though Manasseh had seized a twenty-ton wrecking ball, fastened it firmly to the end of a hundred-foot-long iron chain, and persisted in smashing up everything good and godly that had previously existed in the Kingdom of Judah.

Manasseh overturned all the reforms of his God-fearing father, Hezekiah, whom he was so unlike. He imported into the Temple the paganism of the surrounding nations and indulged in them. We can read the lurid descriptions: pagan fertility rituals with all the shrine prostitution that these involved; worship of the heavenly bodies; fortune-telling; necromancy; witchcraft; black magic; and even the burning of his own son as a human sacrifice—an offering to pagan gods (2 Kings 21:6).

What made this so deplorable was that all this idolatry was carried out in Jerusalem, the city of God, against the backdrop of the established worship of the LORD and the covenants and promises made to David and Solomon. 2 Kings 21:9 tells us that 'Manasseh led them astray to do more evil than the nations had done whom the LORD destroyed before the people of Israel.'

Chapter 2

The judgement on Manasseh and Judah is spelt out most comprehensively in 2 Kings 21:10–15, which is worth quoting in full:

> And the LORD said by his servants the prophets, 'Because Manasseh king of Judah has committed these abominations and has done things more evil than all that the Amorites did, who were before him, and has made Judah also to sin with his idols, therefore thus says the LORD, the God of Israel: Behold, I am bringing upon Jerusalem and Judah such disaster that the ears of everyone who hears of it will tingle. And I will stretch over Jerusalem the measuring line of Samaria, and the plumb line of the house of Ahab, and I will wipe Jerusalem as one wipes a dish, wiping it and turning it upside down. And I will forsake the remnant of my heritage and give them into the hand of their enemies, and they shall become a prey and a spoil to all their enemies, because they have done what is evil in my sight and have provoked me to anger, since the day their fathers came out of Egypt, even to this day.'

Here, for the first time in the whole Bible, was a clear and specific announcement of what God was going to do in judgement against his people: to 'forsake the remnant of my heritage and give them into the hand of their enemies' on account of this sin of idolatry: in brief, the

Babylonian exile. By the time Jeremiah was prophesying in Judah, Manasseh had long been dead. But his evil legacy remained and, at the conclusion of Josiah's reign, we read the following:

> Still the LORD did not turn from the burning of his great wrath, by which his anger was kindled against Judah, *because of all the provocations with which Manasseh had provoked him.*
>
> (2 Kings 23:26)

This is the context in which we must understand not only Jeremiah 15:2, but the whole ministry of Jeremiah, and indeed other prophets who spoke of 'pestilence', 'sword', 'famine' and 'captivity' as judgements of God which could no longer be averted. If we look back at 15:1, we can see that even if Moses and Samuel—notable men of prayer in Israel—had stood before the LORD and begged him not to bring these plagues on his people, still the LORD would not have relented.[5]

But why this insistent, unyielding, divine determination to act in judgement? We have to go back further in the Old Testament to find out.

Law enforcement

The Old Testament is often referred to in the New Testament as 'the Law and the Prophets'.[6] This is because there is an umbilical cord linking the Law of Moses with

Chapter 2

the prophets who followed. Through Moses, the Lord gave his Law to Israel: supremely the Ten Commandments but also, inseparably attached to them, all the statutes and rules which were given by God to be observed by Israel.

One key function of the prophets, who were sent to Israel in the centuries which followed, was to convict Israel of their sin and faithlessness in relation to God's Law. In that sense, the work of the prophets, such as Jeremiah, was one of 'Law Enforcement'.

This comes to a climactic expression in Deuteronomy 28, which is not only one of the longest chapters in the Old Testament (sixty-eight verses), but one of the most important. It lists, very comprehensively and graphically, the blessings that the Lord would bring to Israel if they obeyed his commandments, and the curses he would bring if they disobeyed. But it is a very asymmetric list: the blessings take up just fourteen verses, and the curses the remaining fifty-four verses. Here is an indication of how the history of Israel was going to play out in the centuries which follow, and of why it is that Jeremiah's ministry, like that of the other prophets, was so tear-streaked. The plucking up and breaking down, the destroying and overthrowing, would overshadow the building and the planting.

Pestilence, *sword*, *famine* and *captivity*: we find a great deal of all these throughout those fifty-four verses. It is not always easy to trace a clear division between these four categories. One reason for this is that in lived-out experience, both in biblical history and in the world today, one or more of them frequently overlap. A careful reading of Deuteronomy 28:15–68 will reveal this to be true.

Nevertheless, there are some sections where one of these judgements is especially brought to the fore, as I will try to demonstrate below:

Pestilence (verses 58–62)

> If you are not careful to do all the words of this law that are written in this book, that you may fear this glorious and awesome name, the Lord your God, then the Lord will bring on you and your offspring extraordinary afflictions, afflictions severe and lasting, and sicknesses grievous and lasting. And he will bring upon you again all the diseases of Egypt, of which you were afraid, and they shall cling to you. Every sickness also and every affliction that is not recorded in the book of this law, the Lord will bring upon you, until you are destroyed. Whereas you were as numerous as the stars of heaven, you shall be left few in number, because you did not obey the voice of the Lord your God.

Sword (verses 47–52)

> Because you did not serve the Lord your God with joyfulness and gladness of heart, because of the

Chapter 2

abundance of all things, therefore you shall serve your enemies whom the Lord will send against you, in hunger and thirst, in nakedness, and lacking everything. And he will put a yoke of iron on your neck until he has destroyed you. The Lord will bring a nation against you from far away, from the end of the earth, swooping down like the eagle, a nation whose language you do not understand, a hard-faced nation who shall not respect the old or show mercy to the young. It shall eat the offspring of your cattle and the fruit of your ground, until you are destroyed; it also shall not leave you grain, wine, or oil, the increase of your herds or the young of your flock, until they have caused you to perish. They shall besiege you in all your towns, until your high and fortified walls, in which you trusted, come down throughout all your land. And they shall besiege you in all your towns throughout all your land, which the Lord your God has given you.

Famine (verses 38–40)

You shall carry much seed into the field and shall gather in little, for the locust shall consume it. You shall plant vineyards and dress them, but you shall neither drink of the wine nor gather the grapes, for the worm shall eat them. You shall have olive trees throughout all your territory, but you shall not anoint yourself with the oil, for your olives shall drop off.

Captivity (verses 64–68)

And the Lord will scatter you among all peoples, from one end of the earth to the other, and there you shall serve other gods of wood and stone, which neither you nor your fathers have known. And among these nations you shall find no respite, and there shall be no resting place for the sole of your foot, but the Lord will give you there a trembling heart and failing eyes and a languishing soul. Your life shall hang in doubt before you. Night and day you shall be in dread and have no assurance of your life. In the morning you shall say, 'If only it were evening!' and at evening you shall say, 'If only it were morning!' because of the dread that your heart shall feel, and the sights that your eyes shall see. And the Lord will bring you back in ships to Egypt, a journey that I promised that you should never make again; and there you shall offer yourselves for sale to your enemies as male and female slaves, but there will be no buyer.

These paragraphs make sobering reading in isolation;

Chapter 2

for some of us the cumulative effect of the whole chapter might seem overwhelming.

But is this God the God of the Bible? Or, perhaps, is the God of the Old Testament different to the God of the New Testament? And is he still the same God today? There are some people, even some professing Christians, who might find this idea of a God of Judgement objectionable and even repulsive. At this point we, therefore, need to step back and address some fairly weighty issues: the character of this God who judges, and what his judgement is all about.

3 The God of Judgement

> *At last met my Lord Mayor in Canningstreet, like a man spent, with a handkercher about his neck. To the King's message he cried, like a fainting woman, 'Lord! what can I do? I am spent: people will not obey me. I have been pulling down houses; but the fire overtakes us faster than we can do it.'*[1]
>
> Samuel Pepys

Throughout the whole Bible, God is presented to us as the Sovereign Ruler of the universe, the King of kings and Lord of lords, in distinction to all the 'gods' of the nations.

Nebuchadnezzar, ruler of the Babylonian Empire, who was himself referred to as 'king of kings' (Dan. 2:37), learned this lesson through bitter and memorable experience. Having been greatly humbled, and then exalted once more, this was his testimony about God:

> At the end of the days I, Nebuchadnezzar, lifted my eyes to heaven, and my reason returned to me, and I blessed the Most High, and praised and honoured him who lives forever,
>
> for his dominion is an everlasting dominion,

Chapter 3

> and his kingdom endures from generation to generation;
>
> all the inhabitants of the earth are accounted as nothing,
>
> and he does according to his will among the host of heaven
>
> and among the inhabitants of the earth;
>
> and none can stay his hand
>
> or say to him, 'What have you done?'
>
> (Dan. 4:34–35)

The God of the Bible 'does according to his will among the host of heaven and among the inhabitants of the earth'; his rule is a universal rule, with no one and nothing to prevent him. This is what it means for God to be the Sovereign God; to put it as simply as possible, *this is what it means for God to be God.*

Man[2] in his rebellion pushes back against this, but this is the reality, indeed the ground of all reality: God is Sovereign Ruler. The apostle Paul draws our attention to the same truth in his great Letter to the Romans. Paul's foundational assumption is that God does whatever he pleases, and he does so in perfect justice. 'Let God be true though everyone were a liar,' (Rom. 3:4) is the apostle's starting point when he speaks about the judgement of God. In facing down objectors, who suggest that God might be unrighteous in inflicting wrath on them, Paul responds with vehement indignation: 'By no means! For then how could God judge the world?' (Rom. 3:6). The Sovereign God who created the world and everything in it has the sovereign right to judge that world and all its creatures, you and me included. This is the apostle Paul's starting point, and it must be ours if we are to be humble and teachable students of Scripture. We need to relearn, or perhaps learn for the first time, the fear of God—the fear of the God of Judgement.

God, the Judge of the earth

If we want to stand in the mainstream of historical, orthodox Christian faith, we will be of one mind with the apostle Paul. We will accept without hesitation that God is the righteous, authoritative judge of the whole earth and the present tense is important. It is not sufficient to say that he *will* judge the earth one day, though he will; he is also that Judge *today*, as he always has been.

The prophet Habakkuk understood this well, as he anticipated the impending judgement that God would bring against his people by means of the Babylonian armies. 'But the LORD is in his holy temple', writes the prophet; and on that account, 'let all the earth keep silence before him' (Hab. 2:20). And how is this judgement enacted? 'His brightness was like the light; rays flashed from his hand; and there he veiled his power. Before him went pestilence, and plague followed at his heels' (Hab.

Chapter 3

3:4–5). This was no distant occurrence far beyond the horizon of Habakkuk and his compatriots; these words describe events that God was soon to unleash.

Prominent men of God have, down the ages, understood that 'his judgements are in all the earth' (Ps. 105:7). Among them, few have been more conspicuous or influential than Jonathan Edwards (1703–1758), arguably America's greatest theologian and indeed philosopher. In his outstanding biography of Edwards, George M. Marsden describes the sermons Edwards preached in the spring and summer of 1739, which came to be published under the title, *A History of the Work of Redemption*:

> He took for granted, as did most of his religiously minded contemporaries, the spiritual significance of the politics of Christendom. Every stage, or 'dispensation', in the coming of Christ's kingdom involved a dark time when Christ or his saints suffered deeply at the hands of Satan, followed by a victory in which Christ the righteous judge avenged the cause of justice ... as heir to more than a thousand years of 'Christendom' and to two centuries of Reformed politics, Edwards took for granted that God was working through national religious wars and revolutions that would facilitate the preaching of the Gospel.[3]

The whole concept of 'Christendom' might seem archaic

and foreign to many of us today—perhaps even wrong-headed and offensive at a time when spiritual life is so weak in many parts of the world which once constituted 'Christendom', and when churches in the 'global south' are experiencing far more visible blessing. But this should not blind us to the more substantial point: in the realm of the political and the military, and numerous other realms besides, God is working out his judgements in this world.

On a rather more prosaic level, we could consider the response of J. C. Ryle (1816–1900) to the outbreak of foot-and-mouth disease in Britain in 1865. Further outbreaks took place in 1967 and 2001, and Ryle's words were recalled at those subsequent seasons, though perhaps not sufficiently taken to heart. This is how Ryle answered the question, *'Where does the cattle plague come from?'*

> I answer, unhesitatingly, that it comes from God. He who orders all things in heaven and earth—He by whose wise providence everything is directed, and without whom nothing can happen—He it is who has sent this scourge upon us. It is the finger of God.
>
> I shall not spend time in proving this point. I refer anyone who asks for proof to the whole tenor of God's Word. I ask him to mark how God is always spoken of as the governor of all things here below. Who sent the flood on the world in the days of Noah? It was God. (Gen. 6:17.) Who sent the famine

in the days of Joseph? It was God. (Gen. 41:25.) Who sent the plague on Egypt, and specially the murrain[4] on the cattle? It was God. (Exod. 7:5; 9:3.) Who sent disease on the Philistines, when the ark was among them? It was God. (1 Sam. 5:7; 6:3-7.) I cannot understand how anyone can be called a believer of the Bible who denies God's providence over this world. I believe that wars, famines, pestilences, cattle plagues, are all His instruments for carrying on the government of this world. And therefore, when I see a scourge like the cattle plague, I have no doubt whatever as to the hand that sends it. 'Shall there be evil in a city, and the Lord hath not done it?' (Amos 3:9). It is the finger of God.[5]

We need to take a closer look at this subject, and so we turn to one of the more memorable and famous disasters to ever strike Britain, and to the works of a preacher-commentator who exemplified the approach being recommended here: that God's judgements are indeed in all the earth.

London's burning

In the heart of the City of London stands the 202-feet-tall (61.5 metres) Monument commemorating the Great Fire of London. Like St Paul's Cathedral, a few minutes' walk to the west, and many other adjacent structures, the Monument was designed by Sir Christopher Wren and Dr

Robert Hooke. These days it is dwarfed by the massive commercial skyscrapers that have sprung up around it: the Walkie Talkie, the Gherkin, the Cheesegrater, Heron Tower, the TwentyTwo, with several more in the planning pipeline. But climbing its spiral staircase, all 311 steps of them, is still a 'must do' experience for visitors to London who want to taste its history. For many years it has been an imposing landmark memorializing the devastating conflagration that consumed so much of the medieval city between 2 and 6 September 1666.

Four years later, in 1670, the Puritan pastor and preacher Thomas Brooks (1608–80), who had ministered at St Margaret's Church, New Fish Street, very close to the spot where the Fire started, unveiled his own imposing landmark—one we might do even better to pay attention to today. Brooks published a work with a short and memorable title, *London's Lamentations*. It also had a rather longer title:

> *A serious Discourse concerning that late fiery Dispensation that turned our (once renowned) City into a ruinous Heap. Also the several Lessons that are incumbent upon those whose Houses have escaped the consuming Flames.*[6]

Even these two sentences suggest that Brooks believed the causes of the Great Fire, and the lessons to be learned from it, extended far, wide and deep. It is hard to imagine

Chapter 3

a present-day Government Inquiry using this kind of language. Brooks goes on to make the claim:

> [s]o far as the late fire was a heavy judgment of God upon the city, yea, upon the whole nation, the ends of God in inflicting that judgment are doubtless such as respect both sinners and saints, the righteous and the wicked, the profane and the holy, the good and the bad.[7]

He then proceeds to show how this 'heavy judgment' was executed, first of all, against the 'wicked and ungodly', and provides seven reasons why God had chosen to act in this way:

1. That he may evidence *his sovereignty, and that they may know that there is a God.*
2. God inflicts great and sore judgments upon the sons of men, that *the world may stand in awe of him, and that they may learn to fear and tremble before him.*
3. God inflicts great and sore judgments upon the sons of men, and upon cities and countries, *to express and make known his power, justice, anger, severity, and indignation against sinners and their sinful courses, by which he has been provoked.*
4. God inflicts great and sore judgments upon the sons of men, and upon cities and countries, *that they may*

cease from sin, receive instruction, and reform and return to the most High.

5. God inflicts great and sore judgments upon the sons of men, *that he may try them, and make a more full discovery of themselves to themselves.*
6. God inflicts great and sore judgments upon persons, cities and countries, *that others may be warned by his severities to break off their sins, and to return to the most High.*
7. God inflicts great and sore judgments upon persons, cities and countries, *to put the world in mind of the general judgment.*[8]

Having explained all these rather exhaustively, Brooks then moves on to list 'those high and holy ends, in respect of the people of God, that God aims at by his inflicting of great and sore judgments upon persons, cities and countries.' This list has a little more structure, with four points, the last two being subdivided into four sections, in good Puritan fashion:

1. *To bring about those special favours and mercies that God intends them.*
2. God inflicts great trials and sore judgments upon persons and places, *that he may awaken his own people out of that deep security that oftentimes seizeth upon them.*
3. In respect of his people's sins, God has several special ends that he aims at by all the fiery trials

and smart[9] providences that he exercises them and others with. As,

- First, God by these means designs *a further and a fuller discovery of their sins.*
- Secondly, By severe providences and fiery trials God designs *the preventing of sin.*
- Thirdly, By severe providences and fiery trials God designs *the imbittering of sin to his people.*
- Fourthly, By severe providences and fiery trials, God designs *the mortifying and purging away of his people's sins.*

4. By severe providences and fiery trials, God designs these four things, in respect of his children's graces:[10]

- First, He designs *the reviving, quickening, and recovering of their decayed graces.*
- Secondly, God, by severe providences and fiery trials, designs *a further exercise of his children's graces.*
- Thirdly, by severe providences and by fiery trials, God designs *the growth of his people in grace.*
- Fourthly and lastly, by severe providences and by fiery trials, God doth design *the trial of his people's graces, and the discovery of their sincerity and integrity to the world.*[11]

In summary, Brooks believed that God himself had ordained the Great Fire of London for certain reasons which affected both (1) the unbelieving world and (2) God's own people. Although the effects of the Fire itself did not discriminate between believers and unbelievers— the smoking ruin of a godly home might not look, smell and feel all that different to the smoking ruin of an ungodly home—*the underlying purposes, or to use Brooks' language, the 'designs' of God in bringing it about, were not the same with believers as with unbelievers*. We can see, as a good example, Brooks' use of the expression 'inflicts great and sore judgments' when he speaks about *unbelievers*, and his common phrase 'severe providences and fiery trials' when he deals with *believers*.

Floods, fires and pharaohs

Brooks was not making it up as he went along. He wrote as he did because he knew his Bible inside and out and noted carefully how God had acted in judgement in the past.

The early chapters and books of the Old Testament narrate several historical judgements that God specifically carried out against the ungodly, differentiating them from the godly. Two definitive events in the Book of Genesis are (1) the Great Flood in the time of Noah (Gen. 6-8) and (2) the destruction of the cities of Sodom and Gomorrah in the time of Abraham and Lot (Gen. 18–19).

In both cases, God drew the clearest distinction between

Chapter 3

the righteous, whom he saved, and the wicked, whom he condemned. While Noah and seven members of his family were saved from the Flood, the rest of humanity perished. Lot and his daughters were the only people saved from the destruction of the wicked city of Sodom; the rest, including Lot's wife who turned back, were destroyed. God faithfully answered Abraham's prayer that the righteous would not be swept away with the wicked (Gen. 18:23).

The apostle Peter makes especial mention of both these mighty events in 2 Peter 2:5–9:

> if [God] did not spare the ancient world, but preserved Noah, a herald of righteousness, with seven others, when he brought a flood upon the world of the ungodly; if by turning the cities of Sodom and Gomorrah to ashes he condemned them to extinction, making them an example of what is going to happen to the ungodly; and if he rescued righteous Lot, greatly distressed by the sensual conduct of the wicked (for as that righteous man lived among them day after day, he was tormenting his righteous soul over their lawless deeds that he saw and heard); then the Lord knows how to rescue the godly from trials, and to keep the unrighteous under punishment until the day of judgement.

Peter draws attention to the Flood and to Sodom and Gomorrah to assure his faithful readers that *God*

The God of Judgement

continues to draw a distinction between the righteous and the unrighteous.[12] Although in this present life God might bring the same outward afflictions upon both groups, his divine purposes differ in each case. God will 'rescue the godly from trials', but he will 'keep the unrighteous under punishment until the day of judgement'. For the time being, believers and unbelievers may well be living cheek-by-jowl in the cities, towns and villages of the world, but a Day is coming when there will be a final and fixed separation between them.

If anything, this lesson becomes even clearer as we move into the Book of Exodus and the ten plagues that God brought on the land of Egypt. As plague follows plague, the degree of differentiation between the Egyptians and the Israelites become more marked. In relation to the Fourth Plague, the flies, God tells Pharaoh that 'I will put a division between my people and your people' (Exod. 8:23). By the time we reach the announcement of the Tenth Plague, the death of the firstborn, that division has widened considerably and the message to Pharaoh is even more pronounced: 'But not a dog shall growl against any of the people of Israel, either man or beast, that you may know that the Lord makes a distinction between Egypt and Israel' (Exod. 11:7).

This distinction reaches its climax in the destruction of Pharaoh's chariots and horsemen at the Red Sea. It is spelled out for us in Exodus 14:26-29:

Chapter 3

> Then the Lord said to Moses, 'Stretch out your hand over the sea, that the water may come back upon the Egyptians, upon their chariots, and upon their horsemen.' So Moses stretched out his hand over the sea, and the sea returned to its normal course when the morning appeared. And as the Egyptians fled into it, the Lord threw the Egyptians into the midst of the sea. The waters returned and covered the chariots and the horsemen; of all the host of Pharaoh that had followed them into the sea, not one of them remained. But the people of Israel walked on dry ground through the sea, the waters being a wall to them on their right hand and on their left.

Like the Great Flood and like Sodom and Gomorrah, this final destruction of Pharaoh's host portends the final day of judgement when there will be an everlasting separation between those who are God's people and those who are not. We could add several other biblical examples to this list: the destruction of Jericho and other cities in the time of Joshua (Joshua 6), the slaying of Goliath and other Philistines in the time of David (1 Sam. 17), and the striking down of 185,000 Assyrian soldiers in the time of Hezekiah (2 Kings 19:35; Isa. 37:36).

Distinct divine designs
For the most part, we cannot look at afflictions, disasters

and catastrophes today, or in history, and say 'this happened to Christians *so that* ...', or 'this happened to non-Christians *because* ...'. The outward effects of these trials may look very similar in terms of their impact on the 'righteous' and the 'unrighteous'.

But this does not mean that God himself does not have *distinct purposes* in these events—some purposes directed towards believers and others towards unbelievers. Thomas Brooks understood this well and laboured to know both the Bible he believed and preached, and the times he was living through. Like him—if not quite as painstakingly and compendiously—we need to attempt to trace out 'the several Lessons that are incumbent' in a time of Covid-19, Ukraine, Cost-of-Living Crises and whatever else may lie ahead of us.

My focus in this book is on the divine judgements of 'pestilence', 'sword', 'famine' and 'captivity', or as Brooks would put it, 'those high and holy ends, *in respect of the people of God*, that God aims at by his inflicting of great and sore judgments upon persons, cities and countries.'[13] It is God's judgements as they affect *Christians* that I want to deal with in the main.

'But wait a minute', someone might say. 'This all sounds very harsh, very severe, very bleak. And all you've done so far is quote the Old Testament at length, then illustrate largely from the seventeenth century, when life was far more stringent than it is today. But you're forgetting

Chapter 3

two rather important factors: firstly, we have the New Testament; and secondly, we're living in the twenty-first century!'

Indeed we have, and indeed we do. But we now need to ascertain whether these two factors make any substantial difference.

4 Why is God judging the church?

In my reading of philosophy, I saw that there were innumerable problems that nobody was giving answers for. The Bible, it struck me, dealt with man's problems in a sweeping, all-encompassing thrust.[1]

Francis Schaeffer

We now come to the heart of the matter. Should believers today, New Testament Christians, think in terms of God's judgement being applied to *them*? In particular, should we not insist that judgement has been carried out in full at the cross of Jesus Christ, and should we not rejoice in that wonderful knowledge? If Jesus said, 'It is finished,' as he was about to give up his spirit (John 19:30), then how can we possibly speak of judgement being executed against Christians? Are they not finally and fully delivered from judgement?

We need to answer this question very carefully. Most certainly we must shout it from the rooftops that believers are delivered from the wrath of God in the *final* judgement. Jesus himself pronounces that 'whoever hears my word and believes him who sent me has eternal life. He does not come into judgement, but has passed from death to life' (John 5:24). That is a cast-iron promise from the Saviour:

Chapter 4

not one of his own blood-bought people can be lost. Their names are written in heaven and cannot be erased.

But the same Saviour is the one who says to his followers, 'Judge not, that you be not judged' (Matt. 7:1); whose Father prunes the vine—the Church, the body of Christ—so that it will bear more fruit (John 15:2); who himself walks among the golden lampstands, reproving and disciplining those he loves (Rev. 3:19); even judging, with sickness and death, the members of the Corinthian church who despised their brothers and sisters in Christ (1 Cor. 11:30–32).[2] Sometimes the language of 'discipline' and 'chastisement' is used rather than 'judgement' (Heb. 12:5–11), but we must not soften the impact of the clear teaching of the New Testament. It is corrective discipline, but it is discipline nevertheless, and it does not seem pleasant to us while it is happening.

The biblical evidence is compelling: there is a present, ongoing 'judgement' from God which applies to New Testament *believers* during their lives on earth, in these 'last days' between Christ's first and second coming.

It starts with the church.

I have entitled this book, *Time For Judgement*. The reference here is to the words of 1 Peter 4:17:

> For it is time for judgement to begin at the household of God; and if it begins with us, what will

be the outcome for those who do not obey the gospel of God?

The apostle Peter, like Paul and like Jesus himself, spoke very clearly about 'judgement' being visited on 'the household of God' during this present age. At the time he was writing, probably in the early to mid-60s, the world and the church were on the threshold of unprecedented turbulence and upheaval. The Great Fire of Rome (AD 64) would have far wider and more terrible repercussions than the Great Fire of London. A season of violent persecution against Christians would soon be unleashed. The Roman Emperor, Nero, would shortly fall on his sword at the age of thirty, to be succeeded by four men within the space of little over a year: Galba, Otho, Vitellius and Vespasian. Shortly afterwards, the Temple and indeed the whole city of Jerusalem would be destroyed at the hands of Vespasian's son Titus.

It seems likely that the 'fiery trial' to which Peter refers (1 Peter 4:12) had more than a passing reference to the nature of the suffering that Christians would endure. In that sense, Peter was like a New Testament Jeremiah, ministering at a time when the world was about to be violently convulsed, even turned upside-down. In the light of the reasons why this book is being written—the pestilence, sword, famine and captivity that appear to be striking us—could the same be said about us today?

Chapter 4

Peter is, of course, a New Testament Christian. He preaches the crucified, risen and ascended Jesus to both Jews and Gentiles. He was the first to proclaim openly that God had made Jesus 'both Lord and Christ' (Acts 2:36). But Peter, like Paul and the other apostles, knows that the God of the Old Testament and the God of the New Testament are one and the same Divine Being. His words in 1 Peter 4:17, quoted earlier, are redolent with the cadences of Jeremiah himself.

This becomes abundantly clear as we compare 1 Peter 4 with Jeremiah 25, where the prophet is charged by the Lord to prophesy 'the sword' among many nations. Essentially, a time of violent warfare is about to come upon the world. It is in that context that the prophet speaks these words:

> 'For behold, *I begin to work disaster at the city that is called by my name*, and shall you go unpunished? You shall not go unpunished, for I am summoning a sword against all the inhabitants of the earth,' declares the Lord of hosts.
>
> (Jer. 25:29)

Jeremiah was to prophesy to many nations, all of which would be greatly affected by the disturbances that the Lord would bring upon the world. But where was this 'disaster' going to *begin*? Answer: 'at the city that is called by my name'—with Jerusalem itself. Hence the vast bulk of Jeremiah's prophetic burden concerned Jerusalem and Judah, the covenant people of God. God's actions of judgement, beginning from Jerusalem, would then ripple out into the surrounding nations. The Church of God should take careful note today.

Big judgements are not usually final judgements

These words from Jeremiah follow hard on the heels of his announcement that the people of God are about to be exiled to Babylon for seventy years, while their own land will become 'a ruin and a waste' (Jer. 25:11); this is all part of the same prophetic package.

Four chapters later, we read Jeremiah's letter to the exiles in Babylon. The interesting feature of this letter is its surprisingly upbeat tone. Whereas we might have expected a good deal more weeping and wailing, Jeremiah positively encourages these exiles:

> Build houses and live in them; plant gardens and eat their produce. Take wives and have sons and daughters; take wives for your sons, and give your daughters in marriage, that they may bear sons and daughters; multiply there, and do not decrease. But seek the welfare of the city where I have sent you into exile, and pray to the LORD on its behalf, for in its welfare you will find your welfare.
>
> (Jer. 29:5–7)

The people were not merely to sit on their hands as

Chapter 4

they wept by the Rivers of Babylon, refusing to sing as their harps hung from the willows. They were to engage and interact very positively and proactively in their exiled residence; they were to be fully functioning citizens, heartily devoted to the prosperity of Babylon and their own increase. As we might say today, they were not simply to 'survive' but to seek to 'thrive'. What is more, they were to eagerly anticipate the completion of those seventy years and the ending of their exile.

The key message is this: *these judgements were not final for the people of God in the time of Jeremiah; and we have no reason to conclude that today's judgements are final for the Church in the twenty-first century.* Are we living in the last days? Yes, we are, in the proper biblical sense that we are living in the interval between the first and second coming of Christ. But, if by the 'last days' we mean the very last days—the dying embers of human history before the final judgement—we can never say more than, 'none of us know'.

In practical terms, what this means is that we should live and plan in the expectation that the world will still be here when our children, grandchildren and great-grandchildren are as old as we are now. As Bible-believing Christians, we must hold this in tension with the expectation that the Lord could return at any time. But while the world still turns, while summer and winter, springtime and harvest continue, we must also continue to seek the good of the generations who are younger than us, and even those who are yet to come.

The whole counsel of God

The proposition being put forward in this book is that, in the light of these present judgements which God is bringing on the world, *this is a time for churches and Christians to think very deeply, and very biblically, about the most radical and foundational realities which concern God, man and the whole universe*. It is a time to work out a mature, robust and wholly biblical, Christian worldview, and to shepherd a rising generation, equipping them for the great tasks which face them.

We need, in other words, far more than the preaching of a 'simple gospel message'. We must never abandon preaching Jesus Christ and him crucified, resurrected, ascended and glorified. We must declare these things fervently and frequently. Woe to us if we preach not the gospel!

But, if I can put it this way, we must preach a 'thick' gospel rather than a 'thin' gospel; I mean that we must do exactly what Paul did during his three years in Ephesus—'I did not shrink from declaring to you the whole counsel of God' (Acts 20:27). What does this mean? How big is that 'whole counsel'? Probably bigger now than it has been for several centuries; by which I mean that we cannot assume,

Chapter 4

even in our churches, a level of biblical and theological literacy that we could even twenty years ago.

What are the building blocks of this Christian worldview? We need to begin, unapologetically, at the very beginning. A flimsy grasp of the importance of the doctrine of Creation; confusion around the truth of God as the Creator of a good creation, which was made from nothing—a creation which is altogether distinct from the Creator himself—is like a house of cards that is built on quicksand.

For that reason, what are often called God's 'creation ordinances' need to be rigorously upheld, taught and embraced: the human race created uniquely in the image of God, as male and female; the institution of marriage and the family; the dignity and honour of all our work and rest; the establishment of the Sabbath.

We must go further still; our field of view must be considerably wider than what is explicitly taught in the first two chapters of Genesis. We need to survey what we might call *the entire divine architecture*, which comprehends not only the Creation in its Adamic, pre-fallen state, but the world as it has become, both as a result of the Fall, and as a result of the Redemption which comes through Jesus Christ.

We need a realistic understanding of the many and terrible ways that sin has affected the human race and the whole world, which include sickness—both physical and mental—death and war; we need a fully-fledged understanding of how humanity is constituted, not only in terms of each individual, but in the many and complex relationships in which we all operate. This means we need a clear grasp of how God has established the family, the Church and the nation state.

We need to be in a position to evaluate the currents of thought which are eroding the confidence of many Christians in the Western World today, including the momentous debates about climate change and the future of the earth, with all the profound theological, as well as economic, implications.

The weapons of our warfare

But it is not only 'doctrine' that we need, if by that we mean information only. The whole of God's revelation is given to us, not only that we should know what to *think*, but know how to *live*, how to function and to interact while simultaneously being citizens of God's heavenly Kingdom and the earthly 'Babylon', where we are found. For too long, 'doctrine' and 'ethics' have inhabited separate houses; it is time to marry them together and knock down the dividing wall of partition.

To give one very prominent and pressing example: in an increasingly polarized and acerbic culture, which is especially evidenced on certain social media platforms, God's people need to learn how to wage war with alertness,

Chapter 4

courage and grace. Paul tells us that 'the weapons of our warfare are not of the flesh but have divine power to destroy strongholds' (2 Cor. 10:1-4). There is a great battle to be fought, and it needs to be fought with love and integrity—but also, at times, with subtlety and wit.

For example, with the Corinthians, there were times when Paul employed 'the meekness and gentleness of Christ' (2 Cor. 10:1), when his heart was 'wide open' (2 Cor. 6:11); but on other occasions he found it necessary to employ irony, as when he tells them:

> For you gladly bear with fools, being wise yourselves! For you bear it if someone makes slaves of you, or devours you, or takes advantage of you, or puts on airs, or strikes you in the face. To my shame, I must say, we were too weak for that!
>
> (2 Cor. 11:19-21)

In a similar manner, Paul expresses his wish that the Judaizers, who have misled the Galatians, should emasculate themselves (Gal. 5:12)—we presume this is not a literal desire on Paul's part, but rather a forceful and memorable way of ensuring that his argument in relation to circumcision would gain greater traction in his readers' minds. On other occasions, Paul is not afraid to name and shame his opponents, as in 2 Timothy where he calls out Hymenaeus and Philetus (2 Tim. 2:17) and Alexander the coppersmith (2 Tim. 4:14).

The Lord Jesus urged his disciples to be 'wise as serpents and innocent as doves' (Matt. 10:16). Whether we more closely resemble one or the other of these creatures will depend on our evaluation of circumstances, the conflicts in which we are engaging, and the character of those with whom we are interacting.

Entering through the side doors

To attempt the task of setting out a biblical worldview for the twenty-first century, in a comprehensive and systematic fashion, would be a major undertaking, and also an unrealistic one. This book is no such attempt. To enter this vast mansion through the front door, as it were, would simply be too daunting and demanding; to be exhaustive would certainly be exhausting, for both author and readers. Instead, I will be using the present judgements of *pestilence*, *sword*, *famine* and *captivity* somewhat like side-doors into a building, venturing through these entrances to consider how these significant events, and above all responses to them, shed light on the spiritual and moral health of Christians and churches, and what lessons we might learn at such a time as this.

So, this is what I will attempt to do, and my starting point is the early months of 2020, when the world began to change as it had not for a very long time.

Part two:
Pestilence

5 Disease and Death

This is the reality: the virus is there. We have to face it, but face it like a man ... not like a kid. We'll confront the virus with reality. That's life. We're all going to die one day.[1]

Jair Bolsonaro, President of Brazil

Like a cloud the size of a man's hand which erupted out of a clear blue sky and ominously expanded to dominate the entire firmament, Covid-19 seemingly sprang from nowhere and in a matter of weeks filled our horizons, before making us all run for cover.

My weekly diary entries in February and March 2020 document this inexorable trend; I include excerpts here exactly as I recorded them at the time; they have not been exaggerated in the editing process to which this book has been subjected!

> *Monday 3 February*: 'The spread of the Coronavirus from Wuhan has been a major item in the news for over a week now.'

> *Monday 10 February*: 'Meanwhile the Coronavirus continues to spread, with nearly a thousand fatalities now confirmed.'

Chapter 5

Monday 17 February: 'But the continued spread of the Coronavirus seems to grow in significance.'

Monday 24 February: 'But the Coronavirus continues to dominate, approaching 80,000 cases worldwide and rocketing to 155 in Italy alone. More and more experts are speaking of it as a "pandemic" which may be impossible to contain.'

Monday 2 March: 'But the Coronavirus assumes ever greater proportions, with the number of cases rocketing in South Korea and Italy, rising sharply in France and Germany, and increasing from 23 to 36 yesterday in this country. Today, as the Government's Cobra meeting is convened, all sorts of measures might be discussed as the "containment" phase seems to be over.'

Monday 9 March: 'This was the week in which Coronavirus ceased to be simply "news" on the media and began to affect day-to-day life. The number of recorded cases in the UK soared from 23 on Monday morning to 272 by Sunday afternoon. Our local primary school was closed because the mother of a child had contracted the virus, but it opened again on Friday. By Saturday, large empty spaces had begun to appear on supermarket shelves; there was huge demand for toilet roll, cleaning products, medication for colds and 'flu, and ready meals. As far as possible, life kept going for us as normal.'

Monday 16 March: 'We now seem to be approaching a kind of war footing, although life here in the UK goes on much more normally than it does across much of Europe, where schools, workplaces, restaurants and many shops have been shut, and borders are being closed. Even so, it is eerily quiet this morning on a clear and still day, with fewer planes than usual rumbling their way towards Heathrow. Indeed, a travel ban between the United States and the whole of Europe has been imposed, the UK and Ireland now included. Yesterday it was revealed that there have been 1,372 positive results for COVID-19 in the UK, with 35 deaths. Ventilators will be mass-produced, and many private beds commandeered. Many are arguing that the UK Government is not acting stringently enough; there is an idea that a certain proportion of the population ought to be exposed to the virus in order that "herd immunity" might be developed, whereas in countries where a "lockdown" is imposed, numbers of infections should (as reportedly in China) dramatically reduce. One feature of this crisis is how it accentuates different opinions on

CHAPTER 5

either side, as with Brexit—but life and health are at stake, adding a whole new dimension.'

Monday 23 March: 'This was the week when everything changed. It was a week unlike any other in living memory, a week more extraordinary and far-reaching in its consequences than any other, surely, since the outbreak of world war. Indeed, a number of the restrictions which began to be imposed this week went further than anything in the Second World War.

'It was a week in which events moved at breakneck speed and yet, perhaps for that very reason, it felt interminably long. It hardly seemed possible that just last weekend, 14–15 March, everything in Britain was still going on as normal. But now the country has moved into new measures: even the "elbow-bumps" of last weekend seem a distant memory. Boris Johnson, who when elected last December with a strong overall majority must have thought that Brexit would be front and centre of government policy throughout his term in office, now finds that Coronavirus has not so much dwarfed Brexit as rendered it almost entirely irrelevant. Rishi Sunak, the new Chancellor, will ever be associated with this present crisis. He has responded in a way that would seem incredible at any other time—

directing hundreds of billions of pounds not only to keep businesses afloat, but to guarantee the wages of millions of employees who would otherwise see their earnings vanish. What was called "austerity" under the Coalition Government of 2010–15 will seem laughable compared to what must surely lie ahead.

'Boris' daily press conferences at 5 pm have become a regular feature of life. As the week progressed, pubs, cafes, restaurants, theatres, cinemas and gyms were firstly discouraged and then completely closed down. Schools across the country closed, with only children of "key workers" being allowed to attend. "Social distancing" became the order of the day; for the time being, people are still free to leave their homes and enjoy the fresh air and the parks, but those freedoms look as if they might be withdrawn soon, because too many people are not taking the threat seriously enough. And serious it is, undoubtedly. Officially Britain now has nearly 6,000 cases and about 280 deaths, but that puts us only two weeks behind Italy with its nearly 60,000 cases and over 5,000 deaths. We are probably only a day or two from "lockdown". With or without this, we will surely see, very soon, our National Health Service being stretched to breaking point, with agonizing decisions needed to

Chapter 5

be taken by hospital staff. The mass production of ventilators is now being requested from various manufacturing plants, not unlike the munitions industry of the world wars.'

Monday 30 March: 'And so last Monday evening, at 8.30pm, the Prime Minister announced that the nation was going into lockdown. All shops except "essentials" are closed, and people may only leave their homes for exercise once per day, and not in groups of more than two unless they are part of a household. This had become absolutely necessary.

'Perhaps the novelty factor meant that this week was not as trying or testing as it could have been, and the fine, cloudless weather certainly helped. But it will not be easy. The number of cases and of deaths—1,228 in the UK at the last count—is growing inexorably. For my own part, I was preoccupied a good deal with technology this week: getting ... [the online video conferencing platform] to work successfully for prayer meetings and finding video-recording software that I could combine with ... [a well-known video sharing website]. This has been challenging, and it is a steep learning curve for me and for others, but by Sunday there were two quite passable videos ready for the congregation—and others—to watch.

'Prince Charles, Boris Johnson and Matt Hancock, the Health Secretary, have all tested positive for Covid. As yet, no one personally known to me by name has tested positive, but this will surely change before long. There is open talk now about the lockdown continuing for as long as six months, which hardly bears thinking about.'

What on earth was going on? Did Covid-19 qualify as a biblical pestilence, and what exactly is 'pestilence' anyway?

What is 'pestilence'?

'Pestilence', as we have seen, is a word which is found frequently in Jeremiah, as well as Ezekiel. Jeremiah 15:2 is somewhat unusual in that the Hebrew word translated as 'pestilence' is *mavet*, rather than the more common *dever*.

Whereas *dever* is generally used for a plague, a disease, such as the one which struck the livestock in Egypt (Exod. 9:3), *mavet* has the more basic thrust of 'death' and may not always be as a result of disease. It is the 'death' which Pharaoh pleads to be taken away by the LORD, as he surveys the disaster caused by the locusts (Exod. 10:17). It is the 'death' which is set before the people of Israel as the opposite of 'life', between which they are to choose (Deut. 30:15, 19). It is often understood as a death penalty, whether administered through human instrumentality, as in Deuteronomy 21:22 when a man was hanged for a

Chapter 5

crime, or here in Jeremiah 15:2, as the execution of God's own displeasure and wrath.

The placing of *mavet* alongside the words for 'sword' and 'famine' make it most likely that this 'death' is because of disease, so that 'pestilence' is a plausible translation. It is not that *dever* describes a pestilence that does not result in death—Exodus 9:6 tells us bleakly that 'all the livestock of the Egyptians died'—but the emphasis is more on the plague than on the death.

At any rate, a biblical 'pestilence' is a disease which leads to death. And, although the word 'pandemic' does not appear in any English versions of the Bible, this is the force of both *dever* and *mavet*: a widespread disease, affecting a sizeable number of people, if not necessarily the entire human race, and one which in many cases will lead to *death*. When Covid-19 came along, people began talking about death more than they had for many decades.

But what *is* death?

Pestilence which leads to death

Death is always a tragedy; death should never be brushed aside as something that is 'natural' in any sense. When people—whether Christian or non-Christian—speak glibly about human death as if it were comparable to a washing machine or an old car breaking down, they suppress the inner voice –the evidence of eternity in their hearts (Eccles. 3:11), which screams 'No, no, never! Death is always wrong, always horrible, always unnatural!' Death is 'the last enemy' (1 Cor. 15:26), the foul, ugly, destructive stalker and snatcher of human life.

Death brings bereavement, and bereavement brings tears. No words in the Bible are more moving than the description of Joseph's grief after his father Jacob had 'breathed his last and was gathered to his people'. We read that 'Joseph fell on his father's face and wept over him and kissed him' (Gen. 49:33–50:1). There is nothing sentimental or merely cultural in Joseph's expression; this was manly as well as human grief, a right and indeed righteous expression of deep visceral pain at the parting of death.[2]

And in case we wonder whether the cross and empty of tomb of Christ utterly transforms the pain of bereavement for Christians—after all, has not death lost its sting? (1 Cor. 15:55–56)—we are directed to the account of the martyrdom of Stephen. The words of Acts 8:2 are no less poignant than those of Genesis 50:1: 'Devout men buried Stephen and made great lamentation over him.' That meant a lot of noise, and many tears. The knowledge that Stephen had been received into heaven by the risen Jesus did not dull the dreadful loss and pain felt by his companions.

As is well known, Jesus himself wept (John 11:35) at the tomb of Lazarus. Since he was about to raise him to life, we might wonder whether these were akin to crocodile tears.

CHAPTER 5

We need not wonder. All confusion is removed at a stroke by what we read two verses earlier, that 'when Jesus saw her [Mary, Lazarus' sister] weeping, and the Jews who had come with her also weeping, he was deeply moved in his spirit and greatly troubled' (John 11:33). The righteous, holy soul of the Son of God was deeply assaulted and repulsed by the incursion of death and bereavement into human life.

Death is a tragedy. But we need to know how to handle it; not simply deaths which happen 'out there' somewhere, but death itself—above all, your and my inevitable death.

Disease, death and data

Some weeks before the imposition of lockdown in Britain, the statistics industry was in full swing. As a former teacher of mathematics and statistics myself, it was difficult to resist the appeal of the numbers, however macabre they may be. The *Worldometer* website continues to clock up the Covid data: it tells me today that so far there have been 695,336,700 cases and 6,915,752 deaths. Rather encouragingly, it also informs me that 667,391,148 people have recovered from Covid-19.[3] I cannot be certain whether my own recovery in January 2021 has been included in that figure; I suspect not. I do not recall anyone ever asking me.

From very early on, it was clear that the data generated by Covid-19 would need judicious interpretation. In the

Worldometer listing of countries, for example, Iceland and India were found quite close together, by virtue of beginning with the same letter. But even a passing acquaintance with the cultures of these two countries—the most obvious one being that for every one Icelander there are around four thousand Indians—would suggest that the interpretation of Icelandic Covid data and the interpretation of Indian Covid data might not be identical disciplines.[4] The true death toll from Covid-19, at any point in time, must always be a matter of substantial conjecture. The 6.9 million *Worldometer* figure, quoted above, seems to be well on the conservative side; the World Health Organisation suggested a figure of 15 million.[5]

Statistical analysis of pandemics, particularly of the number of deaths that took place during them, can only be a very inexact science. We have records of plagues in the ancient world: the Antonine Plague, the Plagues of Cyprian and of Justinian, which carried off substantial proportions of the Roman populace. The Black Death of the mid-fourteenth century, according to a number of authorities, wiped out between a third and a half of the European population. When the Spanish and Portuguese Conquistadores penetrated Central and South America in the following centuries, they brought with them a cocktail of European diseases—among them smallpox, which ravaged the native peoples who had never had any

Chapter 5

exposure to such infections. It appears that *pestilence*, and not *sword*, slew the Aztec and Inca civilizations.

Coming to more recent times, the 1918–20 Flu Pandemic, known rather misleadingly as the 'Spanish Flu',[6] is reckoned to have infected as many as 500 million people with the H1N1 virus, and to have killed around one-tenth of this figure, with an alarmingly high death rate among people under the age of forty. The later flu pandemics of the twentieth century, occurring in 1957–58, 1968–69 and 1977–79, respectively known as 'Asian Flu', 'Hong Kong Flu' and 'Russian Flu', pale by comparison; as far as we can ascertain, none of them claimed more than 4 million lives worldwide—considerably below the most cautious estimate for Covid-19.

If the severity of a disease is measured by the number of deaths, then Covid-19 made some alarming inroads, especially during March and April 2020. The vastly increased death rate in British care homes has been well documented: there were as many as 6,331 excess deaths in the week ending 24 April.[7] This followed a much-criticized policy of discharging patients to care homes from overflowing hospital wards without testing being administered; and the care homes which received them were, in these early stages, often under-resourced in terms of both testing kits and PPE (Personal Protective Equipment).

In summary, it seems fair to conclude that Covid-19 has

been a significant pandemic, even on a large enough scale to warrant the biblical tag, 'pestilence'.

Universal death

When Covid-19 struck, death and bereavement became part of media reporting and everyday conversation in a way that was unprecedented, certainly in my lifetime. The UK daily death tally from Covid-19, ripping through the one-thousand barrier in April 2020, then pushing two thousand the following January, somehow produced an impression that death itself, from any and every cause, was some new, strange and terrifying and phenomenon.

The reality has been that something in the region of 1,500 deaths per day, from all causes, has been the norm for several years. But relatively few people gave this any thought pre-Covid. The impression given was that deaths from Covid-19 belonged to a separate category to every other kind of death. While dying from Covid-19 may be a very nasty experience—especially if death took place without any medical intervention which might ameliorate its unpleasantness—the fact remains that unpleasant deaths had been happening for centuries, affecting people of all ages, long before March 2020.

But what is an 'unpleasant' death? Can any death be described as 'pleasant'?

The point is that the *cause* of death, or the circumstances of death, should never be allowed to eclipse the inescapable

Chapter 5

brute *fact* of death. The fact that we are all going to die is, at the end of the day, of far greater importance than questions about the way we die. Will I live to a great age, or will I die relatively young? Will my death be lingering, or will it come quickly? Will I die in some tragic accident, or it will it be as the result of 'natural' causes? It would be heartless, as well as unrealistic, to entirely dismiss these types of questions. When a young child dies, for example, it is a heart-breaking tragedy for everyone concerned; only a person of bloodless insensitivity can remain unmoved at such a time. From time to time, we hear of the brutal and sadistic torture of small children, leading to their deaths, and every few months, it seems, sometimes more frequently, we receive harrowing reports of the latest 'school shooting' from the United States.[8]

But whether George Bernard Shaw ever said that death was 'the ultimate statistic—one out of every one person dies', is irrelevant; the incontestable but widely overlooked fact is that death is universal. The Bible says it best of all: 'it is appointed for man to die once, and after that comes judgement' (Heb. 9:27). The Covid pandemic might have brought that realization closer to home for many people, but there is little evidence that it led to a profound level of reflection about matters of ultimate importance.

It was not all that different in Jesus' time. In Luke Chapter 13, we read about two tragic and violent events:

the massacre of some worshipping Galileans by the Roman governor Pontius Pilate, and the collapse of a tower in Siloam, killing eighteen people. These were the 'headlines' of the day, attracting a great deal of attention. And Jesus anticipated the questions that people were asking at the time:

> Do you think that these Galileans were worse sinners than all the other Galileans, because they suffered in this way? No, I tell you; but unless you repent, you will all likewise perish. Or those eighteen on whom the tower in Siloam fell and killed them: do you think that they were worse offenders than all the others who lived in Jerusalem? No, I tell you; but unless you repent, you will all likewise perish.
>
> (Luke 13:2–5)

The parallels between these incidents and Covid-19 are not exact. We did not hear many people suggesting that people died from Covid because they were 'worse sinners' than others. But in this respect, there is a parallel: some deaths appear to be more newsworthy than others.

When a 'pestilence' like Covid-19 strikes—when God brings such a judgement upon the earth—what is the number one lesson he might be teaching us? It can only be this: that death, every death, is a tragedy and that all deaths are newsworthy, starting with my own. I need to

Chapter 5

know why I must die, why everyone must die, and whether there is anything at all I can do in the face of it.

Eternal death

Jesus gets to the very heart of the matter on another occasion, as he speaks to a crowd of people—many of them hostile to him—in Jerusalem at the time of the Feast of Tabernacles. In John 8:24, he speaks words of breathtaking earnestness: 'I told you that you would die in your sins, for unless you believe that I am he you will die in your sins.'

We should notice the solemn repetition: 'die in your sins'. When a doctor has some difficult news to tell a patient, he must not talk around the problem or speak opaquely. He must give the message as clearly and unmistakably as he can. The same is true of a judge who is about to pass sentence on a criminal. If this is the case with a doctor or a judge, it is far more so when Jesus, the Son of God, speaks to people about matters of eternal destiny.

What does Jesus mean by 'you will die in your sins'? He means to die *in a state of sin*; to die and to remain dead without forgiveness and pardon; to die outside the saving love of Christ, with all the terrible consequences that will follow, which Paul describes in his Second Letter to the Thessalonians: to 'suffer the punishment of eternal

Disease and death

destruction, away from the presence of the Lord and from the glory of his might' (2 Thes. 1:9).

This is not annihilation. This is not even unconscious existence or semi-existence. It is an experience of unending conscious torment, of agonizing regret and sorrow, of desperate isolation and above all of utter hopelessness; there is no way out, no way back, no way forward. Everything good and pleasant is banished from this existence. To 'die in your sins' is to be in a place where there are no smiles, no laughter, no sunshine, no blue skies, no skies at all, no friends, no family, no music, no beauty, no pleasure; and what is more, no relief, no comfort, no second chance, no 'maybes', no hope. The Bible does not allow us to entertain any 'get out clauses' from hell, once the sinner is there.

The consequences of sin are infinitely more dreadful than the consequences of Covid-19. But the big point is that they are one hundred percent certain, and one hundred percent universal. So why are they not more newsworthy? It is because Satan, the author of sin, has 'blinded the minds of the unbelievers, to keep them from seeing the light of the gospel of the glory of Christ, who is the image of God' (2 Cor. 4:4).

The prayer of many Christians, when the first wave of Covid struck, was that many souls would be alerted to the brevity of life and the certainty of death. Has this prayer been answered? Maybe, at a local level, it has; perhaps you

Chapter 5

are acquainted with striking instances of people who were awakened from their spiritual slumber as a direct result of the Pandemic. But I would venture to say that this has not been a widespread phenomenon. It might take another pandemic. It might take something more.

'The wages of sin is death', says Paul in Romans 6:23. Yes it is, and not just the first death but what the Book of Revelation calls 'the second death' (Rev. 2:11; 20:6, 14; 21:8), eternal death.

But that is not the whole of that verse, and neither should we quote it as if it were. To my shame I admit that I have often done exactly this, which is like preaching Good Friday without mentioning Easter Sunday. The verse continues: 'but the free gift of God is eternal life in Christ Jesus our Lord.' We must not preach death in isolation or preach the fear of death as if it were the only or even the main motivation for people to come to Christ. We must proclaim instead that Jesus Christ, by his death *and* resurrection, 'abolished death and brought life and immortality to light through the gospel' (2 Tim. 1:10).

If Covid-19 drew *death* to people's attention, our prayer must certainly be that it will also cause people to think a little more deeply about what *life* really is.

6 Life or liberty?

The power of community to create health is far greater than any physician, clinic or hospital.[1]

Mark Hyman

At eleven o'clock on the morning of Tuesday 17 March 2020, as Britain accelerated towards inevitable lockdown, I stepped out of our house, turned left, and gaped with amazement at the empty pavement stretching a quarter of a mile ahead with not a single soul to be seen. I had never seen it so utterly devoid of people. This was not only eerie; it felt nothing less than dystopian.

A few minutes later I walked past our nearest fast-food burger restaurant; seeing someone I knew sitting there, enjoying her coffee, I went in and urged her to get up and leave as quickly as she could. What if every surface in that restaurant was contaminated with Covid-19? It would be an exaggeration to say that I bundled her out, but only a slight exaggeration.

'Scared New World'?

Has any landscape ever been altered so dramatically, so completely, so rapidly? New vocabulary became part of our everyday speech: the previously unfamiliar

Chapter 6

'Coronavirus', which back in February we had to keep looking up on our mobile devices, gave way to the far briefer and more permanent 'Covid' by the middle of March. 'Social distancing', 'herd immunity' and 'self-isolation', terms which would have made most of us blink with incomprehension a few weeks earlier, were common currency by the end of the month. Soon we would become acquainted with SAGE (Scientific Advisory Group for Emergencies), bubbles, PPE, testing kits, super-spreaders, contact tracing, mask mandates, variants, vaccines (see how many of the drug companies you can remember?), the rule-of-six, PCR, lateral flow, Alpha, Delta, Omicron ... let the reader compile his or her own Covid glossary yet further still.

That warm and sunny spring, as horse chestnut trees blossomed and furtive souls ventured out into parks for their daily exercise, remarkable new phenomena emerged: the taped-off park benches and children's playgrounds; the little shimmies that pedestrians performed when they passed each other, as if they were negotiating a narrow precipice; the newly-eroded track running parallel to the tarmacked footpath, and exactly two metres away from it; sharp and disapproving glances directed towards people with the temerity to stop and sit on the grass for a few minutes; the mutual uncertainty and unease when a familiar face approached. Were we or were we not allowed to stop and talk? For how long, and at what distance from each other?

Indeed, what were we now 'allowed' to do? Certain practices had become *verboten*, whether by explicit government decree or by implicit social expectation. Leaving your home to take a walk for more than hour, driving fifty miles or so to the coast, sitting on a beach, hugging, singing, buying something other than food from the supermarket; if these activities were not all expressly banned, we certainly sensed that they were being frowned upon.

The world had been hit by something that it had never expected. Yes, this was surely an 'Act of God', like the Armenian earthquake of 1988, or the more recent Boxing Day Tsunami of 2004. But this was different, this was global, this was universal. We were all caught up in it together. Governments across the world sensed that they had no choice but to act, and to do so swiftly.

It is not easy, several years on, to recall just how unnerving the early weeks of the pandemic were: the fear that in Britain the National Health Service would quickly be overwhelmed and that, without intervention, 510,000 people would die in the first three months of the pandemic. But in March and April 2020, very few voices were being raised in strong protest. Television footage of Covid victims gasping for breath outside overcrowded Italian hospitals would have unnerved anyone.

Chapter 6

But, for all that we were told to 'follow the science', this was not Aldous Huxley's *Brave New World*. Instead, it was the Scared New World.

'I love you—so keep away!'

Among the new words entering our vocabulary was the sinister, clanging 'lockdown'. If I had ever used that word in the pre-Covid era—and I am not altogether sure that I ever did—I would have understood it to mean the locking down, or perhaps locking *up*, of violent prisoners in their cells to guard against the risk of riot or something similar. That such restrictions might be imposed on peaceful citizens in whole cities or countries, due to illness, was a completely alien concept.

During the Swine Flu pandemic of 2009, a five-day lockdown was imposed in Mexico, but this barely caused a stir in the international media.[2] Yet, the implementation of travel restrictions in Wuhan on 23 January 2020, followed by its extension to other cities in Hubei Province the following day, set the stage for the massive expansion of lockdown policies. By 3 April, just ten weeks later, more than 3.9 billion people—over half the world's population—were under some form of lockdown.[3] If it worked in the Peoples' Republic of China, then it could work in the democracies of Western Europe.

How did people in Britain respond? The answer is that they accepted lockdown—or at least they did so publicly—

with a good deal less resistance than the Government had initially anticipated. It came to be seen as a matter of corporate duty, expressed very audibly by the way in which people stood at their windows and doors at 8 o'clock every Thursday evening, not only to 'clap for carers', but to bang pots, pans and even wheelie-bins.

A new dimension was being added to the concept of civic virtue. Although the choice of two metres as a minimum for social distancing was an arbitrary figure— it was only one metre in France and in other countries— people sought to stick to it rigidly, to the point where it became acceptable to criticize people if they shared a photograph of themselves with a friend in which the separation between them appeared to be something less than two metres. We had all suddenly adopted a 'new normal' (horrible expression!) in which the way to express care and concern for other people was to keep as far away from them as possible.

And all this ran completely contrary to every healthy human instinct. Tenderness between human beings is an attractive gravitational force, not a repulsive one. Love, affection, concern, the desire to help and to encourage others; all these find natural expression in physical closeness. But during lockdown, the only way grandparents could get close to their grandchildren was if they ensured that a windowpane divided them. There were pictures of elderly residents in care homes hugging

Chapter 6

their relatives—but only doing so when separated by a sterilized (and sterile) layer of transparent plastic.

That instinctual human yearning to embrace a loved one now had to be stifled. If you gave in to that urge, you might find yourself the victim of dirty looks, the meddling of 'curtain-twitchers', or even a call or a text from a well-meaning comrade who felt it necessary to administer a personal rebuke. This whole state of affairs ran completely counter to the way in which human beings are wired, so as to be quite unnatural and, inevitably, unworkable.

'Look them in the eyes.'

We now know all too well that some of the highest authorities in the land, the very legislators of these Covid restrictions, eventually fell afoul of the laws they had themselves established. There was widespread and wholly justified anger at the blatant hypocrisy that was uncovered: at the very time that socializing, drinking and partying were going on in the loftiest corridors of political power, millions of people conscientiously stuck to the 'rules' and were prevented from being at the bedside of their dying relatives, or indeed at their funerals.

But was it not inevitable that it would come to this, eventually?

In January 2021, as daily Covid-19 deaths soared to new pinnacles in the weeks before the earliest vaccines had taken effect, the Government launched its hard-hitting

'Look Them In The Eyes' campaign.[4] They explained the rationale behind it:

> Everyone across the UK is being asked 'Can you look them in the eyes and tell them you're helping by staying at home?' in a new government advertising campaign which will act as a stark reminder to the public of the ongoing impact of COVID-19 and the extreme pressures facing frontline workers.
>
> The powerful new campaign will run across TV, radio, press, digital, out-of-home advertising and social media, looking into the eyes of NHS staff and COVID-19 patients and documenting their emotions. It will air for the first time on Friday evening (22 January 2021) on ITV and Channel 4.

Startled eyes looked out helplessly from faces covered by oxygen masks, creating the sense that you and I, members of the public, were to be held personally responsible for that poor individual's present predicament. What if they died? Perhaps some of their blood might stain your hands and mine. There were other forms of wording which were even more probing: 'Look her in the eyes and tell her you never bend the rules!'

Brutal honesty is needed here. Is there a single person in the country, indeed in the world, who could 'look' every other member of the population 'in the eyes' and assure them they had never failed to do everything in their

Chapter 6

power to halt the spread of the Covid virus? How many people nodded vigorously when asked if they supported lockdown measures, but later, when they thought no one was watching, contradicted their words by their actions?

It should have come as no surprise at all to discover that people *did* bend the rules, *did* break the rules, *did* flout the rules—yes, some more subtly, some more egregiously. Some broke the rules more conspicuously by virtue of the high office which they held and criticism of their actions is undeniably warranted, the more so if they were publicly urging people to 'follow the rules' at the very time they were privately disregarding them.

But why *were* these 'rules' so difficult to follow—indeed, we might maintain, frankly impossible, if followed to the very letter? It all has to do with what it means to be a human being, made in the image of God.

We are all lepers now.

Yet surely these regulations—face coverings and social distancing being the obvious examples—were for our good ... were they not? Did it not make sense to follow them?

There is one clear instance in the Bible where both face coverings and social distancing were strictly mandated: in the case of the leper. We see them both being commanded in Leviticus 13:45–46, where instructions are given to 'leprous persons':

Life or Liberty?

> The leprous person who has the disease shall wear torn clothes and let the hair of his head hang loose, and he shall cover his upper lip [face covering] and cry out, 'Unclean, unclean.' He shall remain unclean as long as he has the disease. He is unclean. He shall live alone. His dwelling shall be outside the camp [social distancing].

To be sure, no Government guidance ever went quite as far as this. But we should notice two obvious features of this Mosaic legislation: (1) the 'leprous person' was an *exception*, not the rule, and was separated from the rest of society; and (2) the 'leprous person' was unclean *only for a time*: 'as long as he had the disease'.

When Covid restrictions were introduced, the whole population effectively became 'leprous people', not just those who were known to be infected. Every human being you saw outside your home was a potential spreader of Covid-19—someone to be feared and shunned. And that situation persisted for many weeks and indeed months, not only through the first lockdown of March–July 2020, but into the second, third and fourth lockdowns which followed.

People understood why they were doing this. It seemed to make sense. Whether it was 'flattening the curve', or subsequently buying some time until the vaccines took effect or trying to dodge the hyper-infectious Omicron

CHAPTER 6

variant of the winter of 2021–22—even when we had been jabbed once, twice, three times—we were prepared to live this way for as long as was needed. It was all about saving lives, after all.

Some of our ancestors, in the two world wars, nobly and heroically sacrificed their lives to secure freedom for their children and their grandchildren. Perhaps, now, the situation was reversed: the Covid generation willingly gave up their *freedoms* to save other people's *lives*. Was this not equally noble and heroic? We could go on living like 'leprous people' far longer than anyone told us to, if it might save an extra life or two.

But is this a symmetrical arrangement? It all depends on what we understand by human life. If every life is understood to be essentially biological, like the life of the pet hamster, or the life of the hydrangeas growing in my back garden, then we should all be satisfied as long as our stomachs are filled, our hearts are beating and we are able to breathe like every other living organism. The hamster needs feeding every day or two and could also do with his cage being cleaned. My hydrangeas benefit from a shady position, plenty of watering, and soil of whatever pH is conducive to the desired colours.

As long as I am well-watered and fed, so that I am medically alive, and in sufficiently robust physical health, so that I am not in agony of body, that is what really matters. Perhaps that is all that matters?

'One More Day', all on my phone[5]

Covid lockdowns meant that a huge proportion of people stayed at home behind closed doors for most of the time and that included children, teenagers and young adults, in addition to the elderly and the vulnerable. These people ate, they drank, they slept, they even obtained a modicum of exercise; by and large they remained *alive*. But what kind of life was it?

On 16 May 2022, the BBC aired a documentary, *Facing My Childhood*, featuring Joe Wicks, 'the nation's favourite PE teacher'. In the course of the programme, Wicks stated:

> I receive hundreds of letters and messages a day from people telling me about their mental health struggles and their worries for their children. I thought by making this and sharing my story, I could uplift and help other families going through similar situations.[6]

A few weeks earlier, the *British Medical Journal* had reported some alarming data in relation to this same issue of mental health among children. Three of their key findings are given here:

> The impact of covid-19 (sic) has led to an unprecedented increase in demand for mental health services for children and young people in England, most notably for eating disorders.[7]

Chapter 6

> Between April and September 2021, there was an 81% increase in referrals for children and young people's mental health services compared with the same period in 2019. The increase for adults (19 years and over) in the same period was 11%.
>
> The number of children and young people waiting to start treatment for a suspected eating disorder quadrupled from pre-pandemic levels to 2083 by September 2021.

What Covid lockdowns appear to have revealed, then, is that children and teenagers do not exactly thrive under such conditions. Being stuck behind four walls all day, with minimal social interaction—except through screens for several hours—appears to affect their mental and emotional equilibrium. And it seems to have a particularly detrimental impact on their eating patterns.

Taped-off playgrounds, cancellation of sports fixtures, the substitution of the virtual for the physical; it may be some years before the full cumulative effect of lockdowns, on the younger generation especially, are fully known, but the total cost is likely to be incalculable. Why is this? It is because twenty-first-century secular governments, like twenty-first-century secular society in general, do not appreciate the inestimable value, indeed the divinely created and multifaceted glory, of every human life. The value of life is cheap and not held dear, as our Creator God intended.

Facing up to reality

Before March 2020, heads generally turned if someone wearing a surgical-style face mask made their way along the supermarket aisle. They might be worn routinely in cities like Beijing, owing to industrial pollution, but not in western cities. Although they were not made obligatory in indoor spaces in the UK until July of that year, they quickly became commonplace. And social distancing became *de rigueur* in the early stages of the pandemic.

In London in the autumn of 2023, it is still quite common to see people walking in the open air with a pale blue mask covering their face. There are no laws which forbid the wearing of face coverings, and neither should there be. And the amount of physical space that people maintain from others is entirely a matter of their choice. But that does not mean that masks and distances are morally and spiritually neutral matters. Far from it!

When God was about to create human beings, he heralded this great and climactic work with these words: 'Let *us* make man in *our* image, after *our* likeness' (Gen. 1:26). Discussions have continued throughout the centuries as to whether the first-person plural reflects the Trinitarian nature of God. This is a rich, fascinating and rewarding subject, and to my mind the evidence of

Chapter 6

the implicit Trinity in these words is compelling. But what matters here is that the God whose very nature is social and relational, creates human beings who are likewise social and relational. And social beings have *faces*. I cannot see my own face, except in a mirror, or perhaps in a selfie. Why do I have a face? So that other people can see me. My face is what I present to others. If you are told to 'look at' someone, you do not look at their left elbow or their right knee. You look at their *face*.

The human face matters, it is who we are; and the deliberate covering of it should be seen as a partial, but substantial, repudiation of our humanity. Wherever there have been free societies across the world, the whole human face has been shown unashamedly. The entire face—with eyes, nose and mouth clearly visible—is an essential part of the image of God in humanity. Our faces include our mouths for breathing and eating, but also for speaking and singing, for smiling and laughing, for a thousand-and-one expressions. Yes, you can partially gauge a person's emotions by looking at their eyes when their noses and mouths are covered, but it is a deeply frustrating experience—a bit like watching a football match in which one half of the pitch is hidden from view. Ask any preacher: the day the masks came off and I could see the congregation's mouths once more was a day of significant rejoicing on my part.

Nihilism and despair

Joe Wicks suffered from childhood mental health problems long before Covid-19 and its associated lockdowns. He is far from alone, because so did many other children in Britain and other countries, as did many adults. Since 2020, we have witnessed a steep rise in incidences of mental illness, so that it is not inaccurate to speak of a 'mental health pandemic'.

What Covid lockdowns did was to accentuate, and to throw a spotlight on, a crisis that had been brewing for generations. The root cause of the problem ultimately boils down to this: the way in which we answer the question, 'What is human life?'

In the previous chapter, we thought long and hard about the question, 'What is death?' Covid itself made us confront this question head on, or at least it should have done. But when the 'history of Covid' is written in future years, it will consist of far more than a series of studies in epidemiology, just as the best histories of World War Two are far more than narratives of military campaigns. 'Covid' is not simply a disease; it is a complex of tightly interrelated events, interpretations and responses, and the sociology of Covid will be scrutinized at least as much as its biology. The 'theology of Covid', too, deserves attention.

The predominant worldview of our present day, the

Chapter 6

worldview with which Covid has interacted, is that of scientism, materialism and evolutionism. By *scientism* I mean 'the view that the hard sciences—like chemistry, biology, physics, astronomy—provide the only genuine knowledge of reality'.[8] I do not mean *science*, which is a noble pursuit, its nobility enshrined in such biblical texts as Psalm 111:2: 'Great are the works of the Lord, studied by all who delight in them.' But scientism closes its mind to the possibility of an intelligent Creator and Designer. If the universe appears to exhibit the 'works' of a Higher Being, then this is nothing more than our own human interpretation, and an illusory one at that. Scientism breeds *materialism*, so-called 'nothing buttery'—the idea that there is 'nothing but' atoms and molecules, the various subatomic particles and associated forces. It is also the bedfellow of *evolutionism*—the theory that there is no purpose, no narrative, no intelligent personality behind the workings of the universe.

These are the assumptions that have directed scientific endeavour, more or less, for the best part of two centuries, and human life in today's society is interpreted through this grid, if it is interpreted at all. It is not that children and young people, or even most adults, articulate their worldview using vocabulary of this kind. But it is a fair description of where a great number of people stand in the early twenty-first-century Western World.

What is human life according to this perspective? It is

ultimately random, meaningless, arbitrary and pointless. There is no higher or deeper purpose to my life other than what I choose to make of it. And who am 'I' anyway? Are not 'I' and 'me' social constructs with no objective value? I might choose to assign certain subjective significance to myself and my life, but how can I be sure that anyone else will stand alongside me and support my claim to significance? I am all alone in this universe, with no solid place to stand. This is nihilism, this is nothingness, and this is ultimately despair. The surprise, if anything, is that there are not far *more* people of all ages with serious mental health disorders.

God of life, God of love

Into this desperate void, Christians need to speak with certainty, with confidence and with hope. This is the preaching of the 'thick' gospel which I described in Chapter 4. We must begin with the God who is the Creator and therefore the Designer, Owner, and Ruler of humanity, and of every human individual. We must explain passionately that our lives are not accidental, evolutionary, meandering streams which ultimately lead nowhere; life is the good creation of the God who has life in himself (John 5:26). 'Life' is not the accidental result of certain chemicals being found in a certain concentration, subject to certain atmospheric temperatures and pressures. Life is the creation of a personal God who has

Chapter 6

that life in himself; life originates only in the God who *is* our life.[9]

And this personal God is, as we have seen, a *tripersonal* God. As well as being the God who is life, he is the God who is love (1 John 4:8, 16)—Father, Son and Spirit united in mutual, eternal, perfect love. Nothing is more foundational to our created nature in God's image than this: that we are relational beings, created both to know and to be known. The epidemic of loneliness and societal and familial fracture long predates the epidemic of Covid. We are made for relationship, with one another as human beings, but ultimately to know and love God himself. Fathers and mothers may forsake us, but the Lord will take us in (Ps. 27:10).

This message of certainty, confidence and hope has been entrusted by God to his Church, and it is to the witness and worship of the Church that I now turn.

7 Connection and Communion

The true problem with virtual reality is that orientation is no longer possible. We have lost our points of reference to orient ourselves. The de-realized man is a disoriented man.[1]

Paul Virilio

Nearly four years on, it is not easy to recapture the complex swirl of responses and emotions that were circulating in our minds during that spring of 2020. There was heady excitement of an apocalyptic nature alongside a considerable level of fear. Would this virus sweep away most of the elderly members of our churches by Christmas? That dismal prospect was more than offset by the way in which many people, particularly the older ones who appeared to be most at risk, were asking, 'What might God be teaching us through all of this? What is he about to do with us, and in the world?'

In those early prayer meetings and discussions—adjusting to the new technology—we talked a good deal about the Lord shaking the heavens, the earth, the sea, the dry land and all the nations (Hag. 2:6–7). Our prayer was that this severe shaking may distinguish between the

Chapter 7

good and the bad fruit, and reveal who truly belonged to the Lord.

It was striking how many pastors chose to preach from Psalm 46:1–2 in the first two Sundays of lockdown:

> God is our refuge and strength,
> a very present help in trouble.
> Therefore we will not fear though the earth gives way,
> though the mountains be moved into the heart of
>   the sea.

This is exactly what seemed to be happening in the world—the very 'giving way' of the whole earth—and the people of God were responding with an attitude which was altogether healthy and God-honouring. The early signs looked promising. In the initial weeks of lockdown, many churches found that virtual prayer meetings were better attended than physical prayer meetings had been a few weeks earlier, and that new people were being reached via online ministry—people who might never have made contact without the intervention of the pandemic. We heard striking testimonies of conversions across the world. In a strange way, Covid seemed to be not only bringing the world together but bringing the Church together.

However, the novelty quickly wore off, and before April had turned to May, 'Covid fatigue' and 'lockdown fatigue' were already setting in. We were yearning to see one another's faces again—not on the screen, but in the flesh. Social interaction via randomly assigned video-conferencing-platform 'breakout rooms' might mean that you found yourself talking to people you would otherwise miss on a Sunday, but the limitations and frustrations of online conversation were keenly felt; when two people try to talk at the same time on these platforms, one is silenced by another, which is dispiriting for those who like to think a little longer before opening their mouths!

Church-lite

If Covid had struck in 2000, or perhaps even in 2010, the developed world could not have responded the way it did in 2020. The technological means simply did not exist. You could not simply 'Work From Home', take part in online school lessons or university lectures, or have a virtual appointment with your doctor. But the progress of the digital revolution meant that a wide variety of technological solutions to the Covid-19 crisis now presented themselves, and it seemed, quite frankly, a 'no-brainer' that they should be used to the full.

And churches fell in line with this; of course they did! Christian ministry moved online along with so many other human activities. Hardly any pastors paused to consider whether to stop holding services in their buildings. That decision had been taken for them. 'Church-lite' became the norm; even now a residue of it remains.

Chapter 7

But if we ask some probing questions, we may find that the experience of many Christians had been 'church-lite' for rather longer than the last three or four years. In the previous chapter we explored what it means to be a living human being; life is more than animal biology, we have faces and souls as well as femurs and cells. We need to pick up this argument and take it further: *what does it mean to belong to God's Church?*

To be quite specific, when 'Church' went from being a community—a society, a 'village' made up of diverse, physically-present people—to just one screen among many others, was anything vital and essential lost?

Even today, if a church member tells a pastor, 'I wasn't there on Sunday morning but I joined you online', can that pastor be wholly satisfied? It is better than nothing, yes; but did that member really 'join' with God's people? I am not speaking now about an elderly or infirm member who is housebound, for whom coming to church presents real physical challenges; I am addressing the able-bodied individual who, pre-Covid, would never have considered staying at home on a Sunday morning but is now inclined to do so because the option exists.

We earnestly need to recover both deep *theology*— the truth about God—and also the most profound *anthropology*—the biblical teaching about man. These come together in a robust and healthy doctrine of the

Church which is anchored in Scripture, as well as in historical understanding and practice.

Gnostic nonsense

Human beings are not pure spirits, as God is;[2] they are composed of body and soul, or flesh and spirit.[3] Essentially, man has a material part to his nature as well as an immaterial part, but the material and the immaterial are so closely intertwined that they cannot be separated, though they ought to be distinguished. We are embodied souls, psychosomatic wholes. To deny one or the other, or even to elevate one above the other, is to disparage human nature in its entirety as a good creation of God.

In the earliest centuries of the Christian era, the Church had to do battle with the Gnostic heresy. There are clear hints—for example in Colossians, 2 Timothy and 1 John—that an incipient version of Gnosticism was already corrupting the apostolic Church.

Full-blown Gnosticism taught that God, being pure spirit, had no part in the creation of physical matter, including humanity. Man was created not by God but by a lesser god, a so-called 'demiurge'. In Gnosticism, matter was viewed as necessarily evil, and therefore salvation was 'to escape from the bondage of the material existence and travel back to the home from which souls/spirits have fallen.'[4] Such an understanding of salvation had fundamentally catastrophic consequences for their

Chapter 7

doctrine of the Saviour, Christ himself; they viewed the Son of God as a heavenly messenger but denied every aspect of his embodied humanity: his incarnation, his physical suffering on the cross and his bodily resurrection.

A heretical view of Jesus Christ will inevitably result in a heretical view of the *Church* of Jesus Christ. We should not be surprised that the New Testament strenuously opposes this kind of dualism held by the Gnostics, whether we term it body-soul, flesh-spirit, or material-immaterial. The apostle Paul takes strong issue with the Corinthians, telling them that their bodies are temples of the Holy Spirit, that they are not their own and that, having been bought with a price, they are to *glorify God in their bodies* (1 Cor. 6:19–20). Their bodies are not incidental, they are to be redeemed along with their souls, and what believers do with their bodies matters in this present world. This is an essential part of their sanctification.

Therefore, New Testament worship and fellowship was wholly *embodied*. When the Church of God was enjoying the first vigorous flush of post-Pentecost youthfulness, their activities were communal and very physical: 'Day by day, attending the temple together and breaking bread in their homes, they received their food with glad and generous hearts' (Acts 2:46). Eutychus would not have fallen out of the window, been taken up dead, and then raised to life again, had he been lying alone in his bedroom, under his duvet, watching the apostle Paul preach on YouTube or

Vimeo (Acts 20:7-12). Everywhere, the Church is spoken of as a body, as a gathering of people, 'all together in one place', whether in Jerusalem (Acts 2:1) or in the houses of Lydia, Priscilla and Aquila, Philemon, Nympha and plenty of others whose names are not recorded.

When Paul is torn away from his brothers and sisters in Christ, despite the fruitfulness of his prison ministry, he tells the Philippians, 'God is my witness, how I yearn for you all with the affection of Christ Jesus' (Phil. 1:8). There is a joy for Paul as he remembers the Philippians when he prays for them, but it is a joy tinged with deep personal longing that will not be wholly satisfied while he remains at a physical distance from them.

John speaks in a similar vein as he closes his Second Letter to 'the elect lady and her children' (2 John 1). He says:

> Though I have much to write to you, I would rather not use paper and ink. Instead, I hope to come to you and talk face to face, so that our joy may be complete.
>
> (2 John 12)

He uses almost identical language in his Third Letter, 'to the beloved Gaius, whom I love in truth.'

> I had much to write to you, but I would rather not write with pen and ink. I hope to see you soon, and we will talk face to face.
>
> (3 John 13-14)

Chapter 7

Why is this? Why the depth of feeling and longing to be with people, to see their faces, feel their embraces, sit down and eat with them, talk with them, laugh, cry and pray with them?

The answer is that God himself has given the ultimate 'nod' to the physical and the material, through the wonder of the incarnation, sending his Son into this world in our human nature; and as our great high priest, Jesus remains truly human forever, as he remains wholly divine.

The man of the manifest

The same apostle John, contending with the Gnostics or at least the proto-Gnostics of his day, tells us as much:

> That which was from the beginning, which we have heard, which we have seen with our eyes, which we looked upon and have touched with our hands, concerning the word of life—the life was made manifest, and we have seen it, and testify to it and proclaim to you the eternal life, which was with the Father and was made manifest to us—that which we have seen and heard we proclaim also to you, so that you too may have fellowship with us; and indeed our fellowship is with the Father and with his Son Jesus Christ. And we are writing these things so that our joy may be complete.
>
> (1 John 1:1–4)

Jesus Christ—born, living, dying and raised to life—was the man of the manifest: the one who was heard, seen and touched; known, enjoyed and loved by the people among whom he lived.

But did that joy and fellowship between Jesus and the apostles last during the few short years of Jesus' earthly ministry, only to end abruptly when Jesus ascended into heaven? Not at all. John is writing about a continuing fellowship which 'you too'—those like you and me, who have never seen Jesus in the flesh—can enjoy.[5]

It was for the Church's good that Jesus should ascend into heaven (John 16:7). Only after he had ascended and then poured out his Spirit upon the Church could his people, all over the world, cling to him, as the body clings to the head; before the ascension, Mary Magdalene was forbidden to do so (John 20:17). It is by the Holy Spirit that Christ is united to the Church, just as Paul tells the Corinthians: 'in one Spirit we were all baptized into one body' (1 Cor. 12:13).

'OK', someone might say, 'we need to be connected to Christ if we are to function as the Church. But I still don't see why that means that we need to meet together, to be together in one place, especially now that video sharing platforms have dealt with the issue of physical distance. The Holy Spirit is big and powerful enough to maintain that one-body union over the internet.' This sounds like

Chapter 7

a compelling challenge to the necessity of physically gathered fellowship.

'When you come together'.

A very obvious way to answer this question is to consider the Lord's Supper. Throughout lockdowns it was possible for churches to carry out much of the work of ministry at a distance. Preaching, praying, pastoring, transacting church business, even singing—with uneven and unsatisfactory results—all was reasonably doable over laptops, phones and other devices. But communion presented a problem. It is true that some churches attempted to observe it via online means, but for many more pastors and congregations this seemed quite unthinkable.[6]

The very essence and character of the Lord's Supper is that it is corporate and gathered. The phrase 'when you come together' appears five times in 1 Corinthians 11, most tellingly in a letter to a church that was riven by factions (1 Cor. 1:10–12). Paul berates the church in Corinth because some of them were going ahead and eating and drinking without being mindful of others who were not present or were humiliating people who had far less. By acting in this way, they were despising the Lord's body, not rightly discerning it and, as we have already seen in Chapter 3, this led to their being judged (1 Cor. 11:20–22, 27–30).

Connection and communion

As churches returned to corporate worship after lockdown, communion resumed with various additional features that would have seemed bizarre a few years earlier: strict social distancing, copious amounts of hand-sanitizer, latex gloves, tongs, face-coverings sometimes pulled below the mouth for a fraction of a second, just long enough to admit the bread or wine into the mouth. Strange and overly clinical as this may have appeared to some, it was better to be demonstrating our unity as Christ's body in the specific way he had commanded (Luke 22:19) than either to avoid celebrating the Lord's Supper at all, or to attempt to do so online, in a way that would undermine the essentially physical and corporate dimension of the Church.

But this discussion about the Lord's Supper is a window into other areas of ministry, not least the act of preaching.

Again, had 'church-lite' become the norm in our churches years and even decades before most of us had heard of Wuhan? Had our experience of 'church' become limited to the hearing of the sermon and little more? Take the massive number of hits recorded on sermonaudio.com long before March 2020: how could this be explained? Were all these people, listening to these preachers, doing so because they were genuinely prevented from being with the Lord's people, 'all together in one place'? A likelier explanation is that 'going to church' had become, for many, an activity that was largely, if not wholly,

Chapter 7

intellectual and cerebral, in which physical involvement and the whole notion of 'when you come together' had become an optional extra.

This whole area needs further examination, so that Christians are delivered from 'church-lite' and begin to appreciate and benefit from a far more robust, substantial explanation of what is really happening 'when you come together'.

Look them in the eyes ... again!

When a preacher addresses a congregation, and especially when that preacher also happens to be the pastor, or an elder—as should be the case the majority of the time—that preacher has a relationship of pastoral authority towards that congregation. He has the God-given right to look every member in the eye and say, 'God has given me this word to address to you, in these present circumstances.' Just as Paul's letters to various churches and individuals were composed with definite, local situations in view, so it is with the responsible preacher and the attentive congregation.

Yes, you may very well feel like listening to a different preacher next Sunday, ideally a bit of a celebrity preacher who will give you a lift. Perhaps you could search for a sermon on your favourite passage or favourite theme, whatever that might be—the second coming of Christ, spiritual gifts and their continuation or cessation, the

Connection and communion

meaning of the thousand years of Revelation 20. You feel that you are lacking understanding in a specific Christian doctrine or ethical issue and, in all honesty, you believe that your pastor has been going through Ephesians quite long enough. You might even, by your absence, send him a tacit message that it is time to move on to another area of ministry!

But God calls his people to specific congregations, a specific local expression of his body, to submit to the godly pastoral authority that he has established in these churches. You are called to be physically present, 'not neglecting to meet together, as is the habit of some, but encouraging one another, and all the more as you see the Day drawing near'; and all this is in the context of 'how to stir up one another to love and good works' (Heb. 10:24–25). You do need to sit under your minister preaching that series in Ephesians, and you *do* need to be there to hear it, and to be seen hearing it with all your brothers and sisters, lest you discourage them!

Long before the screens of Covid descended, many invisible screens had already formed between preachers and congregations. The man that was preaching was being seen and heard; but did his physical presence in the same room amount to anything significant? Because we, and a younger generation in particular, have grown used to playing, pausing, skipping, fast-forwarding, and switching off altogether, a 'zoning in and zoning out' mentality has

Chapter 7

crept into churches, as if listening to preaching were a recreational activity.

In our present post-Covid era, pastors and churches need to recapture the chemistry, dynamism and immediacy of genuinely interactive *preaching*. A gifted and experienced preacher gains the feel of his congregation; he can sense the 'vibes' that are circulating among them. This comes about because he, as a godly undershepherd who is being modelled after the pattern of the Good Shepherd, knows his flock (John 10:27); he has spent time with them, and he regularly prays for them. True preaching can be truly 'interactive' in this sense without ceasing to be largely, if not wholly, monologue in form.[7]

Orwellian

One day in September 2020, as the second wave of Covid-19 was gathering relentless momentum, I happened upon a rectangular yellow street sign, with a black border and bold type. I will reproduce exactly what it said:

CORONA VIRUS-19

Help Us Help You

Always Practice Social

Distancing

Please Maintain 2 Metre Apart

I could not resist sharing a photograph of it on social media, and adding comments which I share here in full:

> Aside from the spelling and punctuation: 'Coronavirus' is one word, not two; the correct terminology is 'Covid-19' and not 'Coronavirus-19'; 'metre' should be plural rather than singular—the message 'Practice Social Distancing' by itself is unobjectionable, although the pedant within me (?) would prefer the English spelling, 'Practise', and indeed the terminology 'Physical Distancing' because that is a more accurate description of what is being urged.
>
> But we all know what 'Social Distancing' means, and a reminder to maintain social distancing in public spaces is completely reasonable. However, we may interpret the specific applications, there is little doubt that conscientiously maintaining a certain distance between people reduces the risk of person-to-person transmission.
>
> My big concern, however, is with the words, 'Help Us Help You'. Who is the 'Us'? It doesn't say anywhere on the sign. Is it the owner or proprietor of the building behind? If so, the boarded-up door gives little confidence! There is something sinister and Orwellian about the 'Us'—the Society, the Big State, the 'Party' which has no name but to which

CHAPTER 7

we all belong. 'Us' has no recognizable face or identity but we all surely know that 'Us' is everywhere, all the time, watching everyone.

And we are called on to 'Help Us'. We are to be servants of 'Us'. We are enlisted, Kitchener-style, into this army of 'Us'. What kind of help, exactly, does 'Us' require of me? The short and obvious answer is that we 'help' by practising social distancing ourselves. But if that is it, why doesn't the simple instruction 'Practise Social Distancing' suffice?

The conclusion must be that the anonymous 'Us' seeks to convince me that its existence and agency is necessary; but at the same time, it is unable to execute its purpose without me rolling up my sleeves and lending it a hand.

But what service will 'Us' perform on my behalf? The answer is clear: helping 'Us' will enable 'Us' to 'Help You'. So it's a reciprocal arrangement, a Mutual Aid Contract, whereby as I help 'Us', 'Us' will generously come to my support. 'Us' is here to 'Help You'. But again, how exactly? It doesn't say anywhere. So I have to surmise that 'Us' might be delivering a programme of education or training in how I practise social distancing. As a matter of fact, this sign must itself be a key resource in that curriculum.

There are very few clues about the content of this educational programme, other than perhaps the word 'Always'. 2 Metre (sic) Apart 'Always'. That 'Always' isn't qualified, so maybe I should take it at face value. 'Always' and therefore, presumably, 'Everywhere', even at home.

OK—someone might say that I'm being ridiculously fussy and yes, pedantic, and that this notice was probably scribbled down on the back of a fag [cigarette] packet in less than nine seconds. But words matter, and the public notices which are put up in streets and cities provide a powerful window into the mindset of a society.

And I might even go to the bother of finding out who put this sign up.

I never did find out. And you might argue that some of what I wrote above was a teeny bit supercilious, not engaging with the message seriously enough. Context matters! But the question still remains: who is 'Us', and what authority does 'Us' have to dictate all our actions?

The church, 'as the church'.

For fifteen weeks, from late March to early July 2020, church doors across the UK were shut fast—a level of restriction that was quite unprecedented in this country. Whether such a course of action will ever be repeated seems unlikely, but by no means impossible.[8]

Chapter 7

Churches and pastors followed these regulations, often to the letter and, in many if not most cases, they did not seriously consider any alternative course of action. That was entirely understandable at a time when the eventual devastation caused by the virus was unknown. But, in the second half of 2020 and into 2021, that general sense of unanimity began to fray at the edges. Does the civil government have the unchallengeable right to tell churches that they cannot meet, cannot sing, cannot greet each other with hugs, quite apart from decreeing that all weddings must be halted, and attendances at funerals reduced to a bare minimum?

To express very serious concerns about this level of government action does not make one a conspiracy theorist; in terms of Government policy, 'churches' were probably jotted down on a list somewhere between casinos and cinemas. And for churches to consent to these constraints does not necessarily imply that their pastors were lily-livered 'yes men', not willing to think through these issues. Some churches—including the one I pastor—closed voluntarily for several weeks when the rate of infection seemed perilously high.

But we need to grasp this thorny nettle. It appears that a majority of Christians in this country, perhaps without realizing it, accepted that the Church—*as the Church*—was required to submit to the governing authorities, in this case the British Government. The Government told churches that they had to cease public worship, and churches closed simply because the Government told them to.

But wait a moment: is that not exactly what should have happened? Does Romans 13:1 not tell believers to 'be subject to the governing authorities'? Is it not the case that 'there is no authority except from God, and those that exist have been instituted by God'? Does this not put an end to the argument?

It does not, because this passage is not addressed to churches, *as churches*, but to individuals.[9] The Church is not under the authority of the state and does not meet, or carry out any of its activities, on the basis that it is granted permission by the state government. Christ alone is the head of the Church, and his rule in the Church is not mediated through secular rulers. It is true, of course, that God has appointed these secular rulers, but they are not to exercise authority in the Church, *as the Church*.

This phrase, 'as the Church', is vitally important, which is why I keep adding emphasis to it. Every believer is required to submit to 'the powers that be' in relation to civil matters, like paying taxes. But those secular powers have no jurisdiction over matters that pertain to the Church, *as the Church*. They have no authority to determine where or when the Church gathers, who is admitted to membership or appointed to office, what is preached or taught, how the sacraments are administered or how discipline is

Chapter 7

exercised. These responsibilities belong to those whom God has appointed to authority in churches: which in biblical vocabulary means elders—men given by Christ and called to be overseers and undershepherds of the flock of God.

This should not mean, of course, that those with the authority in the church bury their heads in the sand and pay no attention to what is taking place across the land during a time of difficulty, such as a public health crisis on the scale of Covid. They are to use all their skill, wisdom and experience to arrive at the best course of action, weighing up every consideration. We can say more: they will act wisely and properly before outsiders (Col. 4:5; 1 Thes. 4:12), thinking carefully before they do anything that looks as though they are granting themselves special privileges.

To take another example, most churches in the UK voluntarily consent to the regulations imposed on them by the Charity Commission. This being a voluntary arrangement, churches are clearly under an obligation to honour their side of the bargain. But should the Charity Commission begin to impose requirements that a church could not follow in good conscience, that church is free to terminate its status as a charity, charitable company, CIO (charitable incorporated organization), or whatever position it previously had. The key issue is that churches should not regard themselves as accountable to state authorities for their decisions. They are directly answerable to Christ, the Head of the Church.

The years of Covid have given churches the opportunity to reflect on their identity and robustness. The next major crisis that affects the Church may not be an infectious disease. It may be a wave of persecution in which for Christians to say, 'we must obey God rather than man' (Acts 5:29), is far more costly and sacrificial. The question is whether churches and believers have sufficiently strong biblical convictions, especially those relating to the importance of the gathered local church, as well as the resolve and the courage to stand in an 'evil day' when the testing may be far more fierce and exacting.

PART THREE: SWORD

8 Sunlit uplands?

I have seen war. I have seen war on land and sea. I have seen blood running from the wounded. I have seen men coughing out their gassed lungs. I have seen the dead in the mud. I have seen cities destroyed. I have seen 200 limping, exhausted men come out of line—the survivors of a regiment of 1000 that went forward 48 hours before. I have seen children starving. I have seen the agony of mothers and wives. I hate war.[1]

Franklin D. Roosevelt

To say that Europe had been free from war for nearly seventy years, from May 1945 to February 2022, might seem to be true at a casual glance, but it ignores the horrors of the Yugoslavian civil wars that blighted the continent in the 1990s. It would be an inexcusable oversight if I were to make no mention of these brutal conflicts.

Yugoslavia, meaning 'Land of the Southern Slavs', had never been anything like an ethnically homogenous nation following its creation from the wreckage of collapsed empires after World War One. Under Marshal Josip Tito, President from 1953 to 1980, who followed

Chapter 8

his own divergent brand of communism, the various nationalities—Serbs, Croats, Slovenians, Bosnians, Montenegrins, Macedonians, Kosovars, and numerous others—had been held together with an iron fist. When communist governments in Eastern Europe began to topple, and especially when the Soviet Union disintegrated in 1991, Yugoslavia itself began to unravel.

The independence of Slovenia and to some extent Croatia, lands which for long centuries had belonged to the Roman Catholic Habsburg Empire, was gained relatively painlessly. But in the rest of Yugoslavia, territory which had been ruled over by the Ottoman Turks, it was a very different story. The war in Bosnia lasted over three years and it was as a result of atrocities committed there in 1992 that the phrase 'ethnic cleansing' became common currency. The violence plumbed its lowest depths in the massacre of Srebrenica in July 1995, when over 8,000 Bosnian Muslim men and boys were slaughtered by Serbian militants. The Kosovo War of 1998–99, in which Albanians were targeted, was not on the same scale, but it was a continuation of similar aggression on the part of Serbs towards an ethnic minority.

In the 1990s we saw scenes on our televisions that we thought had been consigned to history following the liberation of Auschwitz, Belsen and Treblinka. 'Never again', they said at the time. But how wrong they were, and how naïve.

Fin-de-siècle

Teenage years are very formative years, and my own teenage years coincided with the decade of the 1980s. As I look back to those times, I remember being struck by certain divisions and hostilities in the world which seemed to be beyond resolution. There were three prominent crises, in particular, which had the appearance of being permanent.

- Firstly, there were the 'Troubles' in Northern Ireland which had been raging since 1969, though the underlying tensions went back much further. At a simplistic level it was Catholics/Republicans/Nationalists against Protestants/Unionists/Loyalists; it involved provocative 'marching seasons' and colourful murals among the barbed wire and barricades. News of bombs and bullets, both in Northern Ireland and in Britain, featured very regularly. For the best part of three decades there seemed to be no solution in sight, no possibility of any rapprochement.
- Secondly, there was apartheid in South Africa—the legally embedded system of racial separation that caused that nation to be an international pariah, with frequent television coverage of rioting and violence, often brutally supressed by the 'white only' police. Nelson Mandela, the symbol of the

Chapter 8

> struggle for equality, had been in prison since 1964 and the expectation was that he would die there.
> - And thirdly, of course, there was the Cold War—the East-West split between communism and capitalism, with the Soviet Union and the Warsaw Pact countries stuck in a deep freeze behind the Iron Curtain which had descended following World War Two. The nuclear arms race and the reality of Mutually Assured Destruction (MAD—never was an acronym more appropriate) surely meant that here we had the Ultimate Stalemate. There seemed to be only two plausible possibilities: the situation would remain the same in perpetuity, or else a spark would light a fuse which would quickly escalate to 'MADness' and inevitable global catastrophe.

But, by the end of the 1980s, and into the decade that followed, we witnessed changes which many thought would be impossible. In the Soviet Union, Mikhail Gorbachev's reforming doctrines of *perestroika* (economic reform) and *glasnost* (openness) paved the way for truly democratic elections in Eastern European countries. In June 1989, for the first time in over forty years, a non-Communist party was elected to power in Poland. Around the same time, the Hungarian government opened their western border with Austria. This was the beginning of a chain reaction which led inexorably to the fall of the Berlin Wall in November 1989 and to the reunification of Germany eleven months later. Then, in August 1991, an attempted seizure of power by hard-line communists in Moscow failed, and a further train of events was set in motion which led to the break-up of the Soviet Union. Boris Yeltsin became the President of a new Russian Federation. In the West, people rubbed their eyes in disbelief. Could it really be that Russia had become a democratic, capitalist, freedom-loving nation?

At the same time, stirring events were happening in South Africa. President F. W. de Klerk, evidently influenced by events in Eastern Europe, held lengthy talks with Nelson Mandela and with other exiled leaders of the African National Congress (ANC) and, in February 1990, he announced a lifting of the long-term ban on the ANC and other political parties. A week later Mandela was released, signalling the inevitable dismantling of apartheid. It would be another four years before Mandela became President, but South Africa had been transformed from the Land of Apartheid, with all the diplomatic and cultural isolation which that had brought, into the 'Rainbow Nation'.

Events in Northern Ireland did not move quite so quickly, and the 1990s witnessed further terrorist attacks, including a massive explosion in Bishopsgate in the City of London in April 1993. But a determined 'peace process' was already underway, culminating in the Good Friday Agreement, or Belfast Agreement, which was

Chapter 8

signed on 10 April 1998 and approved in two referendums the following month. This led to the creation of new, power-sharing institutions, the decommissioning of weapons held by paramilitary groups, the early release of paramilitary prisoners and police reform. The effect was not quite instant: the Omagh bombing of August 1998, carried out by the so-called 'Real IRA', resulted in twenty-nine deaths—the largest figure for any single atrocity during the Troubles. But the streets of Northern Ireland, following the Good Friday Agreement, became, in general, very much safer.

The end of history?

It was during this era, in 1992, that Francis Fukuyama published his famous book, *The End of History and the Last Man*. His basic thesis was that humanity had now come of age, had evolved to its ideological pinnacle, and that the culture of liberal democracy which had developed in the Western World was here to stay. To be fair to Fukuyama, he did not insist that there could never again be a lapse into dictatorships and other forms of totalitarian government, but he did believe that, in the long run, there would be a general trend towards stable democracy. He wrote:

> At the end of history, there are no serious ideological competitors left to liberal democracy. In the past, people rejected liberal democracy because they believed that it was inferior to

monarchy, aristocracy, theocracy, fascism, communist totalitarianism or whatever ideology they happened to believe in. But now, outside the Islamic world, there appears to be a general consensus that accepts liberal democracy's claim to be the most rational form of government, that is, the state that realizes most fully either rational desire or rational recognition.[2]

It certainly seemed to look this way at the end of the twentieth century. The world seemed a bright and hopeful place. The expression, *fin-de-siècle*, generally refers to the closing years of the nineteenth century, not the twentieth, but there was an unmistakable sense of optimism as the new millennium dawned—so long as the dreaded 'Millennium Bug' did not bite too hard! Violent events like wars, revolutions and terrorist attacks were fading into the pages of history. Humanity was ascending into what Winston Churchill called the 'broad, sunlit uplands',[3] and we could all rest assured that the whole globe would soon enjoy the freedom, peace, prosperity and democracy that had developed in Western Europe and in North America—those regions of the world which had led the way in establishing these blessings.

The problem was that the original *fin-de-siècle*, one hundred years earlier, had not been one of undiluted confidence, as anyone can discern from reading Rudyard

Chapter 8

Kipling's famous poem, *Recessional*, published in 1897—the year of Queen Victoria's Diamond Jubilee. Kipling's third stanza is worth citing here:

> Far-called, our navies melt away;
> On dune and headland sinks the fire:
> Lo, all our pomp of yesterday
> Is one with Nineveh and Tyre!
> Judge of the Nations, spare us yet,
> Lest we forget—lest we forget![4]

This was controversial, but it was prophetic. The uncertain note of disquiet which Kipling sounded contrasted with the confident, swelling pride of late Victorian British imperialism, and it heralded a twentieth century that began with the decadence of the Edwardian period and then exploded into the mass slaughter of the Somme and Passchendaele.

Thus it also proved in the twenty-first century, only it all began to happen far more rapidly. The new century had barely got underway when the terrorist-hijacked planes crashed into the World Trade Center and the Pentagon. Subsequent efforts to import western-style democracy into Iraq, Afghanistan and Libya all failed. The Arab Spring of 2011 proved to be, almost completely, a false dawn. The civil war in Syria still rages on, as does violence in another Arab nation, Yemen, which has been vastly underreported by comparison. Sudan erupted into internecine conflict in April 2023. Iran appears to be quickly developing its nuclear capabilities, with potential consequences that hardly bear thinking about.

Shadows from the wild east

The Utopian idealism of the turn of the millennium has long since shed its lustre. It feels more like the 1980s now, than the 1990s, even though the circumstances have changed.

The future of Northern Ireland is extremely precarious, following Brexit complications, backstops and protocols and, at the time of writing (September 2023), the work of the political institutions remains suspended, although mercifully there has not yet been any significant upsurge in violence.

South Africa has not been able to find a ruler of the calibre of Nelson Mandela in the last decade, and the country's economy and general well-being have been in free fall ever since, with Covid exacerbating an already desperate situation. A wave of lootings in July 2021, sparked by the imprisonment of former President Jacob Zuma for contempt of court, caused the most serious outbreak of violence since the end of apartheid.

And from the Wild East of Russia, a shadow has gradually been encroaching, Mordor-like, upon the West. The up-and-coming democracy, which we scarcely believed could emerge, never *did* emerge. Well before

Chapter 8

the end of Yeltsin's presidency, and before the advent of former KGB man, Vladimir Putin, Russia could accurately be described as a kleptocracy—an economy and society characterized by corruption. Incursions into Georgia in 2008 and Crimea in 2014, and the menacing use of nerve agents at home and abroad, presaged the present crisis in Ukraine.

So, in February 2022, war came to Europe. The Yugoslav tragedy should have reminded us, if nothing else did, that European conflict was always a possibility. For the time being, at least, Churchill's 'sunlit uplands' still seem out of our grasp, and Fukuyama's comfortable thesis seems to hang in the balance at best.

Images that had long been associated with war—specifically the two World Wars—and which we thought had been deposited in the archives of the Imperial War Museum, reappeared in digital formats, broadcast on our TVs, laptops, tablets and smartphones: prisoners of war with their hands in the air, being frogmarched away by their captors at gunpoint; the eerie sound of wailing air-raid sirens; weeping women holding out their hands in bitter grief as they surveyed their bombed homes or stooped over the graves of their husbands and sons; railway carriages crammed with evacuated women and children, their tearful men waving them goodbye, uncertain if they would ever meet again; civilians crammed into underground shelters, doing their best to lay their hands on anything comfortable or colourful to adorn their bleak surroundings; motorways lined with the shells of bombed-out tanks; ashen, cadaverous-faced children playing on rubble heaps; mass graves discovered in Bucher; the growing resemblance between Stalingrad 1943 and Mariupol 2022—to that we might now add Bakhmut 2023[5]; the large-scale manufacture of prosthetic limbs in Ukrainian factories; the forced deportation of Ukrainians thousands of miles to the east; and even lines of trenches, dug along Europe's new Eastern Front, replete with duckboards and barbed wire.

All of this in the age of instant, digital, social media.

Passions at war

Why do wars happen? The apostle James, brother of Jesus, pulls no punches as he answers this exact question:

> What causes quarrels and what causes fights among you? Is it not this, that your passions are at war within you? You desire and do not have, so you murder. You covet and cannot obtain, so you fight and quarrel.
>
> (James 4:1–2)

Wars between nations are nothing more than the arguments and vendettas between individuals and groups of people, writ large. Dig a little deeper, and we see that

Chapter 8

war is simply the most visible, violent and destructive manifestation of human sin in the world.

The Greek word James uses for 'quarrels' and 'quarrel' is *polemos*, from which we derive the adjective 'polemic', meaning belligerent or combative. Moreover, the Greek verb which is translated 'at war' is *strateuo*, from which we obtain the English word 'strategy', implying that, within the hearts of sinful people, a type of military conflict is going on: invisible, but nevertheless real.

As long as this world continues to be inhabited by sinful human beings whose internal passions are at war, there will necessarily *be* war at every level: from petty quarrels to bullying in the workplace, to domestic abuse, to violence on our streets, right up to full-scale military invasions and conflicts. Wars that make the news are the ultimate expression of the wars that rage within the human psyche and then boil over into strife and anger against other people.

Desire and rule

When our first ancestors fell into sin, not only did they become alienated from God, but they also became alienated from one another. Adam and Eve hid from God, being terrified when they heard him walking in the Garden of Eden (Gen. 3:8). They should have run gladly to be in the presence of their Creator and Lord, but their souls had immediately become disordered and conflicted;

already their passions were at war within them. But in direct consequence of that, Adam and Eve were also alienated from one another. The beautiful harmony of their blissful fellowship, the 'one flesh' unity of body and soul so powerfully and succinctly described in Genesis 2:25—'the man and his wife were both naked and were not ashamed'—was now irretrievably fractured. The man immediately blamed his wife when God asked him what he had done (Gen. 3:12).

A discussion of marital strife, and the long history of the 'battle of the sexes', is outside my present scope. It is enough for now to discuss the *desire* in the woman which God speaks about in Genesis 3:16. As God brings judgement on the first man and woman, in the immediate aftermath of the first sin, he tells Eve, 'Your desire shall be for your husband, and he shall rule over you.' The Hebrew word for 'desire', *teshuqah*, describes an ardent longing or passion, or even an intense lusting which can only be resisted with great strength.

One possible interpretation is that the woman will be moved by a deep romantic longing for her husband. However, the second half of the verse, 'and he shall rule over you', makes it much more likely that the woman will be motivated by a desire to *rule*—to usurp her husband's authority.[6] But God the Creator had appointed the husband, and not the wife, to rule within the marriage. It was Adam's *failure* to rule which led to the first sin.[7]

Chapter 8

Eve's longing to rule is improper and unsuitable for her; she will need to counter that desire by recognizing that her husband has been called to this position.

This interpretation is certainly borne out by a comparison of Genesis 3:16 with Genesis 4:7, where Eve's son, Cain, is himself addressed by God.[8] I will cite verse 6 as well as verse 7:

> The LORD said to Cain, 'Why are you angry, and why has your face fallen? If you do well, will you not be accepted? And if you do not do well, sin is crouching at the door. Its *desire* is contrary to you, but you must *rule* over it.'

The Hebrew verbs for 'desire' and 'rule' are the same as in 3:16. Cain's spirit is disturbed and convulsed by 'passions at war'. He is riled and infuriated by the way that his brother Abel's offering has been accepted by God, while his own has been refused. But that 'desire', like Eve's, is one that needed to be strenuously opposed. Cain's longing to get even with his brother is shown to be what it is: not morally neutral surges of his animal spirits, but 'sin crouching at the door'. Sinful passions must be countered and overcome by righteous, responsible self-rule.

Cain failed to rule, just as Adam failed to rule. Nothing is more fundamental to the whole theme of ruling than *self-rule*, self-control.[9] Cain's inability to achieve mastery over his sinful passions caused hatred to manifest itself as murder, exemplifying some other verses from the Letter of James: 'But each person is tempted when he is lured and enticed by his own desire. Then desire when it has conceived gives birth to sin, and sin when it is fully grown brings forth death' (James 1:14–15).

Once murder has gained a foothold in Cain, it begins to multiply in extent and in audacity in his offspring. Sin is the seed which gives birth to murder; murder is the child who grows up into massacre and war. We see this in the arrogance displayed by Lamech five generations later, when he boasts to his two wives—notice in passing that polygamy, another instance of warring passions, began in Cain's line—that he has killed a man, and will be avenged seventy-seven times as compared to Cain's seven (Gen. 4:23–24).

There but for the grace of God

This, in a nutshell, is the history of the origin of war. Every aggressive act of war is an enlargement and a development of the violence meted out by Cain against his brother Abel, violating the peace and unity in which God's image-bearers were intended to live. I very carefully choose my words: every *aggressive* act of war. No consistent biblical Christian can be a thoroughgoing pacifist, arguing that it is never right to take up arms under any circumstances whatsoever.[10] War, in this sense, is similar to divorce; it is an unhappy but necessary feature of a fallen world, one in

Chapter 8

which some individuals and nations will not, realistically, co-exist in harmony.

The vital lesson we need to learn is that we cannot afford to be naïve about the human propensity to violence against other people, of which war is the most devastating manifestation.

But it may not always be the most shocking manifestation. In February 1993, the British public were appalled to hear about the murder of two-year-old James Bulger on a railway line in Bootle, north of Liverpool. What was sickening about this incident was not simply that it was a murder—in the early 1990s, these were happening at a rate of about 700 per year, or two per day—or even the murder of a young child. It was the fact that the murderers *themselves* were children, two boys aged ten at the time, Robert Thompson and Jon Venables, who became, on 24 November 1993, the youngest convicted criminals in Britain in the twentieth century. More recently, the case of Lucy Letby, found guilty of murdering a number of premature babies at the Countess of Chester Hospital, has horrified the British people.

'Surely I was sinful at birth, sinful from the time my mother conceived me' (Ps. 51:5, NIV). No truth is more inconvenient to us, nor to our fellow human beings. But no truth is more painfully necessary for us all to be thoroughly acquainted with. 'There but for the grace of God go I,' is an established English proverb, and its origin is uncertain.[11] It means that without the imposition of

God's goodness and mercy in my life, I might have gone to far greater lengths of sin and violence than in fact I did. It is a wise, accurate and disarmingly honest saying.

We are all capable of actions of astonishing brutality and barbarism: the mother who cannot get her crying baby to sleep; the wronged, bitter and jealous husband; the power-intoxicated playground bully; the ex-student or ex-employee who believes that he has been overlooked or ill-treated and now nurses a spirit of murderous revenge. These are just a few examples of how anger can, and sometimes does, easily boil over into physical violence, resulting in injury and even death when restraints are cast off.

When we began to think about Covid-19, we had to start with the inevitability of death for us all. In looking now at the subject of war, we need to begin by probing even deeper, to the sin which infects all our souls, of which death is the wages (Rom. 6:23). Or, as Paul puts it in Romans 3:10–12:

> None is righteous, no, not one;
>> no one understands;
>> no one seeks for God.
> All have turned aside; together they have become worthless;
>> no one does good,
>> not even one.

The uplands may not always be as dreary and cloud

Chapter 8

covered as they might seem at the moment, but they will never be permanently sunlit during this present age. We will have to contend with our own sin and the sin of others—sometimes sin which expresses itself on a vast scale, as in aggressive acts of war between nations. We are not yet in Immanuel's land, where there is no more curse (Rev. 22:3). That day of eternal light lies in the future, and it will surely come. While we live in this world, we must do everything within our power to live peaceably with everyone else (Rom. 12:18), yet all the time realizing that a present-day violence-free Utopia is nothing more than a pipe dream.

9 Blood and soil

Patriotism is a lively sense of collective responsibility. Nationalism is a silly cock crowing on its own dunghill and calling for larger spurs and brighter beaks.[1]

Richard Aldington

Once it became clear that a major conflict in Europe was underway, one of the first things I did was to buy myself a USB plug-in memory stick.

I had owned several of these before, of course, but had never used them consistently. What if the electronic 'cloud' was assaulted by cyber-attack? Is this not what a twenty-first-century war would look like? Less in the way of guns, tanks, bombs and missiles, and instead a new era of remote warfare, cyber warfare, even space warfare. Perhaps someone in the Kremlin was already eyeing up some of my sermons and was about to delete them all or corrupt all my files.

As it happens, my memory stick is still sitting idly on my desk and all my files are still saved on the 'cloud'.

Boots on the ground

The war in Ukraine, at least in the first year-and-a-bit of its duration, has been an old-fashioned territorial war,

Chapter 9

fought in the air and on the sea, but predominantly on land, involving tanks, guns, rocket launchers, shells, boots on the ground and armies of occupation. It is about blood and soil, about disputes over land between two historical nations. Such has been the history of warfare since time immemorial.

When George W. Bush declared a 'War on Terror' in the immediate aftermath of 9–11[2], it began to look as though territorial wars between Nation A and Nation B were a thing of the past. Those sorts of wars happened during years that began with a 1, not years that began with a 2. The difficulty with such a declaration of war was not immediately obvious: when could comprehensive victory over an enemy as diffuse as 'International Terrorism' be pronounced with any confidence?

When martial language began to be used in relation to Covid nearly two decades later, it seemed as though definitions of warfare were becoming even more tenuous. It is frankly even more difficult to declare full and final victory over a microscopic virus than it is to claim conquest over international terrorism. At least Osama bin Laden was cornered and killed. SARS-CoV-2 is a somewhat slipperier opponent.

But, since 24 February 2022, the world has been witnessing a 'traditional', bloody, violent war between two sovereign nations, Russia and Ukraine. This is not the place to go into any depth about the historical and geographical roots of this conflict, and by the time you read these words, the situation may have developed a good deal further than it has at the present time of writing; these chapters on the 'Sword' concern a fast-changing situation, unlike those covering the 'Pestilence' which now lies pretty firmly in the past. For that reason, I will avoid, as far as possible, detailed comment about the progress of the Russia-Ukraine war.

The important historical point to be made here is that in general, wars have been fought between *nations*, whether a one-on-one struggle or a larger conflict involving two or more nations forming alliances. Sometimes those nations have been city-states rather than extensive territorial areas, as in the Peloponnesian War (431–404 BC) where Athens and Sparta were the main combatants. And of course, there have also been numerous civil wars throughout history. But for the most part, the history of warfare has been the history of international warfare.

Bearing all this in mind, perhaps nations are not such a good idea? If nations keep on going to war against each other, would it not have been better for humanity if there had never been any nations in the first place?

Clans, languages and lands

Why use the specific vocabulary of 'nation'? There are plenty of available synonyms, like 'country', 'people' and 'state'. The first of these emphasizes territory, the second

Chapter 9

ethnicity, and the third draws attention to political organization. But the word, 'nation', includes elements of all three of these, at the very least. What is more, our English translations of the Bible speak of 'nations', so we need to be clear what nations are.

There is no mention of any nations in the world until after the Flood in the time of Noah, so we can only speculate as to how people living before the Flood organized and governed themselves. The Bible speaks of mounting violence and tyranny as the time of the Flood approached; we read in Genesis 6:11 that 'the earth was corrupt in God's sight, and the earth was filled with violence'. It was because of this corruption and violence that God determined to bring the Flood upon the ancient world.

After the Flood, once God had established his covenant with 'all flesh that is on the earth' (Gen. 9:17), there would be no further divine act of global destruction and people would multiply to fill the face of the earth. Under this new global economy, it would be *nations*, represented by their rulers, which would carry out God's purposes of restraining violence across the world. So, in Genesis 10, we have the first mention in the Bible of 'nations' (10:5, 20, 31, 32). The first three of these references describe the descendants of Noah's three sons: Japheth, Ham and Shem respectively. The final reference is a summing up of the whole chapter.

It is helpful for us to see how these nations are introduced. In each of the first three references in Genesis 10, the nations are mentioned alongside 'clans', 'languages' and 'lands'. From very early on, these were the factors which determined and defined the world's nations. Nations were identified according to *kinship*; they could trace their roots back to a common ancestor. Nations also became distinguished according to the *language* that they spoke. And nations were also demarcated by the specific *territory* that they occupied.

The long history of the world has, of course, witnessed the constant shifting and reshaping of nations across the globe. Of all the many names listed in Genesis 10, only one is an unambiguous nation in 2023—Egypt (10:6), the original Hebrew, *Mizraim*, being one of the sons of Ham. The names and the boundaries of nations undergo constant flux throughout human history.

Even so, 'clans', 'languages' and 'lands' have tended to shape nations across the millennia. Sometimes these three characteristics have been very clearly defined in a nations' identity, sometimes less so, but at the risk of over-generalization, history teaches that the more clearly defined these three have been, the greater the longevity and security of the nations.

As in an earlier chapter, we can take the contrasting examples of Iceland and India. In the case of Iceland, a racially homogenous Nordic people, the Icelanders have

Chapter 9

made up the great majority of the population for many centuries, speaking their distinctive Icelandic language, and inhabiting a very clearly defined territory—a volcanic and glacial island in the North Atlantic situated just south of the Arctic Circle.

India, of course, could not be more different: its vast population of well over a billion comprises of numerous people groups—among them Hindi, Bengali, Punjabi, Gujarati, Kashmiri and Tamil, each of which speak their own distinctive languages. But, as we pan further into that vast nation, the most populous on earth, we see that the same pattern is true at a more local level: the peoples of Northeast India—Assamese, Khasi, Nissi, Ao, Manipuri, Mizo and Nepali—form their own ethno-linguistic patchwork which is probably more complex than in an average-sized nation. Moreover, the borders of India, which have existed as an independent nation only since 1947, are far less well-defined, especially in the northern region of Kashmir, where there has been a long-running dispute with Pakistan—the two countries often being on the brink of military conflict if not actually taking up arms against each other, as in 1947, 1965, 1971 and 1999.

Nevertheless, both Iceland and India are acknowledged 'nations', certainly insofar as they are numbered among the 193 (currently) internationally recognized member states of the United Nations.

Nations are complicated, to say the least. I am writing

these words at a time, of course, when the makeup, integrity and identity of the United Kingdom is subject to a huge amount of scrutiny and discussion. For how much longer will Northern Ireland remain part of the Union? Will a second independence referendum in Scotland take place any time soon? Is Wales a 'nation' or is it simply a principality and therefore part of a larger nation? Is that nation England, Britain or the United Kingdom? Such questions cannot be answered without a huge amount of thought, tact, and the occasional running for cover!

It is safer to go back to Genesis. The description of these nations which 'spread abroad on the earth after the flood' (Gen. 10:32) is followed by the narrative of the Tower of Babel, which is essential in any discussion of how the world's nations came into being.

Communication problems

If Genesis 10 tells us *what* happened, Genesis 11 explains *why* it happened. The account of the Tower of Babel in Genesis 11:1–9 shows us why God determined to disrupt the unity of the human race, which had existed hitherto. Because this passage is relatively short, I have cited it all here in one place:

> Now the whole earth had one language and the same words. And as people migrated from the east, they found a plain in the land of Shinar and settled there. And they said to one another, 'Come, let us

Chapter 9

make bricks, and burn them thoroughly.' And they had brick for stone, and bitumen for mortar. Then they said, 'Come, let us build ourselves a city and a tower with its top in the heavens, and let us make a name for ourselves, lest we be dispersed over the face of the whole earth.' And the Lord came down to see the city and the tower, which the children of man had built. And the Lord said, 'Behold, they are one people, and they have all one language, and this is only the beginning of what they will do. And nothing that they propose to do will now be impossible for them. Come, let us go down and there confuse their language, so that they may not understand one another's speech.' So the Lord dispersed them from there over the face of all the earth, and they left off building the city. Therefore, its name was called Babel, because there the Lord confused the language of all the earth. And from there the Lord dispersed them over the face of all the earth.

What were the people seeking to do which provoked God to take decisive action in judgement? The clue is found by looking at verse 4; notice the prominence of 'us' and 'we'. They sought prominence, fame, and security for themselves *without reference to God*. They wanted to concentrate their numbers and their power in one place by building up and massing together, rather than to obey the divine mandate to fill and subdue the entire earth.

Left to themselves, these people would speedily have constructed a godless tyranny of the kind that had developed in the days preceding the Flood.[3] God confused their languages to call an abrupt halt to their self-aggrandizing megaproject of world domination. As Philip Eveson explains in his commentary on Genesis:

> Human beings, precisely because they are created in the divine image, are capable of planning and executing incredible projects. Because they are sinners such planning or plotting has to be restrained. God puts a brake on human rebellion. He will not allow it to reach the proportions evident before the Flood. No similar worldwide judgement is to take place before the Second Coming of Jesus Christ. In this respect, the judgement at Babel includes a gracious provision for the long-term provision of life. God sent the communications problem as a restraining influence in a world bent on acting contrary to God.[4]

How did God disrupt and destroy the Babel initiative? By confusing the speech of the people who were working at it together, and no judgement could have been more effective. In verse 1 we read that 'the whole earth had one language and the same words.' This means more than

CHAPTER 9

that everyone happened to be competent in the same language. It means that their speech was so uniform that there could never be any danger of misunderstanding. While these linguistic circumstances prevailed, any kind of mutual co-operation would take place at breakneck speed.

We cannot overstate the blessings and advantages of common speech. Imagine you are waiting on the phone, hoping to talk to someone representing, say, a bank or a utility company. You have selected several different keypad options, but you are massively relieved when the human person on the other end not only speaks your own language but does so fluently. It is frustrating to deal with someone who has learned to speak it only as an additional language and only for limited professional purposes; you are so much more comfortable talking to a person who appreciates the cadences, allusions, and proverbial sayings of your own language.

If you are speaking to someone who has 'one language and the same words' as you do, that person will be able to read between your lines and will immediately 'get the gist' of what you are communicating. Resolution of the initial problem will be far speedier than it would be if you needed to keep pausing and spelling out what you were attempting to say. A common tongue, easily understood by every member of a nation, will be a major factor in ensuring efficiency, progress and prosperity. Communication is key; communication is king.

Patriotism good; nationalism not so good

So, to check the overweening pride of man, and to safeguard the world against global tyranny, God acted as he did in relation to the Tower of Babel, setting limits on what humanity could do. From Babel onwards, the division of people into nations is part of his good divine will and purpose.

The Bible, by and large, tends to encourage smaller nations, ones where kinship, language and territory are well-defined and understood. Empire building, the haughty pride of the king of Babylon (Isa. 14:3–23), is a manifestation of the spirit of Babel-Babylon, as exemplified in the judgement against King Nebuchadnezzar (Dan. 4:28–33). None of the nations mentioned in Genesis 10 spanned whole continents from ocean to ocean. The same is true of the nations listed in Acts 2:9–11, when their various languages were spoken by the apostles on the Day of Pentecost.

God made the division of nations clear when he spoke through Moses in Deuteronomy 32:8: 'When the Most High gave to the nations their inheritance, when he divided mankind, he fixed the borders of the peoples according to the number of the sons of God.' Whatever the precise meaning of 'the sons of God' in this context,

CHAPTER 9

this verse should be seen as programmatic in terms of God's overall plan to divide the world into nations.

The apostle Paul may well have had this passage in mind when he addressed the Athenian philosophers on Mars Hill: 'And he made from one man every nation of mankind to live on all the face of the earth, having determined allotted periods and the boundaries of their dwelling place' (Acts 17:26).

It is important to emphasize here that the 'allotted periods' and 'boundaries of their dwelling place' refer not to human beings individually, but to 'every nation of mankind'. Nations are an essential part of God's unfolding plan in this world; nations have divine sanction. The specific boundaries of each and every nation state, at any point in history, should not be viewed as arbitrary or up for grabs; they are in place by divine appointment. This is why the current conflict in Ukraine matters: the boundaries of that nation have been violated.

In summary, nations are God's good purpose for the world in its fallen state. Had it not been for Babel, Nuclear Armageddon or its equivalent would surely have taken place millennia ago. While it is true that there would not have been any nations in this world were it not for the sinfulness of the human heart, this does not in any way suggest that nations ought not to exist.

If nations are good, it follows that there is a place for a positive and healthy patriotism, a love for one's nation, which may well combine the features of kinship, language, and territory—indeed many rich and varied aspects of that nation's culture. A heartfelt and even visceral attachment to your nation should not be seen as something unworthy of a Christian, provided that love for that nation does not become an idol. Patriotism should be distinguishable from the type of nationalism which regards other nations as inferior to your own, although not all kinds of nationalism are equally vicious. A true patriot does not only love their own country; they fully appreciate how people of different nationalities love *their* own countries, and when they spend time in different countries, they learn to love them too.[5]

Neither is it wrong to speak about national characteristics—they undoubtedly exist. Every nationality in the world will tell jokes about some other nationality; national generalizations have a basis in observed reality and are not the heinous crimes they are sometimes made out to be. When Paul writes to Titus, he is quite happy to cite a Cretan poet, possibly Epimenides, who wrote that 'Cretans are always liars, evil beasts, lazy gluttons.' Paul then adds, rather tersely, 'This testimony is true' (Titus 1:12–13). We could well imagine accusations of libel being levelled against Paul by 'triggered Cretans' demanding 'safe spaces' if he were writing today; to my knowledge no bookshops in Crete have deleted these words from any Bibles they might be trying to sell!

Chapter 9

The point is that, in God's wise purposes, nations are here in this world, and here to stay until the very end of the present age.

-ocracies and -archies

There is a further aspect to nationhood without which nations could not exist—to which I have already referred—and that is the question of rule and government. Without these, the whole *raison d' être* of a nation is lost; that nation is no longer a *sovereign* nation.

In the Bible, by and large, the nations had kings. There is no specific mention of 'kings' in Genesis 10–11, although we are told in 10:10, in connection with Nimrod, that 'the beginning of his kingdom was Babel, Erech, Accad and Calneh, in the land of Shinar'. Nimrod seems to have been the first individual in Bible history to be recognized as a 'king' in any sense. By the time we get to Genesis 14, we find kings in abundance, with nine of them in the first two verses. Each of these kings ruled a specific nation in the lands surrounding the territory that God was promising to Abram.

For a nation to hold together and to experience any continuation, it must have rule and government. The provision of rule and government is set out, by implication, back in Genesis 9:5–6, where God spells out his requirement for capital punishment to be carried out in the case of murder:

> And for your lifeblood I will require a reckoning: from every beast I will require it and from man. From his fellow man I will require a reckoning for the life of man.
>
> > 'Whoever sheds the blood of man,
> > by man shall his blood be shed,
> > for God made man in his own image.'

The question that would need to be resolved in time is simply this—'Who will authorize the carrying out of the shedding of blood?' This could not simply be in the hands of self-appointed vigilantes without a return to the conditions which prevailed before the Flood. Rule and government are appointed by God to safeguard the people against the encroachment of blood-shedders; the two utterly indispensable functions of government are (1) the proper administration of justice, so that evildoers are punished and those who do good are rewarded (Rom. 13:3–4); and (2) the defence of the people against enemy invasion—the execution of the 'just war' we have already considered in the previous chapter.

The fact that the Bible speaks in so many places of 'kings' rather than 'presidents', 'chancellors', 'emperors' and other kinds of ruler should not be pressed too far. Scripture does not insist that monarchy, not even constitutional monarchy, is the *only* viable form of human government.

Chapter 9

Back in the 1990s, when I was teaching ethical issues to 13- and 14-year-old school students, I would set them an exercise: to tell me as many words as they could ending in -ocracy or -archy. Eventually we would come up with a list, such as the following:

> Democracy, monarchy, aristocracy, anarchy, plutocracy, bureaucracy, technocracy, oligarchy, patriarchy, theocracy, hierarchy, tetrarchy... occasionally others.

My question then was, 'Which of these is the odd one out?' The only right answer was 'anarchy' because that alone describes the *absence* of rule and government. The others in the list might be more or less favoured at various times in history and in various places across the world, but only anarchy is absolutely and uniformly bad all the time.

So, when the Bible instructs us to 'be subject to the governing authorities' (Rom. 13:1), it does not adapt or temper that requirement according to what precise form of governing authority is in power. Any '-ocracy' or '-archy', other than anarchy, could be in place, and none of these forms of governance guarantee, or necessarily jeopardise, the moral rectitude of those who exercise power. None of these factors in any way compromise the sovereign rule and authority which God has established in every nation across the world throughout history; we are to respect all sovereign rule and authority, those *powers that be*, as being instituted by God and invested with his own authority (Rom. 13:1).

Nations and their borders

There are few more emotive subjects than borders, and that emotion is likely to increase rather than decrease in the years ahead as the porous nature of many national borders is challenged. I have already referred in Chapter 1 to the controversy in March 2023 involving Gary Lineker, and the debate about borders and migration will only intensify as the decade of the 2020s advances. But where you have nations, of necessity you also have borders, and the control and oversight of these borders, whether on land or at sea, belongs to the jurisdiction of the governments over those sovereign nations on either side of the borders.

Many vexed questions could be raised in connection with the subject, and are being raised, in ever shriller tones. Could a 'harder' border ever come down between England and Scotland—and even more controversially, between Northern Ireland and the Republic of Ireland? In the case of the latter, who would police it in either direction? Is there, or should there be, a trade border in the Irish Sea, in some sense dividing one part of the United Kingdom (Northern Ireland) from the rest (Great Britain)? And what about the English Channel—does the border between the UK and France have any real meaning or

Chapter 9

force when several hundred migrants cross it each week, without passing through passport controls or customs?[6]

We could travel across the Atlantic and ask similar questions about the USA-Mexico border. In the summer of 2019, the whole world was shocked by photographs of Óscar Alberto Martínez Ramírez and his 23-month-old daughter Valeria, who had drowned trying to cross the Rio Grande from Mexico into the United States. They had been unable to pay the $800 fee which—they had been told—would enable them to jump to the top of the US asylum priority list and, in desperation, tried to swim across the narrowest stretch of river they could find, but the current proved too strong for them.

Some people seized on these pictures as visual evidence of the evil of borders—'Why should there be borders at all?' 'Why should not people of any and every country cross over into whatever country they like, without border controls, immigration checks, customs barriers?' 'Why do people need visas or even passports to travel from one country to another?' 'Would it not be a happier world if there were free and uninhibited movement of peoples, everywhere?'

At this point we need to pause and take a few steps back. There is such a thing as a common humanity that people of all nations share, and the division of the world into nations does not imply a rigid compartmentalization in which the various nations have no communications with one another, or do not come to international agreement as to how the mounting global migrant crisis might be handled.

But when sovereign nations enter into such agreements, they do so freely and voluntarily, in such a way as to retain the sovereign right to manage and oversee the influx and outflow of people through their national borders. To fail to recognize this responsibility is to tip the whole world towards anarchy, and global anarchy is an even more dreadful prospect than national anarchy.

Globalization and its limits

Christians who hold to the authority of the Scriptures need to insist on the divine provision of nationhood and of national sovereign rule and government, no less strenuously than they insist on the division of humanity into male and female, and of the goodness of work and the Sabbath.

We scarcely need to be told that we are living in days of globalization, with a global economy, global companies, global infrastructures and global communications. It would be both wrong and unrealistic to attempt to reverse all these features. The nations of the world, in the best of times, engage in the mass transference of goods, people and capital, preferring not to erect restrictive trade barriers. In 1 Kings 5:10–12, we read of Solomon's altogether legitimate and mutually beneficial trade with

CHAPTER 9

Hiram, king of Tyre. Without this international trade agreement, the Temple in Jerusalem would not have been built.

In areas as diverse as travel, diplomacy, education, technology, the combatting of crime, disease and poverty, international co-operation is an essential good—a blessing to peoples across the globe. Imagine a world without international air traffic control, or without the sharing of best practice in the development of vaccines, and you will appreciate the point: for a nation to cut itself off from these benefits and conveniences would be insanity. North Korea is the best (or worst) example of such a practice.

But, as Christians, we must be wary of a 'mission creep' that drifts towards Babel. We need to distinguish between an increasingly globalized *economy*, on the one hand, and global *government*, on the other. This is because, in the world God has established, no human authority should be permitted to override the decisions of the governments of sovereign nations. While there is such a thing as international law, national governments should not be perpetually bound by such laws; they become signatories to them on a voluntary basis and may withdraw from them when they deem it appropriate.[7]

International law is essentially the modern extension of the ancient practice of nations making treaties with one another, in which national governments, representing their nations, act with sovereign determination. But those nations must remain free to enter and to withdraw from the obligations outlined in those various treaties. No international organization, whether the United Nations, the European Union, the World Health Organization, the Intergovernmental Panel on Climate Change, or any other, should be vested with the sovereign authority that belongs to nation states.

The war in Ukraine, along with other emergencies which are rippling through the world at the moment—most notably the various migrant crises—has brought this subject of nations and national sovereignty into the foreground. Some readers may wonder whether the concerns expressed in this chapter are genuinely scriptural, spiritual concerns; surely matters of statehood are about as 'political' as it gets?

Our response should be that the God who rules the earth has ordained that people should live in nations; he has also appointed that prayers should be made for rulers of nations (1 Tim. 2:2) and that such rulers should be honoured (1 Peter 2:13, 17). If we are indeed living through a 'time for judgement', then we should regard this subject as one of crucial importance, affecting the security and well-being of every citizen of every nation on earth.

The nation and the holy nation

One closing thought. That same First Letter of Peter

Chapter 9

speaks of God's Church as 'a holy nation' (1 Peter 2:9). There has never been, and there never will be, a territorial nation in this present world which enjoys uninterrupted blessing and harmony. Not only will nations go to war with other nations but they will experience rupture and discord within themselves. Over recent centuries, nations such as the United States, the United Kingdom, the Netherlands and Switzerland have been relatively 'successful' insofar as they have been havens for people from across the world fleeing war, poverty and persecution. What has been the reason why these specific nations have been so welcoming and tolerant? My unambiguous answer is that their cultures have been greatly affected and infused by biblical Christianity.

But, as the Western World shakes off its Christian past—and vestiges of the old 'Christendom' are increasingly hard to detect—so it is that these nations are being more blighted by intolerance, division and polarization.

There never *has* been a definitive 'Christian nation' in the history of the world; the only entity which answers to that description is the Church of Jesus Christ. In the Church 'there is neither Jew nor Greek, there is neither slave nor free, there is no male and female, for you are all one in Christ Jesus' (Gal. 3:28).

The great calling of the Church, and a calling whose importance will surely only grow in the years ahead, is to be this holy nation, the transcendent and everlasting nation for peoples across all the nations.

> Blessed is the nation whose God is the Lord,
> the people whom he has chosen as his heritage!
> (Psalm 33:12)

10 Rough and Tumble

Be men! In courage; not cowards, turning our back on the foe, or giving way in danger, or reproach, or evil days. In solidity; not shifting or shadowy, but immoveable as the rock. In strength; as the man is, so is his strength. Be strong! In wisdom. Foolishness is with childhood, wisdom with manhood. Speak and act with wisdom, as men.[1]

Horatius Bonar

Where you have nations, you have narratives, and the narratives are just as diverse as the nations that embrace those narratives. A national narrative, in this sense, is a key aspect of that nation's culture. Culture is an indescribably complex entity, both in terms of the influences which generate culture and the multifaceted nature of cultures themselves, but cultures generally give expression to a core narrative of some kind.

When two or more nations come into collision, and especially into armed conflict, there will be an inescapable clash of narratives. That is conspicuously true in the case of the present Russia-Ukraine war. The mainstream opinion in Western Europe and North America, which has been expressed through a majority of media over the last

Chapter 10

two years, is that Russia is the aggressor and that Ukraine is an innocent victim whose territorial integrity has been violated. But that view, of course, is not propagated by the Russian media and is not held by a substantial proportion of Russian citizens, though it may not be possible to determine how sizeable that proportion is.

President Vladimir Putin has spoken several times about the de-Nazification of Ukraine.[2] This is a conviction, a national narrative, to which he conscientiously holds, however ghastly or unconscionable it may seem to many onlookers, including me. But it can only be understood as one expression of his Russian nationalism and the narrative to which he subscribes. From this perspective, Russia has spent several centuries repelling invaders from the West, most significantly Napoleon in 1812 and Hitler in 1941; the Second World War is referred to as the 'Great Patriotic War'. The fertile plains of Ukraine and the warm-water Black Sea coast, especially Crimea, have historically been Russian territory which needs to be defended against any western incursions.

According to this narrative, NATO has expansionist and aggressive intentions towards Russia; if Ukraine were to join NATO, it would be perceived as a threat parallel to that posed to the West in 1962 when the Soviets developed missile launchers in Cuba. If the United States have clung jealously to the Monroe Doctrine since 1823—the policy principle that intervention by any foreign power in the Americas constitutes an act of hostility against the United States—then why should Russia not have its own equivalent 'Moscow Doctrine' in relation to the Eurasian land mass?

It is beyond question that the war in Ukraine has been carried out with brutality and cynicism, and many Russian people manifestly disbelieve Putin and do not subscribe to his version of history. But my point is simply this: that every one of us looks at the world and at the nations of the world through lenses that have been shaped by certain narratives. It is impossible for any citizen of any nation to claim neutrality in this regard. There is only One who sees everything in space and time with a perfect, comprehensive, all-seeing gaze, and he is also the one who has all power over heaven and earth.

The Commander of the army of the Lord

Remember how Joshua, on the eve of the battle for Jericho, was confronted by a man with a drawn sword. Vigilant leader that he was, Joshua demanded to know one thing from this man: 'Are you for us, or for our adversaries?' The answer he receives is remarkable. 'No; but I am the commander of the army of the Lord. Now I have come' (Josh. 5:13–14).

If any battle in history was a clash between the forces of right and wrong, surely it was *this* battle for Jericho. How could it be that this 'commander of the army of the

Chapter 10

Lord'—who is evidently the preincarnate Son of God, as demonstrated by the way Joshua then falls to the ground and worships—would be anything other than *for* Joshua and the people of Israel?

This Divine Commander is not saying that he is for Israel's adversaries, but neither is he simply joining himself to the ranks of Israel's army. He does not want to give encouragement to anything akin to an 'Israelite Popular Front'. This Commander is elevated far above them—the Commander of a Greater Army, a heavenly host. The Lord has joined himself by covenant to the people of Israel, but that does not make God himself a mere Israelite. Neither is God a Ukrainian, or a Russian, or a Brit, or an American or any other nationality.[3]

This is the mindset which we need to cultivate as we look at the world and its many conflicts. It should not stop us from calling out evil as evil, nor from asking that God would bring a just end to wicked acts of cruelty. The Lord acts in judgement when 'the land is full of bloody crimes and the city is full of violence' (Ezek. 7:23). In Psalm 72:12 we read that 'he delivers the needy when he calls, the poor and him who has no helper,' and we have seen the hundreds of thousands of such people fleeing Ukraine. We should use such Scriptures in our prayers when we pray, as we should, for justice and for peace.

But the God who delivers the needy is also the God who told the prophet, Habakkuk, that he was 'raising up the

Chaldeans, that bitter and hasty nation' against Judah (Hab. 1:6). It was revelation from the Lord that caused Habakkuk to confess, 'I hear, and my body trembles; my lips quiver at the sound; rottenness enters into my bones; my legs tremble beneath me' (Hab. 3:16a). God was raising up the Chaldeans in order to chastise his own people for their sin and idolatry; in his own time, he would then bring a 'day of trouble to come upon people who invade us' (3:16b).

Putin's anti-gay war

Very great caution is needed in attempting to answer questions like, 'What is God's purpose in bringing this specific judgement on his people?'

We should adopt an attitude of the deepest humility. As Paul asks in Romans 11:34, alluding to Isaiah 40:13, 'For who has known the mind of the Lord, or who has been his counsellor?' God's ways are far above our ways and attempting to 'second-guess' him is an act of astonishing hubris. Additionally, we must be extremely wary of conflating the people of God with any one nation or culture. In the Old Testament, the nation of Israel constituted the people of God and the judgements that fell on the nation of Israel were divine chastisements against his covenanted people. But that situation no longer persists today; the Church of God is found across all the nations of the world.

Chapter 10

Nevertheless, as we search the Scriptures and survey events going on in the world today, we are bound to ask the 'why' questions. If David was able to pray, 'Search me, O God, and know my heart! Try me and know my thoughts! And see if there be any grievous way in me' (Psalm 139:23–24), then the Church of God, at all times and in all places, must surely follow his example. It is not unreasonable for the Church in the Western World, principally in Western Europe and North America, to ask these kinds of searching questions. And at this point, Putin's narrative in relation to western culture is certainly worthy of our careful attention.

On 14 March 2022, the *Boston Review* published an article by Emil Edenborg, 'Putin's Anti-Gay War on Ukraine', which included the following:

> In the geopolitical worldview of the Kremlin, Russia is standing up for 'traditional values' in the face of a morally corrupt West weakened by sexual liberalism. In numerous speeches, Putin has positioned Russia as an international leader in the defence of 'traditional values'. In this way, gender conservatism contributes to carving out a meaningful geopolitical role for Russia in a world order where LGBT rights have become international politics and increasingly framed as a question of civilization and modernity.[4]

The article also states that:

War is gendered not just in the sense that decisions to go to war are overwhelmingly made by men and that almost all the killing and other atrocities in wartime are performed by male bodies. Gender norms and gendered inequalities also shape how people are affected by war, whether we speak of men not being allowed to leave Ukraine, women being charged with the responsibility for evacuating children and elderly, or trans people whose mobility may be hindered by a mismatch between their gender and what is stated in their passport.[5]

These observations and above all the *interpretations* made in this article should cause Christians a good deal of serious reflection.

Among some sections of the American population, we have seen the recent rise of the 'Alt-Right', a reactionary movement against the left-leaning position exemplified by the *Boston Review*, and many of the Alt-Right would be unreserved supporters of Putin and his war in Ukraine. This reflects the gaping polarization which has been developing in American culture, and it should prevent us from asking too hastily, 'Are you for us, or for our adversaries?'

Reactionism inevitably tends to polarization because reactionaries, in wholly rejecting a certain position, paint their opponents as the very negation of everything good.

Chapter 10

They absolutize their opponents' position as the epitome of everything bad and wrong, and in doing so establishing their own view as the zenith of goodness and truth. This attitude inevitably leads to entrenchment and alienation in which any kind of rapprochement becomes impossible.

But Christian people who follow the Commander of the Lord's Army must not simply file right, or file left, and then dig in. They lift their heads *up*, and see that God alone is the only source of ultimate goodness, truth and beauty. Slavish allegiance, or even prior commitment, to any political or cultural movement as if it were an infallible rule in itself, is to be shunned by disciples of the Christ who is our one Teacher (Matt. 23:8).

'War is gendered'

There is certainly a specific narrative in the Western World in the twenty-first century, one which seeks to dominate and which now controls mainstream media, education, advertising and increasingly politics. It is the narrative that makes the definition of 'sex' to be quite distinct from a definition of 'gender'. While, according to this position, there are indeed such things as 'male bodies', the inhabitants of those male bodies may identify as female, or indeed as transgender; and the number of possible gender identities is so fluid that any computation is meaningless. Someone born with a male body was very likely to be 'gender-assigned' male at birth, but he—or 'they'?—may well choose a different gender identity later in life.

It is impossible to read the *Boston Review* piece without detecting their sense of being on a global moral crusade: it is not enough that 'LGBT rights' should be recognized and accepted in the public arena; individual gender identities should be affirmed and embraced without reservation, because if not then 'civilization' and 'modernity' themselves are at stake.

The inevitable conclusion is that there are *two wars* going on here: the war between Russia and Ukraine, and the war over the subject of gender. We are talking here about a radical gender ideology which will fight tooth and nail to gain universal acceptance, and which will silence all dissent, labelling as 'toxic' anyone who dares to demur from the party line. For these militants, the victory of their gender ideology matters far more than the eventual victory of either Ukraine or Russia. The great offence, in their view, is the fact that 'war is gendered', that the phenomenon of war results in the kind of clear male-female division of roles which the Russia-Ukraine war has highlighted: the men staying in the country to fight, while the women, with their children, are packed onto trains and sent to the relative comfort of nations to the west.

The transgender militants are right to fight their gender war so zealously. The only problem is that they are on the wrong side, ultimately the losing side.

CHAPTER 10

'What is a woman?'

In June 2022, a documentary film was released by *The Daily Wire*, a Nashville-based website and media company which speaks for the voice of what we might call 'conservative America'. The title of the film, presented by Matt Walsh, was *What is a Woman?* It very quickly generated a vast amount of interest; *The Daily Wire* itself claimed that it became 'the single most-trafficked live-stream event' in their history.[6]

Some of the documentary makes for harrowing viewing, especially the descriptions of gender-reassignment surgery and the testimonies of people who endure the lifelong effects of the deepest physical and emotional trauma following transition. Any war has significant casualties; all wars involve the distortion and denial of truth; every war incurs costs which run into millions and billions of dollars. These factors are certainly present in the War of Transgender Ideology.

Over the course of the 94-minute production, Walsh travels across North America and even into Africa, asking a variety of 'experts' that simple question—'What is a woman?' A significant proportion of those he interviews, those representing the front line of gender ideology, respond with a combination of incomprehension and hostility, being grievously offended that such a question should even be posed. Why on earth do you need to know what a woman is? A woman is someone who identifies as a woman—that is all we need to say—end of! Walsh's quest for 'truth' in this whole area is described by one affronted academic as 'deeply transphobic' as well as 'condescending and rude'.[7]

'Comical, yet deeply disturbing' is the way that the documentary is described by *The Daily Wire* itself. The last scene in the film depicts Walsh entering his kitchen at home and asking his wife the question he has been posing all along: '*What is a Woman?*' She tells him, after a short pause, 'An adult human female', and then, handing him what looks like a jar of pickled gherkins, 'who needs help opening this'.

Some viewers may baulk at what they see as the reinforcement of 'gender stereotypes' in such a setting. But Mrs Walsh's answer to her husband's question highlights two essential considerations: firstly, that we need a further definition, that of 'female'; and secondly, that if the question 'What is a Woman?' is worth asking, so is the equally pressing question, '*What is a Man?*'

A quantum shift

It is God the Creator who defines both manhood and womanhood: 'male and female he created them' (Gen. 1:27). The reason that so many academic 'experts' wriggle and wince so uncomfortably when faced with Walsh's question is this: in their blind and obstinate rebellion

Chapter 10

they cannot bear to allow any such thing as objective, transcendent, divine truth and definition. As soon as they answer the question, 'What is a Woman?' by referring to any reality above and beyond subjective selfhood, their own hallowed ground has been swept from under their feet.

God alone has ultimate authority to *define*, to say 'this is the way things are'; when his creatures exercise the right to define, they can only do so legitimately as 'under God'. The man called his wife 'Woman' (Gen. 2:23) in full agreement and harmony with the real event that had taken place—'she was taken out of Man' and was now being reunited with him. But to 'define' anything in defiance of God is an act of high-handed rebellion, the original sin of Satan.

It is also to complicate matters exceedingly; Satan and sin are the agents of confusion and chaos. God made humanity male and female, and he made it remarkably easy for us to determine whether an individual human being is male or female. When Eve gave birth to a baby, Cain, and observed that his anatomy resembled that of the baby's father, she said 'I have produced a man with the help of the Lord' (Gen. 4:1). This child, though an infant, was a man-child. He was a 'man' at birth and would remain a 'man' throughout the days of his life; his identity as male was observed at birth—not 'assigned'!—and could never change. When Eve called him a 'man' she was, in effect, thinking God's thoughts after him. Eve did not need to receive special revelation from the Lord to know that Cain was a 'man'; when she said 'I have produced a man with the help of the Lord' she was confirming the maleness of Cain as an external, objective source of authority which rested on God's original creation of man as male and female. Every parent who has ever said, 'It's a boy!' or 'It's a girl!' is following in Eve's good tradition.

But a quantum shift of devastating magnitude has been taking place and the victims are piling up. What has happened? The seat of authority which makes pronouncements on issues of sex and gender has shifted, from the external to the internal, and from the objective to the subjective. It is no longer the pronouncement of God which is authoritative, but the pronouncement of the self, and that 'self' is beholden to no external, objective authority; the decision to say, 'I am male' or 'I am female', or indeed to reject the whole binary notion of gender, belongs to the individual and to no one else.

Self has become divine, in effect; and this is nothing other than a modern form of paganism—a theme I will return to in a later chapter. If someone contradicts or even queries another person's expression of gender identity, they have, in the view of the offended party, committed an act of gross blasphemy.

Here is the most blatant demonstration of the mindset which Paul exposes in Romans 1:25: people say and do

Chapter 10

such things 'because they exchanged the truth about God for a lie and worshipped and served the creature rather than the Creator, who is blessed forever! Amen.' That creature is *self*. And because 'they did not see fit to acknowledge God,' but believe the lie that gender is a matter of self-identity rather than divine institution, they are propelled to go on and 'do what ought not to be done', having been given over by God to a 'debased mind' (Rom. 1:28). This is the only satisfactory and robust explanation for the horrors that are unfolding around us, distorting and poisoning the minds, and in many cases the bodies, of a generation of children and adolescents.

So, *'What is a man?'* One key consideration here is that it is the man who names the woman, and in Hebrew as in English, the word for 'woman' is derived from the word for man.[8] When Mrs Walsh asks Mr Walsh—or indeed when Mrs Yeulett asks Mr Yeulett, which happens relatively frequently—to open a jar of gherkins, she is taking joy in the fact that husband and wife complement each other beautifully as a team—they need each other! As Matthew Roberts recently put it in his outstanding work on the idolatry of 'self', 'Men, we might say, build houses; women fill them and make them worth living in.'[9]

John Gray was not entirely right. Men are not from Mars, and women are not from Venus.[10] They were both formed on Earth and created to live and thrive on Earth. But notwithstanding the vast range of diversity, which is observed among men and among women, physically, psychologically and emotionally, the Bible requires us to think in terms of distinct categories of manhood and womanhood.

This is the *divine* narrative and consequently it is the only *authoritative* narrative on the subject—'Male and female he created them, and he blessed them and named them Man when they were created' (Gen. 5:2). Any rival narrative, whether that of feminism which seeks to obliterate key aspects of the male/female distinction, or of transgenderism which denies binarism and replace it with a gender-fluid spectrum, is an act of subversion against the Creator and Lord of humanity.

'Male' and 'female' Creation accounts?

It is my conjecture that the male/female distinction finds expression in the very creation narrative itself; that the two accounts, in Genesis 1:1–2:3 and 2:3–25, themselves reflect something of the binary image of God in man as male and female, respectively. For the sake of simplicity, I will refer to these two accounts as Genesis 1 and Genesis 2. The two creation accounts disclose something of the complementary natures and aptitudes of men and women, broadly and generally understood.

Genesis 1 is programmatic, architectonic, comprehensive, universal and all-encompassing—a grand and full-scale view of the whole of creation, viewed as it were from an

Chapter 10

exterior vantage point. It is a timetable and a map with the most extensive coverage. Genesis 2, by contrast, takes as its vantage point the interior of the creation, the Garden of Eden. It has a local, even homely aspect about it: the land, the trees, the rivers, the minerals, the animals, and finally the marriage and the home of marital bliss.

- Genesis 1 depicts the world as a place to work; Genesis 2 depicts it as a place to live.
- Genesis 1 builds the house; Genesis 2 decorates and furnishes it.
- Genesis 1 goes out and obtains the raw materials for food; Genesis 2 takes it and processes it into something delicious.
- Genesis 1 gets the job done; Genesis 2 settles down and enjoys the fruit of the labour.

Moreover, Genesis 2 is interpersonal and relational in a way which Genesis 1 is not. That is, interpersonal and relational at a human level. In Genesis 1 God speaks, but in Genesis 2 the *man* speaks. In Genesis 1:27 the adjectives are 'male' and 'female', but in Genesis 2:23 they are 'woman' and 'man'; in the latter pair the close correspondence of the two Hebrew words communicates the way in which the woman was made from the man and for the man.

Is it as simple as to say that Genesis 1 is a 'male' chapter and Genesis 2 is a 'female' chapter? This would be a crude and a crass way of understanding it. It would be more accurate to say that Genesis 1 presents with the man in his *creaturely* relationship to God, whereas Genesis 2 concludes with both the man and the woman in their *covenantal* relationship to God as well as to one another.

I allow that these observations may be nothing other than flights of speculative imagination, but I offer them here as a basis for discussion. If there is any substance to them, they certainly underline how God establishes male and female, from the beginning, as the only fundamentally embedded distinction and differentiation within humanity.

This much is undeniable: the perversity of our present rebellious culture is that it breaks down the distinction which God has set in place—the clear identification of human beings as either male or female.[11] But it puts up walls and barriers where God has *not* established them, the division and separation of people from one another on the basis of skin colour being the most obvious example.

Martial males

In such corrupted and confusing times as these, it is more necessary than ever to speak quite uninhibitedly of divinely determined male and female characteristics—always allowing for the vast variation *among* males and *among* females which has already been acknowledged. At the risk of being accused of gross generalization, I offer these observations with sincerity and, I hope, sensitivity.[12]

Chapter 10

Most fundamentally, men *beget* children while women *bear* children. Men are the active, penetrative partners in sexual intercourse while the women are passive. Men are generally stronger than women and have a higher proportion of muscle in their bodies; the female body has a higher proportion of fat and is designed for bearing and nursing babies. The physical constitutions of men and women are designed so that men should act as the providers and protectors, while women are nourishers and nurturers. Men, on the whole, are 'wired' so as to focus on tasks, on getting the job done, whereas women have a more developed social facility, focusing more on people.

The traditional symbol for males, ♂, which was first used extensively by the Swedish biologist Carl Linnaeus (1707–78) is also the symbol for Mars, the classical God of war. The symbol appears to represent a raised sword emerging from behind a shield. This takes us back to the theme of these last three chapters: the sword. Over the centuries and millennia, front-line warfare has been understood as a predominantly, if not exclusively, male occupation.[13] The nature of modern warfare being what it is, men, women and children are inescapably caught up in it, but the great majority of the fighting has always been done by the men.

But if the War of Gender Ideology is won by the wrong side—that is, by those who insist that the male-female distinction described in this chapter is an oppressive expression of patriarchal, toxic masculinity, and that the practice of warfare must, like all else, conform to contemporary norms approved by the LGBT movement—then western civilization will be ever easier prey for those who, like Putin, regard western nations as already being largely emasculated.

That they might know war

In the Book of Judges, Chapter 3, and the first two verses, we read this fascinating observation:

> Now these are the nations that the Lord left, to test Israel by them, that is, all in Israel who had not experienced all the wars in Canaan. It was only in order that the generations of the people of Israel might know war, to teach war to those who had not known it before.

We know from Judges that the people of Israel experienced occupation and oppression by foreign invaders because of their unfaithfulness to the Lord. But God had this additional purpose in allowing these armies to harass his people—*that a new generation might know war.* I suggest we may be living in similar times today.

This may or may not amount to physical warfare that affects our lives directly. I will go further; we must pray that it will not. War is a terrible, brutal, devastating evil. The scars of war are deep and horrifying. Like Franklin D.

Chapter 10

Roosevelt, we must say with a passion, 'I hate war'. But it is undoubtedly true that we need to be people—and here I address *men*, and boys, especially—who know what it is to be strong as men. This means being strong in the physical and material world, not a virtual world; it means looking up from *Fortnite*, *Call of Duty* and *Warzone*,[14] and employing skill and courage in the real world.

The apostle Paul tells the Corinthian church, 'Be watchful, stand firm in the faith, act like men, be strong.' Then he adds, as part of the same set of instructions, 'Let all that you do be done in love' (1 Cor. 16:13–14). Genuine biblical manhood scorns popular stereotypes. It is not the hyper-masculine caricature exemplified by contemporary 'influencers' such as Andrew Tate. It is not about being macho, about having a well-developed six-pack, or wrestling grizzly bears and anacondas to the ground; not that physical strength should be despised, because 'bodily training is of *some* value' (1 Tim. 4:8). When the Bible tells men to 'act like men', it addresses *all* men, not only those who are endowed with unusual physical strength, ability or courage. Weak-stomached Timothy is included just as much as lion-tearing, pillar-collapsing Samson.

The manliness that God looks for is, in the first place, strength of heart and mind, resolute will, self-control and self-denial, patterned after the Proper Man[15] who 'set his face to go to Jerusalem' (Luke 9:51) and said to his Father, 'not my will, but yours, be done' (Luke 22:42). The man of God says to himself, above all else, 'I am the servant of the Lord'. No need is greater in the world, beginning in the *Church*, than the need for men of this Christlike spirit and character, who by example and precept, train the next generation to be strong in a world which will make great demands.

PART FOUR:
FAMINE

11 Where have all the Avos gone?

> *'Keep climbing,' he told himself.*
> *'Cheeseburgers,' his stomach replied.*
> *'Shut up,' he thought.*
> *'With fries,' his stomach complained.*[1]
>
> Rick Riordan

When I was a child, I was told that 'hate' was a strong word, not to be used too often. That good advice stayed with me; I try to use the word 'hate' only when I mean it.

'Famine' is also a rather strong word, not one to be bandied about carelessly. Perhaps we should think twice before saying, as we sometimes do, 'I'm famished', or 'I'm starving', when we have only gone an extra hour or two longer than usual without a meal.

Certain teenage children have been known to say, 'There's no food in the house!' They are factually incorrect; the kitchen is well stocked with plentiful food, albeit the specific food that they would like to eat at that precise moment is in short supply.

But 'famine' is a reality for a frighteningly large number of people in the world today. Barnabas Fund, which 'works to provide hope and aid for the persecuted Church, from

CHAPTER 11

Christians, to Christians, through Christians',[2] issues regular updates from around the world, and an increasing number of these speak of famine. In the three months from April to June 2022, there were specific reports of serious food shortages from Madagascar, Sri Lanka, Myanmar, Kenya, Ukraine, and Zimbabwe.

The situation in East Africa is especially desperate, as reported by ReliefWeb:

> Rainfall deficits during the recent March-April-May 2022 rainy season have been the most severe in at least the last 70 years in Ethiopia, Kenya, and Somalia. The ongoing, four-season drought has been the most extensive and persistent event since 1981. Grave concerns are raised by elevated risks of a fifth below-average rainy season in October-November-December.
>
> This exceptional four-season drought, amplified by exceptionally warm air temperatures and increased evaporative demand and desiccation, has been devastating to livelihoods and produced repetitive, debilitating and cumulative shocks to herds, crops, water availability, and household incomes.
>
> More than seven million livestock have died and millions of people face the threat of starvation. The impacts of the severe drought on livelihoods will

intensify rapidly in the coming months due to the effects of the extremely poor March-April-May rains.[3]

Do not say 'hate' unless you mean it, and do not say you are 'starving' unless you mean it, either.

Unimaginably grotesque

The Hebrew word for famine, *ra'av*, could also be translated 'hunger' and is related to the verb, 'to hunger'. It is an intense hunger that is experienced by many people, over extensive territory, and over a lengthy period of time. 'Famine' is a hunger that tends towards death, just as 'pestilence' is a disease that tends towards death. It results in malnutrition, dehydration, bodily wasting and severe weakness. It affects both people and animals, and is both a consequence and a cause of economic hardship.

For me and for probably most readers of this book, famine lies mercifully outside the realm of personal experience. The kind of extreme hunger which leads people to go to extraordinary and desperate lengths, such as resorting to cannibalism (2 Kings 6:28–29; Lam. 2:20; 4:10) is unimaginably grotesque to most of us. Famine resulting in cannibalism is prophesied by Jeremiah himself:

> And in this place I will make void the plans of Judah and Jerusalem, and will cause their people to fall by

CHAPTER 11

the sword before their enemies, and by the hand of those who seek their life. I will give their dead bodies for food to the birds of the air and to the beasts of the earth. And I will make this city a horror, a thing to be hissed at. Everyone who passes by it will be horrified and will hiss because of all its wounds. *And I will make them eat the flesh of their sons and their daughters, and everyone shall eat the flesh of his neighbour in the siege and in the distress*, with which their enemies and those who seek their life afflict them.'

(Jer. 19:7–9)

On this occasion the famine was caused by the besieging armies of Babylon, enclosing the city of Jerusalem so that no inhabitant could exit or enter the city, thus cutting off its supply of food.

The causes of famine are many and various: sometimes natural phenomena alone are the main drivers of famine, whether drought, flooding, extreme temperatures, insect infestation such as locust swarms, or plant disease. Very often, however, there is a human cause behind famine, as in Jeremiah's day. This human agency could be an army of occupation, government mismanagement or corruption, oppression and exploitation on the part of unscrupulous landowners, or indeed, as in today's interconnected global economy, a conflict in a distant country that is a major exporter of foodstuffs. Historically, Ukraine has supplied wheat, maize and sunflower oil to many countries, some of them among the poorest in the world. In 2019, nearly one-third of Ethiopia's wheat was imported from Ukraine; even more precarious situations exist in Yemen and Lebanon, two countries which are also facing quite desperate economic futures.[4]

This is not how it was meant to be.

Whether the causes of famine are seen to be predominantly 'natural' or 'human' or, as is most often the case, a combination of the two, famine should be understood as a judgement that God chooses to bring upon a fallen world, as with pestilence and sword. God's providence means that, although he sometimes works directly as the 'first cause', he often makes use of 'second causes', that is, other agencies, in executing his purposes.[5]

Famine, again, like pestilence and sword, was absent from the pre-Fall world. The Garden of Eden was the diametric opposite of famine; the fruit of all the trees there was found in abundance (Gen. 1:29–30; 2:9). Even in a fallen world, famine should be understood as an abnormal condition, an anomalous state of affairs. The man would have to sweat and toil to extract his bread from the ground (Gen. 3:19), but that is not a description of *famine*. Where famines are described in the Bible (there are three in Genesis alone, introduced in 12:10, 26:1 and

Chapter 11

41:27), they are introduced as the exception to the rule, which is fruitfulness, not famine. 'The earth has yielded its increase; God, our God, shall bless us' (Ps. 67:6) is a description of what usually happens.

There are several verses in Psalm 104, a glorious Psalm of God's creation and providence, which describe what we might call the normal, expected state of affairs:

> You make springs gush forth in the valleys;
>> they flow between the hills;
> they give drink to every beast of the field;
>> the wild donkeys quench their thirst.
>>> (Ps. 104:10–11)

> You cause the grass to grow for the livestock
>> and plants for man to cultivate,
>> that he may bring forth food from the earth
> and wine to gladden the heart of man,
>> oil to make his face shine
>> and bread to strengthen man's heart.
>>> (Ps. 104:14–15)

> These all look to you,
>> to give them their food in due season.
> When you give it to them, they gather it up;
>> when you open your hand, they are filled with
>>> good things.
>>>> (Ps. 104:27–28)

What is especially noticeable about these verses is that they frequently address God himself in the second person—'*You* make', '*You* cause', '*you* give', and so on. God is understood as the Giver of food, the Provider of plenty, and Psalm 104 is a hymn of praise to God for his goodness and generosity, to man and beast.

I have never experienced a famine or anything remotely approaching one. The main challenge for me, and probably for most of my readers, is not 'how to be brought low' and deal with 'hunger' and 'need', but rather 'how to abound' and deal with 'plenty' and 'abundance' (Phil. 4:12).

Food associations

In the prosperous West we must reckon, not with chronic shortage and aching bellies, but with what we might call 'First World' food issues that are a consequence of the materialistic-idolatrous culture which influences us so deeply. And Psalm 104 is a passage that many of us may need to read and meditate on rather carefully.

In order to illustrate how far we have fallen from the spirit of praise and wonder, which the Psalmist expresses, I sat down and brainstormed the whole subject of food; I wrote down all the associations that came to mind in relation to food in 2022, and I came up with the following observations and impressions:

- Food in twenty-first-century Britain is vastly more

Chapter 11

than the daily, tasty, satisfying sustenance for which we are grateful to God.
- People of all ages—especially younger people—are often fussy about what they eat. They tell you there is 'no food in the house' when the cupboards and fridges are bursting at the seams!
- The choice of food is often linked to lifestyle choices and social identities, as well as deeply held convictions: the vegetarian, the vegan, the pescatarian, the flexitarian, the macrobiotic, the non-organic, among others.
- Whereas certain types of food used to be enjoyed 'in season'—the new potatoes and strawberries of June, for example—the sense of seasonal food has now all but evaporated with our global supply lines, and sophisticated methods of storage.
- Avocados used to be regarded as a luxury. To eat an 'avocado pear', as we used to call them, was a treat which you might enjoy if you had the privilege of going to a Mediterranean country on holiday. These days, 'avos' are not only 'crushed', 'mashed' or 'smashed' onto toast or bagels; they over-ripen and darken along with the bananas.
- We have witnessed in the last generation or so an explosion in the variety of allergies and intolerances which people have in relation to food: nuts, dairy, gluten, eggs, yeast, caffeine and so forth.

Where have all the Avos gone?

- There has also been a proliferation of global cuisines; you go the 'food courts' in some service stations as well as shopping malls and find every nation under heaven represented by their food. It is the same when you order food on fast-food delivery apps.
- Eating has become an increasingly individual activity rather than a social one. Even eating a meal as a family watching TV has become outdated. You eat what you want to eat, when you want to eat it, where you want to eat it.
- A large amount of food ends up in the brown food-recycling bin.
- Food is closely associated with health as never before. Sometimes I look at the side of a cereal box. It is plastered with nutritional information from top to bottom. There is little or nothing there telling me that the food is tasty, or suggesting any reason I should eat it other than it being very good for me.
- Food hygiene is a huge industry. Every restaurant or takeaway in Britain will have a food hygiene rating displayed by the Food Standards Agency, on a scale of 0 to 5. When we judge whether or not to enter an eating hostelry we are inclined to ask, not only 'will this food taste good?' but 'will this food make me ill?'

Chapter 11

- There is huge interest in diets. I have tried various diets myself, usually of the intermittent-fasting variety, somewhat ... intermittently; the two-five and the eight-sixteen. How much weight am I losing? How many calories am I consuming? Carbs, protein, fibre; Atkins, Mediterranean, Paleo—the selection is mind-boggling.
- We have also been made conscious of different types of eating disorders: Anorexia, Bulimia, Binge Eating, Compulsive Overeating, Orthorexia, Rumination Disorder, Selective Eating Disorder. Again, the list is growing and seemingly endless, bearing some resemblance to gender identities.[6]
- We are also seeing a large number of TV celebrity chefs, and the preparation and cooking of food has become a growing spectator sport, with many programmes having a competitive element.

The categories above are, of course, personally subjective, but I invite readers to reflect on their overall representative reality.

What should strike us is just how different all this is to Psalm 104, where God is thanked and praised as the giver of all food. The petition in the Lord's Prayer, 'Give us this day our daily bread' (Matt. 6:11; Luke 11:3), and the practice of giving thanks before food, and indeed afterwards, clash with contemporary cultural norms.

'Hurry up and give thanks, the food will get cold, and I'm hungry.'

Ever heard that, thought that, or said that? And *how* hungry?

Enjoyment or entitlement?

It is difficult to escape the conclusion that we are a food-obsessed society; we might even say, in monstrously different circumstances to those in famine-stricken countries, that *we cannot get enough food*. Not because it is scarce, but because it is so abundant. I recall an anecdote about an Indian pastor, visiting Britain back in the late twentieth century, entering a supermarket; when he saw that entire aisles were dedicated to the sale of dog food and cat food, he burst into tears. In his own home, the *people* would not have been nearly so well-supplied with provisions as our pampered dogs and cats.

We do not have difficulty finding food, but we have great difficulty in deciding what food we are going to consume. We are not grateful recipients of the food God gives us; we have become selective consumers of the food we like. Food has gone from being a matter of *enjoyment*—yes, we are meant to enjoy food, because it is God 'who richly provides us with everything to enjoy' (1 Tim. 6:17)—to a question of *entitlement*.

Perhaps the nearest thing to this we find in any biblical narrative is the account of the people of Israel

Chapter 11

in the wilderness, accompanied by the 'rabble' that was with them.[7] In Numbers 11:4-6 we read about their dissatisfaction with the manna which God had given them, and their nostalgic desire for the menus they had left behind:

> Now the rabble that was among them had a strong craving. And the people of Israel also wept again and said, 'Oh that we had meat to eat! We remember the fish we ate in Egypt that cost nothing, the cucumbers, the melons, the leeks, the onions, and the garlic. But now our strength is dried up, and there is nothing at all but this manna to look at.'

They were tired of the sameness of the daily menu; they longed for the varied delicacies of Egypt. They looked at the manna which they received miraculously every day, and they despised it.

But, as we read further, we go on to learn that it is not only God's gift which they despise—it is God himself:

> And say to the people, 'Consecrate yourselves for tomorrow, and you shall eat meat, for you have wept in the hearing of the Lord, saying, "Who will give us meat to eat? For it was better for us in Egypt." Therefore the Lord will give you meat, and you shall eat. You shall not eat just one day, or two days, or five days, or ten days, or twenty days, but a whole month, until it comes out at your nostrils

and becomes loathsome to you, *because you have rejected the* LORD *who is among you* and have wept before him, saying, "Why did we come out of Egypt?"'

(Num. 11:18-20)

The LORD was true to his promise, and he delivered the meat the people craved so much in the form of quail. Even those who 'gathered least gathered ten homers' (11:32)—around two thousand litres, a phenomenal amount!—but 'while the meat was yet between their teeth, before it was consumed, the anger of the LORD was kindled against the people, and the LORD struck down the people with a very great plague' (11:33). The Hebrew name of that place where the people were buried was called *Kibroth-hattavah*—'Graves of Craving'.

These graves were filled, not with the bodies of people who had starved for lack of food, but the bodies of people who had begged for more and more food, had been supplied with a glut of meat, and had eaten themselves to death. It was a 'craving', a lust, an inordinate desire for the kind of food that they, the people of Israel, demanded. It was as though God was saying to them, 'All right then; if you insist on demanding the food you want, rather than the food which I supply for you, I will give you so much that it will make you sick—'*until it comes out at your nostrils*'; not much in the Bible scores more highly on the

Chapter 11

'yuk factor' than this!—'and your overdose of meat will actually kill you.'

Gorging on Netflix

This grotesque narrative is a parable for our times, in an oversupplied, overfed, over-pampered and over-entitled culture. But it applies to much more than food; it can apply to any commodity in the whole created realm.

You can suffer from a surfeit of entertainment. Here is a family sitting down to watch a movie on a Friday night. They decide to choose from the multitudinous options available on one or two of the well-known streaming services. It takes them half an hour, amid several arguments, to settle on a collective decision, but twenty minutes later most of the family agree that this film is 'boring', far too slow, difficult to get into. So, the room half-empties as various family members go to other parts of the house to enjoy their own preferred source of entertainment on their various solitary devices, while the remnant of the household slogs it out through the remainder of the movie. But any enjoyment has long since evaporated. Every individual in that dwelling goes to bed feeling, at one and the same time, dissatisfied with what they have watched, and sick of screens.

'Give me neither poverty nor riches', says Agur son of Jakeh, a wise man; 'feed me with the food that is needful for me, lest I be full and deny you and say, "Who is the

LORD?"' (Prov. 30:8–9). This is the specific danger of riches; the corresponding peril of poverty: 'lest I be poor and steal and profane the name of my God', is not a temptation that I suspect most of the readers of this book have faced.

That may, of course, change. As I write, the economic future of the UK and many other developed countries is decidedly uncertain. Inflation has risen to levels not seen for four decades, with sharp rises in the cost of food and fuel in particular, so that there is increased talk of poorer households being forced to choose between 'heating and eating'. There has been a discernible increase in the number of people begging on inner-city streets, and of the prevalence of prepacked, discounted food parcels in certain shops. Some of these pressures have come about as a result of the hiatus due to Covid, and others because of supply-line disruption connected to the war in Ukraine, though these two crises by no means explain the whole economic downturn. A day may come when the avocados do run out, although it will be rather more serious if apples, potatoes and bread begin to disappear from our supermarket shelves.

Worshipping the creature

This may all sound rather gloomy, and in writing all this, I am not arguing against the enjoyment of occasional treats and luxuries. Anyone who knows me would rightly accuse me of hypocrisy if I did so. And in the following chapter I

Chapter 11

will argue that the pursuit of prosperity, not poverty, is a noble and God-honouring aim. But the very definition of a 'luxury', in the realms of food, entertainment, holidays and so much more, is that it is occasional rather than frequent and commonplace.

This is the distinction that is being lost in an age of consumerism and entitlement. It is the worship of the gift, not the Giver—the service of the creature, not the Creator. It is a misdirected human appetite which both demands more but hates to have more. It is the very essence of addiction. Just as the people of Israel stuffed their faces with quail until chewed-up morsels of meat were dangling from their nostrils, yet kept on eating more and more, never being satisfied, so it is with people today, including so many professing Christians, as we gorge ourselves on everything the world has to offer, but pay lip service, if even that, to the God 'who richly provides us with everything to enjoy' (1 Tim. 6:17).

In the second half of Romans 1, the apostle Paul provides a devastating analysis of the decline of godliness and righteousness in the ancient world. At the heart of that passage is this statement: 'They exchanged the truth about God for a lie and worshipped and served the creature rather than the Creator, who is blessed forever! Amen' (Rom. 1:25).

Sexual immorality rather than gluttony is Paul's focus in this passage. But the essential diagnosis is just the same: when we make created entities the object of our desire and adoration, rather than the Creator from whom all these good things come, we lapse from divine worship to pagan idolatry; we despise 'the Lord who is among you' (Num. 11:20). He is dishonoured, and we, as individuals and as a society, are disfigured. It is better to forego the odd avocado than to spurn the knowledge and salvation of our God.

12 Vows of Prosperity

*If we command our wealth, we shall be rich and free.
If our wealth commands us, we are poor indeed.*[1]

Edmund Burke

If you have just read the last chapter, you might be forgiven for wondering whether I am mounting a denunciation of any kind of prosperity. Perhaps material wealth, in general, is a bad thing, something to be shunned by Christians? Maybe we have something to learn from medieval, mendicant orders such as the Franciscans and Dominicans, who took up their 'vows of poverty'?

Living as we do today, in a mounting Cost-of-Living Crisis that seems to be tightening its grip in many parts of the world, this question demands our serious attention in a way that might have seemed ludicrous only a decade or so ago.

As you will find out in this chapter, I want to oppose, most strenuously, the idea that Christians should renounce the pursuit of prosperity and wealth. Nothing could be more perverse and destructive than an attitude of this kind. But before coming to a discussion of these themes, we need to take a rather deep breath and appreciate the vast and detailed nature of this topic.

Chapter 12

Economics ain't easy

I approach these areas with a significant degree of trepidation; indeed, I would say that this chapter has been by far the most difficult one for me to write, involving several false starts and discarded outlines. The main reason for this is essentially personal and intellectual: I do not regard myself as any kind of economist and hesitate to make authoritative pronouncements on the subject. I have spent a large part of my life trying, and inevitably failing, to get my head around the subject.

Back in the latter days of the twentieth century, when radios were properly radios rather than smartphones, I used to be woken very early in the morning by the Shipping Forecast on *BBC Radio 4*. The wind speeds, storm warnings and visibility conditions in the various maritime regions around the United Kingdom—Viking, North Utsire, South Utsire, Forties, all the way round to Southeast Iceland, became familiar friends to me. I understood what a Force 8 gale in Biscay meant, and the clockwise meteorological journey around the British Isles held my attention; I could *see* it all in my mind's eye. I had no difficulty staying awake during those few minutes.

But this was followed by an early morning financial report, which never failed to send me back to sleep. The complexities of global markets, the performances of international companies, and comments about exchange rates and bond yields, simply caused me to glaze over and drop off very quickly. Strenuous efforts to read the *Financial Times* and the *Economist*, and even easy-to-use guides written for 'dummies' and 'idiots' left me unenlightened and confused.

Perhaps I am not alone and perhaps this is not surprising; perhaps you might be a sympathetic reader! The reason for this, it has dawned on me, is very clear: economics, of all subjects, refuses be reduced to a level which is accessible to 'dummies'.

As Wayne Grudem and Barry Asmus comment in their outstanding biblical treatment of economics, *The Poverty of Nations*, '[E]conomic systems are the result of millions of human beings making millions of choices every day. Who can ever expect to understand all this?'[2] They go on to quote Jay W. Richards, who demonstrates that in the science of economics we encounter high levels of complexity which make analysis all the more challenging:

> In biology ... we enter a higher order of complexity than in physics and chemistry. We are now dealing with organisms, which resist simple mathematical explanations ... From biology we move to the human sciences. Here the effects of intelligent agents appear everywhere. So it's no surprise that it's harder to use math to model human behavior

Chapter 12

than it is to use it to model, say, the movement of a ball rolling down a hill. By the time we reach economics, we are dealing not only with human agents, but with the market exchanges of millions or billions of intelligent agents.[3]

Reducing economic questions down to basic principles is very challenging, and few of us should attempt it. Renowned economic experts, of course, will disagree among themselves. But this does not seem to prevent *non-experts* from giving it a go, usually with a great, and almost uncertainly unwarranted, display of apparent confidence.

Economics quickens the pulse.

Get a group of friends together, let the conversation flow, and before long the discussion is bound to turn to questions of economics, with a fairly generous twist of politics thrown in. Perhaps you have been part of these types of conversations:

'House prices, especially here in London—they're astronomical! How can a young graduate, on a moderate salary, ever expect to get on the property ladder? The government should get involved and do something about it!' Someone else retorts, 'No, you're wrong; it's got absolutely nothing to do with the government. Let the free market decide.'

Or take a look at the National Health Service in the United Kingdom, a cherished institution, celebrated rather bizarrely during the opening ceremony of the 2012 London Olympic Games, and lauded to the skies during the initial months of the Covid Pandemic. 'I absolutely love the NHS', says someone, 'although I did go private last month to get my verruca seen to.' Someone else pipes up, 'That's because the system is broken. Once you actually get to see the doctors and nurses then it's great, but it's getting to see them which is the problem. The government will never fix this bureaucratic monstrosity just by throwing money at it.'

Then a debate might arise as to whether the government should decrease taxes, or increase borrowing, or allow inflation to rise, or exercise more control over central banks. People will articulate their opinions vehemently, but careful, reasoned discussion of underlying economic principles and assumptions seldom takes place.

The time has come for Christian people to give careful attention to the most fundamental axioms regarding wealth. And that means taking many steps back from the immediate issues which confront us, of the kind I have cited in the previous three paragraphs. In order to offer robust and authoritative commentary in such areas, we need to be well-acquainted with the essence and meaning of wealth itself.

The clearest and safest way to do this, it seems to me, is to set out six principles, the first of which is this:

CHAPTER 12

1. God defines and encourages wealth.

What does the word, 'wealth', mean? It comes from an old English word, 'weal', meaning a happy, successful, prosperous state or condition; 'weal' was often set against 'woe', its opposite.[4] Several centuries ago, the 'Public Weal' was understood to mean the general welfare of the nation; today we would mean the same thing by the 'Public Good'.

But what is *good*? No question is more essential now, or at any time, than this. If we can answer this question, we establish the moral compass which guides us. Remember how Jesus replied to the rich young ruler with the words, 'Why do you ask me about what is good? There is only one who is good' (Matt. 19:17). In saying this, Jesus was, at the very least, hinting at his own divine identity. *God alone* is good in the sense that he uniquely defines what goodness is. Or, as the Westminster Confession puts it: 'God hath all life, glory, goodness, blessedness, in and of Himself.'[5]

We then need to see that this good God is the good Creator God. What God creates is necessarily good because *he* is good and, by the time the creative process is completed, it is 'very good' (Gen. 1:31). The Psalmist praises God by telling him, 'You are good and do good' (Ps. 119:68), establishing the essential goodness of the whole created order.

Sin, of course, came into the world and marred it. But

we must strenuously maintain the rightness of speaking of this creation, even now, as *essentially good*. Paul is insistent on this as he writes to Timothy, 'For everything created by God is good, and nothing is to be rejected if it is received with thanksgiving' (1 Tim. 4:4). The food which God gives to you and me to eat—contrary to so much mythology that is peddled around food today, as we saw in the last chapter—is God's good gift to us. The same is true of clothing, housing, land, transport, technological appliances and every other kind of possession imaginable. While the way we use these created entities may be sinful, that sin springs from our evil hearts, and not from the creatures themselves.

2. God the Giver is alone to be worshipped.

To worship the gift, to worship anything that belongs to the created realm, is to commit idolatry. To remember this is a safeguard against the consumerism which I have described in the previous chapter.

Throughout the whole Bible, relying on riches is condemned, and this is as true in the Old Testament as it is in the New. Solomon himself counsels us, 'Whoever trusts in his riches will fall, but the righteous will flourish like a green leaf' (Prov. 11:28). We find the same kind of wisdom in the Psalms, especially in 49:6, 52:7 and 62:10.

Jesus' Parable of the Rich Fool underlines the same point. The man in the parable is a 'fool' precisely because

Chapter 12

he 'lays up treasure for himself and is not rich toward God' (Luke 12:21). Later in Luke's Gospel, in Chapter 16, Jesus directs additional parables to the Pharisees who, Luke tells us, were 'lovers of money' and ridiculed Jesus who told them that they could not serve both God and money (16:13–14). The great irony here, of course, is that the Pharisees boasted in their great devotion to God. It is perhaps no coincidence that Paul, a one-time Pharisee, experienced a point in his life when he was convicted of the specific sin of covetousness (Rom. 7:7–8).

For some decades we have witnessed the phenomenon of the 'Prosperity Gospel', sometimes called the 'Health and Wealth Gospel', or sometimes 'Name It and Claim It'. Essentially, it is the teaching that God's will for his people, which they can claim by faith and through prayer, is that they should be free from sickness and free from poverty. A clear sign of God's blessing is that you are healthy and wealthy—if not necessarily wise. The more you give to God, the more you will get back, in terms of material blessing.

Today, perhaps the best-known preacher who falls into this category is Joel Osteen of Lakewood Church in Houston, Texas. If you go onto that church's website, you will read these words on the front page:

> At Lakewood, we believe your best days are still out in front of you. Whether you are joining us in person

or online, we invite you to experience our services and be a part of the Lakewood family. The Bible says when you are planted in the house of the Lord, you will flourish. Get ready to step into a new level of your destiny![6]

Osteen could claim he is basing these words on Scripture; Psalm 92:13 does indeed say that God's people 'are planted in the house of the LORD; they flourish in the courts of our God.' The question is, what does Osteen mean by 'flourish'? What are the emphases, the currents, the whole character of his ministry? Does it agree with what Paul in verse 3 calls 'the teaching that accords with godliness'? Is God simply a means by which I can get rich, or is God himself my true and greatest treasure? If Osteen were to encounter a believer who was full of faith and the Holy Spirit, but living very modestly in material terms, would he conclude that God had not blessed him?

But we need to respond proportionately to this position, with a third principle.

3. God gives prosperity as a blessing.

As Paul draws towards the close of his First Letter to Timothy, he says a good deal about the subject of wealth. Timothy was labouring in Ephesus, one of the most prosperous commercial cities in the Roman Empire, and he was evidently ministering to some wealthy individuals and families. In 6:17–19, Paul charges Timothy:

Chapter 12

> As for the rich in this present age, charge them not to be haughty, nor to set their hopes on the uncertainty of riches, but on God, who richly provides us with everything to enjoy. They are to do good, to be rich in good works, to be generous and ready to share, thus storing up treasure for themselves as a good foundation for the future, so that they may take hold of that which is truly life.

Paul openly acknowledges that there will be rich people 'in this present age'. The bare fact of their wealth should not be viewed as necessarily wrong. The rich are not charged to renounce their wealth, nor to redistribute it. Paul does not charge them to carry out certain actions, instead he addresses their *attitudes*. They are to guard against a spirit of haughty pride which might lead them to view themselves as superior to poorer believers, and they are to place their ultimate trust, not in anything they possess, but in the God who has blessed them with those possessions. Material prosperity must not, therefore, be viewed with suspicion by Christians, as though it were something evil in and of itself.

Writing in the *Daily Telegraph*, Janet Daley identifies a growing and worrying trend:

> Until quite recently, there has been very little doubt in mainstream political discourse of the inherent value of growth itself. The idea that it was a good

thing for more people to become prosperous, more free from the deprivations and limitations of poverty and so more able to make their own life choices, has generally been considered beyond ethical doubt. The extent to which an elected government has managed to enable the poor and deprived sections of its population to achieve a degree of affluence has been regarded as a chief measure of its success. So morally unquestionable was this aim that every aspiring political leader had to express a commitment to it, and even a plausible programme for achieving it.

Not anymore. There is now quite vociferously among us, an ideological movement which asserts that continuous economic growth with its consequences of widespread popular prosperity and material comfort, is a pernicious thing: that more people having more money is a threat to the survival of everyone.[7]

We can go further: God himself gives people material blessings to *enjoy*, and he wants us to enjoy them! The right response to prosperity is neither greed nor guilt, but gratitude.

In the Bible, no one is condemned for creating wealth; people are not condemned *simply because they are rich*. Abraham, Isaac and Jacob became very rich, and so was

Chapter 12

Job (Gen. 13:2; 26:12–14; 30:43; Job 1:3). They were righteous men, and their wealth did not undermine their righteousness. We are specifically told that Joseph of Arimathea, who took Jesus' body and buried it, was 'a rich man' (Matt. 27:57). It was *because* this man was rich that he had been able to purchase a valuable piece of real estate in Jerusalem, a new tomb, carved out of the rock. This became a fitting burial-place for the Son of God; for one thing, Joseph's wealth became a factor in securing the rich hymnology of the Christian Church. It was a win-win deal in every sense.

4. Private ownership is commanded in the Bible.

The eighth commandment given by the Lord through Moses, 'You shall not steal' (Exod. 20:15), would be meaningless unless it is understood that property was to be privately owned. In the subsequent chapters in Exodus, where the implications of this commandment are spelled out, there are numerous references to different assets which belong to people: oxen, sheep, donkeys, fields, vineyards, cloaks. The various rules about restitution could not be enforced if private property rights were not upheld by God's Law.

But an objection might come. What about the practice of the early church as recorded in the opening chapters of Acts? During these days, 'all who believed were together and had all things in common. And they were selling their possessions and belongings and distributing the proceeds to all, as any had need' (Acts 2:44–45). We go on to read that 'no one said that any of the things that belonged to him was his own, but they had everything in common' (Acts 4:32). Should Christians regard this state of affairs as a template towards which we need to work, or even, in some sense, to enforce?

The most important consideration here is that these early believers were *freely motivated* to act as they did, being 'of one heart and soul' (Acts 4:32). There was no coercion applied, not by the leaders of the church, far less by state officials. The condemnation meted out on Ananias and Sapphira (Acts 5:4, 9) came about, not because of a lack of generosity towards their neighbours, but because of a lack of sincerity and integrity before God.

One reason why this discussion is so important is that we are witnessing a surging interest in a kind of Marxism which is not only cultural, but economic, and many younger people, even professing Christians, are being seduced by this theory. The essence of Marxism is that the state, rather than private individuals and companies, own and control the means of production and indeed the goods and services which are produced. Productivity is engineered, not by the market forces of supply and demand as they play out among individuals and companies who are free to buy and sell as they choose, but through centralized state planning.

Chapter 12

The inevitable consequence of this is the loss of incentive, the evaporation of the resourceful, pioneering, entrepreneurial spirit which has historically driven wealth creation. Marxist policies, or even socialist policies which tend in that direction, with their radical redistribution of wealth, discourage enterprise and cause wealth-creators to flee to more benevolent fiscal environments; and when rich people flee, the poor do not become richer; they become poorer.

Grudem and Asmus explain that:

> ... full-fledged socialism faces the same obstacles as communism: lack of sufficient incentive, loss of human productivity, loss of private ownership of businesses, and a corresponding loss of human and economic freedoms to be productive. Instead of consumers freely deciding which products are best and what should be produced, government officials make all those decisions. Socialism thus diminishes human freedom, choice, and opportunity to excel. No matter the plan, it has not been and cannot be made to work.[8]

Human beings think, plan and work most productively when they realize that their choices have clear, immediate, tangible consequences for themselves, their families and their businesses—whatever form those businesses might take.

If I believe that the free decisions which I take are going to have a definite effect, for better or worse, on my own, my family's and my business' material well-being, then I will be all the more motivated to think and plan carefully before making those decisions. With greater freedom comes greater responsibility—in fact, greater resemblance to the Creator himself in the free and responsible work which he carries out.

5. Prosperity is the reward of work.

Even in a pre-fallen world, Adam had to work the Garden of Eden and keep it, to enjoy its fruit (Gen. 2:15–16). Idleness was never to be rewarded. After the Fall, the same principle was in operation: human labour would result in human enjoyment of the produce of the land, despite it being wearisome, back-breaking and sweat-inducing toil (Gen. 3:17–19).

This remains the *modus operandi* today. In 2 Thessalonians 3:10–12, Paul has some fairly sharp words for individuals, members of the church no less, who imagine there can be such a thing as work-free prosperity:

> For even when we were with you, we would give you this command: If anyone is not willing to work, let him not eat. For we hear that some among you walk in idleness, not busy at work, but busybodies. Now such persons we command and encourage in the

Chapter 12

> Lord Jesus Christ to do their work quietly and to earn their own living.

This biblical axiom is at odds with the welfarism that has been developing, in Western Europe especially, since 1945. By 'welfar*ism*' I do not mean the wholly reasonable expectation that those who are genuinely incapacitated, because of age (very young or very old) or infirmity cannot work and should be materially supported. I mean the general assumption that government agencies are expected to step in and support any individual or business whose level of income falls below what that individual or business believes to be an acceptable level.

To take a current example, in February 2022 the Welsh Government announced that over 500 young 'care leavers' would receive a 'basic income payment' of £1600 per month for two years from the date of their eighteenth birthday.[9] It has been presented as a 'pilot' and its outcomes will be assessed in due time.

It is questionable whether we need to wait very long before finding out what these outcomes will be. One of the stated aims of the project is 'addressing poverty and unemployment and improving health and financial wellbeing'. We should very much hope that young people in Wales will be encouraged to see that the only viable route to 'financial wellbeing' is through gainful employment. *Simply* throwing cash in their direction may not prove to be any more productive than handing out money to homeless drug addicts and alcoholics sitting by the side of the road.

Let us broaden the picture. You do not need a Ph.D. in economic theory to appreciate that the massive government handouts during the Covid Pandemic would have seriously negative repercussions before long. The sight of hundreds and perhaps thousands of people crowding into London's parks, to enjoy the summer afternoon sunshine, would be quite unremarkable during weekends. But in June 2020 this was happening every *weekday*. Millions, employed both in the private and the public sector, were being asked to 'work from home' while the Government paid their wages. Having the flexibility to choose the hours when they might be sitting at their laptop, was it any surprise that many of them would opt to 'knock off' for several hours when the sun was shining?

Government sources reveal the astronomically eye-watering scale of the cost of this support:

> Official figures show that spending in 2020/21 was about £167 billion higher than had been planned before the pandemic for that year.
>
> Most of this extra money was spent on public services (such as the NHS), support for businesses, and support for individuals. Some of the largest schemes include the Coronavirus Job Retention

Chapter 12

Scheme (CJRS, sometimes called the furlough scheme) and NHS Test and Trace.

The departments responsible for the most extra spending were HMRC, the Department for Health and Social Care, and the Department for Business, Energy and Industrial Strategy.[10]

There had to be some comeuppance somewhere down the line. One of the first principles of economics is that 'There's No Such Thing as a Free Lunch'.[11] Millions of people, for several months, were effectively being paid not to work. Where would all this extra money come from? The Government would have to raise that money somehow, through a variety of means, but the essential equation is this: no government can spend what it does not have, and unless a government chooses to default on its debt payments, devalue its currency or declare itself bankrupt, it must find that money from its people.

One way or another, all those millions of people sunning themselves in the parks will have to pay the Government back for that benefit, whether through increased taxation, through reduction in Government spending (which means that the people are denied the benefits they might otherwise have gained through taxation) or through rising inflation (which is an indirect form of taxation), or through a combination of the three.

If, as may happen, the Cost-of-Living Crisis takes a

more stringent hold over the months that lie ahead, the inadequacies of welfarism will be tested to their limits. There can be no welfare safety net without copious tax receipts, but those receipts will not be forthcoming without a corresponding increase in productivity. It is not enough to argue about how to cut the cake—bigger and better cakes need to be baked.

My conclusive and climactic principle is the following:

6. Wisdom should direct and determine prosperity.

The above statement is a condensation of a rather longer one which I will state more fully: *the way in which human beings decide to invest their various assets—assets being defined as broadly as possible—will be the great determinant of their prosperity.*

This comprehensive statement can be divided into its constituent parts and examined from various angles.

By 'human beings' I include absolutely everyone: from the most powerful and influential, whether in government, industry, finance, education and a host of other sectors, right the way down to the individual who has very limited responsibilities and means—but nevertheless has *some* responsibilities and means.

By 'invest' I intend the allocation of time, communication, energy, skills and material resources as well as money, and each of these in turn are rightly to be seen as 'assets'.

Chapter 12

And by 'prosperity' I mean fruitfulness, abundance, satisfaction, or perhaps better, 'succeeding' in what is done, for the benefit of those for whom good is intended, and to the glory and praise of the God who first instructed man to subdue the earth and exercise dominion over its creatures (Gen. 1:28)—a mandate that has never been rescinded.

Psalm 1 describes the wise, righteous man whose 'delight is in the law of the Lord'. He is compared to a tree which never fails to flourish: 'in *all* that he does, he prospers' (Ps. 1:2-3). The Hebrew verb for 'prosper', *tsalach*, conveys the idea of advancing, succeeding, thriving, being in a good condition. It amounts to more than simply material prosperity, though it undoubtedly includes a material aspect.

This picture of the wise, godly and prosperous individual is set before every believer, not simply for our admiration, but for our imitation. From time to time, we see examples of such people in our lives, and we also see them in the Scriptures.

One of the most prominent biblical examples is Joseph who, when he was in Potiphar's house, knew the blessing of the Lord to a remarkable degree. Immediately after learning that Joseph had been sold to Potiphar, we read the following, striking description:

> The Lord was with Joseph, and he became a successful

man, and he was in the house of his Egyptian master. His master saw that the LORD was with him and that the LORD caused all that he did to succeed in his hands. So Joseph found favour in his sight and attended him, and he made him overseer of his house and put him in charge of all that he had. From the time that he made him overseer in his house and over all that he had, the LORD blessed the Egyptian's house for Joseph's sake; the blessing of the LORD was on all that he had, in house and field. So he left all that he had in Joseph's charge, and because of him he had no concern about anything but the food he ate.

(Gen. 39:2–6)

In few other places in the Bible do we find such a conspicuous narrative of what is, essentially, 'economic prosperity'. And what is equally impressive is that Joseph's excellent qualities were put to full use in the next phase of his life, when he was thrown into prison on false charges. The account of the prison-keeper who 'paid no attention to anything that was in Joseph's charge, because the LORD was with him' (Gen. 39:23), resonates strongly with the passage quoted above.

So it was, that when the whole land of Egypt was poised to enter seven years of plenty, followed by seven years of famine, Joseph was the man with the ability, wisdom, character and experience to deal with the crisis. Not

Chapter 12

only did he gather up sufficient food during the years of abundant harvest (41:47–49); much later, when the effects of the famine began to bite, Joseph exercised outstanding prudence and courage in dealing with the mounting crisis, buying up not only the people's livestock but eventually the land itself (47:13–26).

A reader might be tempted to argue that Joseph's economic plan for Egypt was the most radical exercise in wealth-redistribution imaginable, an ancient experiment in proto-Marxism, against which I have been contending! In fact, the abiding legacy of Joseph's policies was nothing more than a twenty per cent income tax in Egypt (47:26), but what is especially noticeable is that the people of Egypt expressed the deepest gratitude to Joseph: 'You have saved our lives; may it please my lord, we will be servants to Pharaoh' (47:25). The prosperity which Joseph's policies generated was such that he would have won a landslide general election that year if Egypt had been a parliamentary democracy!

There is surely a vital lesson for us here, which is that large-scale government economic intervention may be necessary under extreme, life-threatening circumstances, as in times of war and famine, but should not be understood as the norm. What is normal, and what is abnormal? This is where great wisdom and judgement are required.

Countries in twenty-first-century Europe and North

America may not be about to embark on seven years of famine, not just yet anyway. But the lesson for our times is very clear: Christian people need to exercise responsible, resolute and at times radical means of stewardship over all that is entrusted to them.

We need leaders of the calibre of Joseph, but at the same time we are *all* called to be leaders, in one capacity or another; we need to study examples like Joseph, so that we might have the understanding, wit and wherewithal to know how to function at a time when harsh economic winds really begin to blow.

13 THE JANUARY TEST

The Holocene has ended. The Garden of Eden is no more. We have changed the world so much that scientists say we are in a new geological age: the Anthropocene, the age of humans.[1]

Sir David Attenborough

Let me frankly own up to something which may already be apparent: I am, by nature, somewhat inclined to be reactionary. Not necessarily sceptical, and not, I sincerely hope, cynical—I could not do anything 'sincerely' if I were cynical!—but most definitely *reactionary*.

When everyone else in the room is raving about the latest marvellous and life-changing innovation, I am more inclined to shake my head or roll my eyes in disdain. When a salesman knocks at my door, or accosts me in the streets, I want to run a mile. The fact that someone is enthusiastically seeking to persuade me that I need to buy such-and-such a product will inevitably prejudice me against it. I do not think I would have been much of a success if I had gone into the world of advertising.

So when, during the 1990s, more and more people began to make panicky noises about 'global warming', holes in the ozone layer, the greenhouse effect,

Chapter 13

chlorofluorocarbons (CFCs—remember them?), and rising sea levels which would surely inundate large tracts of dry land by the middle of the twenty-first century, my instinctive response was to shake my head and say 'Nah— it's a load of old alarmist scaremongering. It's never going to happen!'

But around that time, I privately set myself a test— one that seemed as objective and verifiable as possible. It was this: if the air temperature, anywhere in the United Kingdom, exceeded a threshold of 20°C during the calendar month of January, then I would give serious consideration to the claim that the world really *was* getting warmer. At the time, certainly in the northeast of England where I then lived, January was a month of frost, snow and ice, punctuated by Atlantic low-pressure spells of wet and windy weather where the temperature nudged up into the low teens, at best. A temperature of 15°C in January was rare, if not unprecedented. A temperature of 20°C was impossibly high. There seemed little danger of losing my wager.

I have not lost it even now; not that I told anyone about it until I wrote it in these pages. According to the Met Office, the record high temperature for January in the United Kingdom is 18.3 °C, recorded in three separate locations—interestingly all in Scotland and Wales, something to do with those Atlantic Lows, no doubt—and even *more* interestingly, in three years which are spaced quite far apart: 1958, 1971 and 2003.[2] The 'January test' has failed to convince me. January remains, for me, the best advertisement there is for the benefits of hibernation.

But the 'February test' might stand a better chance. On 26 February 2019 the mercury hit 21.2°C in Kew Gardens, not a million miles from our neck of the woods. The Met Office says so. That sunny afternoon, in the parks and gardens of South London, the daisies and dandelions were out in force—a rare and welcome sight.

Climate change is not a myth.
So, has it been getting warmer recently? That is the majority report, and it is a fair conclusion. But to make a judgement such as this, we need to know how to handle and interpret the data.

The fact that 1976 remains the hottest summer in my memory, and in the memory of just about anyone who can remember those parched cricket outfields and dry river beds; and the fact that much *later*, in December 2010, the River Severn in Shrewsbury froze over, with the temperature plunging to eighteen degrees below zero—these facts count for little by comparison with the global picture, with long term trends across the whole world, not just in one location.

'Global Warming' in the 1990s has morphed into 'Climate Change' in the twenty-first century. Is the climate really changing? Yes, it seems that it is. I'm

Chapter 13

not *that* reactionary! Anecdotal evidence may not be as highly regarded in some circles as 'scientifically' as statistical data, but human observation and consensus are not without value. Yes, it hardly ever snows in London these days—the 'Beast from the East' in 2018 was quite exceptional—whereas in years gone by a snow-clad capital was not a rarity, even if the snow rapidly melted into ugly brown-and-grey slush. Foggy autumn mornings were once far more common than they are now, not only in built-up urban centres, but in the countryside as well; filters fitted on vehicle exhausts because of various Clean Air Acts, by themselves, can scarcely account for such a change.

The observation that climate patterns do indeed change should not be restricted to the age of the Met Office. Diligent climate historians are aware of both the Roman Warm Period (roughly the first four centuries of the Christian era) and the Medieval Warm Period (950–1300).[3] The agriculture and horticulture of Britain flourished during these centuries, with a booming trade in the produce of vineyards. What made the intervening 'Dark Ages' so dark? It seems likely that the climate must have played a part. More recently, the 'Little Ice Age' (roughly 1300–1870) was a time of shorter growing seasons and no realistic prospect of Berkshire Beaujolais hitting the supermarket shelves. It is well known that there were frost fairs on the Thames in the latter half of the seventeenth century, but what might be less well known is the compelling evidence that there was a general lowering of temperatures across the globe during these centuries. The far greater quantity of sea ice, as well as river ice, for example, affected warfare and exploration as well as agriculture and commerce.[4]

The dominant secular religion

Michael Shellenberger was once a passionate environmental activist. As the dust jacket of his highly readable and informative book explains:

> [Shellenberger] has been fighting for a greener planet for decades. He helped save the world's last unprotected redwoods. He cocreated the predecessor to today's Green New Deal. And he led a successful effort by climate scientists and activists to keep nuclear plants operating, preventing a spike of emissions.[5]

Michael Shellenberger *is still* a passionate environmental activist. But the difference now is that he no longer submits to the creed of what he describes as 'the exaggeration, alarmism, and extremism that are the enemy of positive, humanistic, and rational environmentalism.'[6]

Shellenberger describes a BBC interview in October 2019 with Sarah Lunnon, a zealous spokesperson for Extinction Rebellion, which sought to disrupt life in

Chapter 13

London as much as possible on several occasions. In the course of the interview, Lunnon made the claim that:

> [t]here are a number of scientists who've said that if we get to four degrees of warming, which is where we're heading at the moment, they cannot see how the earth can support not one billion people, but half a billion people ... That's six and a half billion people dying![7]

In subsequent correspondence, it became clear to Shellenberger that Lunnon was basing her conclusions on the views of just two scientists, Kevin Anderson and Johan Rockström—the latter of whom was quoted as saying, in an article in *The Guardian* in May 2019, that a four-degree global temperature rise could not support a billion or even half a billion people. However, further research on Shellenberger's part uncovered, not only that nothing in the IPCC's reports could be found to back up such claims, but that Rockström had been significantly misrepresented.[8] Indeed, a number of Rockström's colleagues at the Potsdam Institute 'found that food production could *increase* even at four- or five-degrees Celsius warming above preindustrial levels.'[9]

In the course of his book, Shellenbeger investigates such diverse subjects as deforestation, polystyrene waste, gorilla conservation, whaling, meat production and nuclear power. He underlines the misinformation, media hype and political pressure which has created the narrative that he now rejects—that climate change is the 'greatest challenge humans have ever faced.'[10]

Shellenberger does not write as a Christian, but he writes with remarkable insight as he describes the 'religious' hold which environmentalism has over large sections of the world's population:

> Environmentalism today is the dominant secular religion of the educated, upper-middle-class elite in most developed and many developing nations. It provides a new story about our collective and individual purpose. It designates good guys and bad guys, heroes and villains. And it does so in the language of science, which provides it with legitimacy.[11]

Is Shellenberger right? Would anyone disagree with him?

The heart of education

In November 2021, as COP26[12] got underway in Glasgow, the following bulletin appeared on the UK Government web site:

> Young people will be empowered to take action on the environment as part of new measures designed to put climate change at the heart of education. Announcing a range of measures in a speech at COP26 today, Education Secretary Nadhim Zahawi

Chapter 13

will set out his vision for all children to be taught about the importance of conserving and protecting our planet. Teachers will be supported to deliver world-leading climate change education through a model science curriculum, which will be in place by 2023, to teach children about nature and their impact on the world around them.[13]

If climate change is 'at the heart of education' then it must be the overriding, pre-eminent concern of education; unless, like certain dinosaurs, education has multiple hearts. The clear messaging is that nothing, absolutely nothing, can be more important in our world, and for children to learn about at school, than climate change. This is worth thinking about.

In England and Wales, statute books still retain the requirement that state-funded schools must conduct daily acts of collective worship which are 'wholly or mainly of a broadly Christian character'. This was undoubtedly the case in the 1940s. It was still true to a large extent in the 1980s. But in the 2020s—though there are notable exceptions—it has largely evaporated. In many schools, perhaps in most, the opening words of the Lord's Prayer, 'Our Father who art in heaven', have been replaced by such invocations as 'Dear Earth.'[14]

The new religion in the UK and in large parts of the world has become Environmentalism. Why do I say 'religion'?

The January test

Because, as Shellenberger explains so clearly, like all religions Environmentalism has its god, its narrative, its sinners, its crisis, its saints, its saviours, its sacrifices, and its moral code.[15]

Once the suffix '-ism' is added to any word, a new narrative emerges, indeed an entire worldview. That worldview then competes with other worldviews including, for our purposes, the biblical and Christian worldview. We need to be able to demonstrate where Environmentalism is fundamentally at odds with the biblical worldview.

Who governs your thinking?

Where do we start? Environmentalism clearly has a moral code, its own version of the Ten Commandments. It has a very definite list of dos and don'ts. *Do* try to compost your throwaway food. *Don't* throw scrap metal into the same recycling box as cardboard. *Do* put on an extra layer of clothing when it's a bit chilly, rather than putting the heating on straightaway. *Don't* build hundreds of coal-fuelled power stations if cleaner energy sources can be used. *Do* try to save endangered animal species from extinction. *Don't* throw millions of plastic bottles into the oceans. *Don't* drive your car through the streets of London. But *do* please ride your bike!

It is not that these may not be reasonable, sensible, and responsible things to do. I follow most of them myself,

Chapter 13

although I really have to scratch my head to remember the last time that I toyed with the idea of building a coal-fuelled power station.

But we must probe deeper than actions. We need to examine our thinking, our underlying assumptions. We need to discern the controlling worldview. And we get at that by asking this question: in all my thought, speech, and action in relation to the environment, who is my ultimate authority? Who governs my thinking and my conscience?

Am I under a moral obligation to agree with every pronouncement made by every media outlet in relation to climate change? For example, the Science and Security Board of the Bulletin of the Atomic Scientists are telling us that it is currently '100 seconds to midnight', the nearest the world has ever been to annihilation.[16] What if I take a different view? Am I permitted to say so? What if someone tells me very earnestly that flying by aeroplane produces vast emissions of CO_2 and that these are mainly responsible for climate change. Do I have the freedom to say, 'I don't agree', or even, 'It's not quite so simple as that'?

In the United Kingdom there is a push to reach 'net zero' by 2050.[17] Am I at liberty to express any misgivings about whether this might be realistic or affordable? Because in the final analysis, 'realistic' boils down to 'affordable.'

My point is that Christian people are free to differ on

questions of this kind. We are under no absolute moral obligation to agree or to disagree; these are matters of opinion, and some opinions are more expert than others. The fundamental issue at stake is not the specific answers we reach in terms of policies and practicalities; it is the underlying convictions and assumptions, the whole worldview, that we bring to this debate. It is whether these convictions and assumptions are built on biblical revelation, which stands firm, or on the shifting sands of public consensus.

At the Diet of Worms in 1521—an environmental-sounding gathering if ever there was one—Martin Luther said, famously, 'My conscience is captive to the Word of God'.[18] Christian people must have the same attitude and mindset as Luther, at this point in our history. Paul's words, in Romans 12:2, are always needed: 'Do not be conformed to this world, but be transformed by the renewal of your mind, that by testing you may discern what is the will of God, what is good and acceptable and perfect.'

That means that we need to think about this whole subject of the environment under a biblical framework. If we have this framework clear in our minds, we will be able to think intelligently as Christians about this subject and indeed every other subject.

What is the biblical, Christian framework? How should we think about the whole of history? What is the big picture, the metanarrative which should govern our

Chapter 13

thinking if, like Luther, we say that 'my conscience is captive to the Word of God'?

I suggest that the best way to start is to consider the fourfold structure of Creation-Fall-Redemption-Restoration.[19] These are the four states or conditions through which humanity, and the earth on which human beings live, pass during the entire course of history. This division has a long and noble history, with deep roots in the theology of Augustine of Hippo (AD 354–430) and given powerful expression in the work of Thomas Boston (1676–1732) and his book, *Human Nature in its Fourfold State*.[20]

Augustine and Boston, among others, focus primarily on the human condition, on our relationship to God, to sin and to righteousness. But our focus here is the condition of the earth; or, more precisely, how human beings should understand and relate to the earth, given this biblical framework. Before proceeding any further, we need to pause and examine, briefly, the relationship between God, man, and the earth.

God, man and the environment

In my schooldays I was taught that geography could be summarized as the study of 'man and his environment'.[21] We could broaden the scope by suggesting that 'man and his environment', and the interaction between them, could be equally descriptive of many other academic disciplines: economics, sociology, geology and biology among them.

But as biblical Christians we need to insist that 'man and his environment' is a partial and inadequate portrayal of reality, of everything that exists. It is more than this; it is entirely blasphemous as well as foolish to believe that is the full story. It rests upon atheistic assumptions: there is no God, or if there is one, he is not significant enough to feature prominently in any serious intellectual pursuit (Ps. 14:1; 53:1). The Christian begins by saying '*God, man and his environment*'. The 'environment'—for our purposes the earth—was created by God and given to man as a dwelling-place. When God had created man, male and female, and placed them on an earth that was ready for them to inhabit, then and only then, God pronounced everything 'very good' (Gen. 1:31). As it says in Psalm 115:16, 'The heavens are the Lord's heavens, *but the earth he has given to the children of man.*'

This means that we cannot understand the environment accurately unless we view its history through the lens of God's existence, his creative work, and his relationship to man. What is more, the whole condition of the earth—physical, meteorological, biological, moral—mirrors the state of the divine-human relationship. The 'very good' description of the earth continued only as long as Adam retained his original righteousness and obeyed God's commandments.

CHAPTER 13

Today we live in a world which still bears the hallmarks of Creation. The continuation of 'seedtime and harvest, cold and heat, summer and winter, day and night' (Gen. 8:22) is the most palpable evidence that the earth we live on is the handiwork of a mighty, wise, artistic Creator.[22] In any intellectual pursuit, as we study every kind of creature—human, animal, vegetable or non-living—we continue to enjoy what God himself first enjoyed. 'Great are the works of the LORD, studied by all who delight in them' (Ps. 111:2).[23]

The fact of the Fall means that every human pursuit is attended with pain and difficulty. When Adam fell into sin, and his whole human posterity with him, the earth came under the curse of thorns and thistles, toil and sweat, disease and death (Gen. 3:17–19). As sin, evil and violence gathered momentum in the earth, the greatest environmental catastrophe in history, the Great Flood in the days of Noah, drew near and was eventually unleashed (Gen. 6:13). The Flood, of course, did not wash away the curse. Frustration and hard drudgery continue to characterize all human work and activity. Vast amounts of time, money and labour are expended on the effects of the Fall. We need police, armed forces, locksmiths, anaesthetists, family lawyers and many other agencies which exist only because man has become a rebel against God—and the longer he goes on saying 'man and his environment' rather than '*God*, man and his environment', the worse that whole environment becomes.

But what about Redemption? This is where the debate becomes especially interesting and important. Exactly who, or what, does God, through the Lord Jesus Christ, redeem?

A category error

The clear answer given by the whole Bible is that God redeems his *people*. While there are passages in the Law of Moses, and in the Book of Ruth, which speak about people redeeming property as well as individuals in the land of Israel, the overwhelming narrative throughout the Old Testament is that the LORD is the Redeemer of his *people*. Isaiah 49:26 stands out among many other verses: 'I am the LORD your Saviour, and your Redeemer, the Mighty One of Jacob.'[24]

There is not the space or time to deal with this question thoroughly in this chapter; suffice to say that there has been a good deal of rather confused and muddled thinking on this subject. In this present age, God is not redeeming art, music, culture, education, politics or whole nations: God has redeemed his chosen *people*.

Most importantly, God has not redeemed the environment; it is wrong and unhelpful to think in these terms. The poignant description of the present world

Chapter 13

given by Paul in Romans 8:19–23 is as palpably true today as it was in the first century AD:

> For the creation waits with eager longing for the revealing of the sons of God. For the creation was subjected to futility, not willingly, but because of him who subjected it, in hope that the creation itself will be set free from its bondage to corruption and obtain the freedom of the glory of the children of God. For we know that the whole creation has been groaning together in the pains of childbirth until now. And not only the creation, but we ourselves, who have the firstfruits of the Spirit, groan inwardly as we wait eagerly for adoption as sons, the redemption of our bodies.

The Bible does not speak about 'the environment'; instead, it speaks about 'the creation'. The point is that this creation is awaiting redemption; redemption is a 'not yet' reality for the creation, even though it is a 'now' reality as far as believers themselves are concerned, in terms of their status—by which I mean that Christians can and should say, 'God has redeemed us'.[25] But God has not yet redeemed the creation, which includes the bodies of believers; verse 23 demonstrates that the redemption of these bodies is a future event. That future event belongs to the fourth category in our framework, *Restoration*. God has done two 'firstfruit' things to assure his people that this Restoration is certain: he has raised the Lord Jesus to life—'Christ has been raised from the dead, the firstfruits of those who have fallen asleep' (1 Cor. 15:20)—and he has given his people his Spirit, as Paul says at the end of the passage quoted above.

What is the implication for the environment and for Environmentalism? It is this: we err when we suppose that care for the environment, including every so-called 'green policy', has some kind of redemptive element. This is to make a fundamental category error. The right perspective is to see that when we care for the environment, we are still carrying out God's original *creation* mandate to Adam: 'Be fruitful and multiply and fill the earth and subdue it, and have dominion over the fish of the sea and over the birds of the heavens and over every living thing that moves on the earth' (Gen. 1:28). Even though the world is fallen, our present stewardship of the earth in its cursed condition remains the outworking of the same command which God gave Adam at the beginning.

Seven activities which are still good

This perspective should be nothing less than revolutionary, and it should impart confidence and courage to Christian people—of all ages—who have grown used to acting as though climate change, or the extinction of Planet Earth, were the ultimate reality to be feared. To live in fear in this manner is nothing other than paganism—modern,

Chapter 13

sophisticated and 'scientific' perhaps, but paganism nevertheless, rather than faith in the God of the Bible. As the apostle Paul would again remind us, we must 'not be conformed to this world, but be transformed by the renewal of your mind, that by testing you may discern what is the will of God, what is good and acceptable and perfect' (Rom. 12:2).

So let me finish this chapter, and this third section of the book, by listing seven human activities, based on Genesis 2, which were good when the world was created, and they remain good right now, as you read about them.

1. *Discovery and investigation are good.* In the land of Eden there were four rivers, and gold, bdellium and onyx stone (Gen. 2:10–14). What was that world like? It was a place to be discovered and investigated. Exploration and curiosity are good; education and research are good; learning and finding things out are good!

2. *Food is good.* There is a great deal about food in the early chapters of Genesis. The plants in the Garden of Eden were 'good for food' (Gen. 2:9). Leaving aside for now the question of diet—whether or not we eat meat, or are vegetarian, or vegan—food remains good. Agriculture—the whole process of producing food from the earth—is therefore right and good. As physical creatures we need to eat, and food is understood as the end product of our work. That is why the main wage-earner in households

The January Test

has traditionally been called the 'breadwinner'. If we do not work, we will not eat (2 Thes. 3:10).

3. *Material production is good.* Notice in verses 11 and 12 of Genesis 2 that the land contained materials: gold, onyx stone and bdellium—an aromatic gum or resin, in case you are wondering. These substances are 'good'; they are good for human usage. Extracting and using raw materials for human use is a right use of the earth's resources.

4. *Wealth production is good.* This underlines the theme of the previous chapter. We are told in verse 12 that 'the gold of that land is good'. Gold is a precious commodity, so find it, get it, make something from it and sell it! To create wealth through industry, business, marketing, enterprise and investment is a good thing for human beings to do. Without this, all our lives would be much harder. This is not an encouragement to be greedy and selfish; instead, it is about being creative and resourceful. Burying gold in the ground and leaving it there is not massively encouraged in the Bible (Matt. 25:24–27).

5. *Beauty is good.* The trees in that land were 'pleasant to the sight', verse 9 tells us. It is a snapshot of just how beautiful that Garden was, and indeed how beautiful the world is even today, although it is fallen. As human beings made in God's image we should appreciate beauty, and we should also create beauty: in fine art, sculpture, architecture, interior design, clothing,

Chapter 13

jewellery, cosmetics, literature, music, dance, sport, cinematography, food; in fact, the list is endless.

6. *Romantic love, marriage and having children is good.* There is a growing idea today that it is wrong and bad to have children—that in the present 'emergency' it is best avoided. Not only are fewer people getting married in many parts of the world, but fewer children are also being born. But God still says to the human race, 'Be fruitful and multiply and fill the earth' (Gen. 1:28). When did God ever tell us to stop doing these things? There are enough resources in this world to feed and supply everyone—our God is good, and where there is wise and responsible stewarding, the whole earth's population can be sustained.

God is still the God who makes us male and female; he is still the Creator of physical attraction and procreation. If a teenage person reading these words wants to get married one day, and have children, it is a good and noble ambition.

7. *It is good to care for the earth and its resources.* It is good to care for the environment, and even better to call it the 'creation'! Adam was put in the Garden to keep it, to care for it—and we have a duty of care for the whole world. All of us are called to exercise that duty of care in an almost infinite variety of ways, depending on the gifts, circumstances and opportunities we are given. And yes, that will mean, for us today, newer, cleaner, more

sustainable and renewable forms of energy. It could even look something like a 'green revolution'. As people invest their time in researching and developing these new technologies, thinking and working it through with God-given wisdom and bearing in mind *all* the costs so that the overall quality of life is enhanced rather than impoverished, that will be good and responsible stewardship.

If 'reactionary' describes someone who sticks to what we might call the 'old paths', then a concern for the environment is genuinely reactionary. We will not save 'Planet Earth' from extinction by any human activity, by any national or international law-making. We must continue to act as wise stewards of the earth and all its resources as long as it continues, just as we care for our own bodies and our own homes. The inevitable fact that body, home and world have an end-date stamped on them should not make us irresponsible.

But God's people have an infinitely better hope guaranteed to them in the Bible: 'new heavens and a new earth in which righteousness dwells' (2 Peter 3:13). Our responsible stewardship in this world is preparation for our greater work in the world which is to come.

PART FIVE:
CAPTIVITY

14 Take me to your captives.

> *I was in misery, and misery is the state of every soul overcome by friendship with mortal things and lacerated when they are lost. Then the soul becomes aware of the misery which is its actual condition even before it loses them.*[1]
>
> Augustine of Hippo

We have now covered 'pestilence', 'sword' and 'famine', linking each of these to specific contemporary events: the Covid-19 Pandemic, the war in Ukraine and the Cost-of-Living Crisis. The connections between the first three categories in Jeremiah 15:2 and present world events jumped out at me almost instantaneously on that very memorable Thursday, 24 February 2022.

But what about 'captivity'? Is there any current world event which clearly relates to this fourth category? Modern-day slavery perhaps? I'm sure a compelling case could be made for the inclusion of this theme. Or addictions of various kinds; surely no experience is more descriptive of 'captivity' than drug or alcohol addiction, or even a gambling addiction? Or maybe, as it is the fourth item in the list, 'captivity' awaits a future

Chapter 14

concrete fulfilment, which we cannot presently predict. Or it may just be that the whole pattern of one-to-one correspondence is just too forced, too contrived. There simply is not anything going on today matching the theme of 'captivity'.

This question exercised me as I approached this final part of the work, and there was a fairly lengthy pause in my writing before I began to tackle this question head-on. Where do we find the captives? The problem with captives is that they are not usually paraded around openly in the streets; they are generally locked up in cells, incarcerated behind multiple walls and doors.

I eventually concluded that the captives *could* be located, but only after going back to the Bible again and examining how the theme of captivity features in the Old and the New Testaments. That is what we will be doing in this chapter, before we begin to identify the present-day captives in the following chapter.

Captivity and exile—are they the same?

The Hebrew word for 'captivity' in Jeremiah 15:2, and in many other Old Testament texts, is sh'vi. It describes a state in which someone is bound and imprisoned, held in custody—someone who is, by definition, *not free*. In this verse the prophet is foretelling the seventy years during which the nation of Judah will be held captive in Babylon; this is first published in Jeremiah 25:11: 'This whole land shall become a ruin and a waste, and these nations shall serve the king of Babylon seventy years.'

'Captivity', however, may not be the word we first tend to think of in connection with this specific historical event. We are probably more likely to think in terms of 'exile'.

In Jeremiah 29, the chapter in which Jeremiah writes to his compatriots in Babylon, the word 'exile' appears six times, but 'captivity' not at all. In historical terms, 'captivity' and 'exile' overlap; when Jerusalem and Judah went into captivity, they went into exile. In the Books of Ezra and Nehemiah, the two descriptions are sometimes used almost interchangeably. For example, in Ezra 8:35 we read that 'Those who had come from *captivity*, the returned *exiles*, offered burnt offerings to the God of Israel.' Similarly in Nehemiah 7:6: 'These were the people of the province who came up out of the *captivity* of those *exiles* whom Nebuchadnezzar the king of Babylon had carried into *exile*.' And, in Ezekiel 12:11, the prophet is told to speak these words in almost the same breath: 'Say, "I am a sign for you: as I have done, so shall it be done to them. They shall go into *exile*, into *captivity*."'

There is historical overlap between these two categories, though the meanings are not identical. The root meaning of exile is *removal*—to be displaced from one's home or usual dwelling place. The exiles in Babylon were certainly not 'captives' in the sense that they were

Chapter 14

physically restricted from pursuing certain activities. They could hardly have followed Jeremiah's instructions—'Build houses and live in them; plant gardens and eat their produce. Take wives and have sons and daughters; take wives for your sons, and give your daughters in marriage, that they may bear sons and daughters; multiply there, and do not decrease' (Jer. 29:5–6)—had they been locked up in jail.

But for God's people in the Old Testament, exile necessarily implied captivity. Why? Because Jerusalem was not simply their homeland, it was the place which the Lord had appointed for his people to worship him. In Deuteronomy 12:5–7 God spoke to his people as they were about to cross the Jordan and enter the land of Canaan:

> You shall seek the place that the Lord your God will choose out of all your tribes to put his name and make his habitation there. There you shall go, and there you shall bring your burnt offerings and your sacrifices, your tithes and the contribution that you present, your vow offerings, your freewill offerings, and the firstborn of your herd and of your flock. And there you shall eat before the Lord your God, and you shall rejoice, you and your households, in all that you undertake, in which the Lord your God has blessed you.

'*There* you shall go ... *there* you shall eat ... and you shall

Take me to your captives.

rejoice'. These words were spoken through Moses several centuries before the Temple was built in Jerusalem in the days of Solomon. That Temple was the appointed 'place' which God had chosen for his holy habitation. So, when the exiles by the rivers of Babylon sat down and lamented, 'How shall we sing the Lord's song in a foreign land?' (Ps. 137:4), they were not good patriotic citizens of Jerusalem simply indulging in mere nostalgia. They were lamenting and grieving very deeply that they had been thrust out from the presence of God himself.

This was no less than the Lord had warned Israel while they were still in the wilderness, as we read in an earlier passage in Deuteronomy, 4:25–27:

> When you father children and children's children, and have grown old in the land, if you act corruptly by making a carved image in the form of anything, and by doing what is evil in the sight of the Lord your God, so as to provoke him to anger, I call heaven and earth to witness against you today, that you will soon utterly perish from the land that you are going over the Jordan to possess. You will not live long in it, but will be utterly destroyed. And the Lord will scatter you among the peoples, and you will be left few in number among the nations where the Lord will drive you.

As we have already seen in an earlier chapter, this

Chapter 14

warning is then re-echoed in Deuteronomy 28—the chapter with 14 verses of blessings and 54 verses of curses. We turn back to that devastating chapter once more.

Exodus goes into rewind.
God had foretold all the curses which would come upon his people 'if you will not obey the voice of the Lord your God or be careful to do all his commandments and his statutes that I command you today' (Deut. 28:15). We saw there that the four themes of pestilence, sword, famine and captivity featured prominently in that baleful list of curses which culminated with verse 68:

> And the Lord will bring you back in ships to Egypt, a journey that I promised that you should never make again; and there you shall offer yourselves for sale to your enemies as male and female slaves, but there will be no buyer.

This might at first sight seem confusing. The seventy years' exile were in Babylon, not Egypt, and no ships were involved in taking them away from their homeland, were they? We should understand that this language is highly symbolic, and the essential meaning is this: if God's people, whom he had redeemed from Egypt by his mighty power, were to turn away from him and worship other gods, then God would effectively reverse the whole Exodus narrative, and return his people to the bitter slavery and captivity of the type they had experienced in Egypt.

These warnings were not merely hypothetical, as if God were saying to Israel, 'I know you're far too smart to ever contemplate turning away from me; but just so that you know, this is what *would* happen to you if you ever did disobey me.' The future rebellion and apostasy of Israel is foretold in devastating fashion before the people have crossed the Jordan, while Moses is still with them. In Deuteronomy 31:26, Moses is making final arrangements for his own death and for Israel's entry into Canaan. He instructs the Levites, 'Take this Book of the Law and put it by the side of the ark of the covenant of the Lord your God, that it may be there,' ... for what purpose? To teach the people? To guide them? To encourage and cheer them?

None of the above! This is what the verse says: 'Take this Book of the Law and put it by the side of the ark of the covenant of the Lord your God, that it may be there for a witness *against* you.' And having issued this command, he goes on to tell the Levites:

> For I know how rebellious and stubborn you are. Behold, even today while I am yet alive with you, you have been rebellious against the Lord. How much more after my death! Assemble to me all the elders of your tribes and your officers, that I may speak these words in their ears and call heaven and

Chapter 14

earth to witness against them. For I know that after my death you will surely act corruptly and turn aside from the way that I have commanded you. And in the days to come evil will befall you, because you will do what is evil in the sight of the Lord, provoking him to anger through the work of your hands.

(Deut. 31:27–29)

In the following chapter, we come to the song which Moses recited in the hearing of all Israel. The first four verses are replete with evocative, lyrical vocabulary: teaching which drops like the rain, distils like the dew, gentle rain on tender grass; the God who is the Rock whose ways are perfect, 'just and upright is he' (Deut. 32:4). We soar to the dizzying heights of divine excellence, glory and grace. But in the following verse we come back down to earth with a jarring thud:

> They have dealt corruptly with him;
> they are no longer his children because they are blemished;
> they are a crooked and twisted generation.
>
> (Deut. 32:5)

The same theme pervades the whole of Moses' song. Moses knew from long personal experience just how corrupt, perverse and indeed idolatrous the people of Israel had been during the forty years' wandering in the wilderness. He knew that more of the same lay in the future.

Baaling out

And so it proved. We can fast-forward to the end of the Book of Joshua, where the people of Israel are all gathered at Shechem and, in response to Joshua's final address, they proclaim their determination to serve the Lord. 'Far be it from us that we should forsake the Lord to serve other gods', they insist (Josh. 24:16). But Joshua confronts them with the cold, hard reality, just as Moses had done:

You are not able to serve the Lord, for he is a holy God. He is a jealous God; he will not forgive your transgressions or your sins. If you forsake the Lord and serve foreign gods, then he will turn and do you harm and consume you, after having done you good (Josh. 24:19–20).

Still the people protest, so Joshua enters into a covenant with the people, putting in place laws and rules for the people and setting a large stone as a witness against them.

But we should know how it all unfolded, and if we do not know we should be able to work it out. The Book of Joshua is followed by Judges, where we read that after Joshua's generation had died, another generation arose 'who did not know the Lord or the work that he had done for Israel. And the people of Israel did what was evil in the sight of the Lord and served the Baals' (Judg. 2:10–11).

Several more centuries would elapse between the time

Chapter 14

of the Judges (roughly 1300–1100 BC) and the days when Jeremiah prophesied (627–587 BC). The reigns of David and Solomon, and the powerful prophetic ministries of Elijah and Elisha, would intervene. But the essential problem remained the same. We skip all this history and come all the way forward to Jeremiah once again as we hear the word of the Lord through him:

> They set up their abominations in the house that is called by my name, to defile it. They built the high places of Baal in the Valley of the Son of Hinnom, to offer up their sons and daughters to Molech, though I did not command them, nor did it enter into my mind, that they should do this abomination, to cause Judah to sin.
>
> (Jer. 32:34–35)

Notice how Baal is referenced in this passage. The people of Israel and Judah were still worshipping Baal in the time of Jeremiah just as they did in the days of the Judges; just, indeed, as they did while they were still in the wilderness (Num. 25:3).

It helps to know a few details about Baal. He was worshipped by the Canaanites and Phoenicians and was often depicted as a bull. Baal was associated with fertility, in relation to both crop-producing and childbearing, and also with the sun, with thunder, lightning and rain. His consorts were Ashtoreth, a fertility goddess, and Anath, a goddess of war. Baal-worship involved both ritual prostitution and the shedding of blood, including at times child sacrifice. All of this needs to be grasped as we read both the historical and prophetic sections of the Old Testament which speak of Baal.

In one sense, however, the gory details of Baal-worship are incidental. Of far more relevance is the very *meaning* of the name Baal, which was lord, possessor, or husband. Baal was understood to be the master and the owner of those who worshipped him. To worship Baal was to be joined to him in marriage, to yield to him as lord and husband.[2]

But the LORD had chosen Israel so that they would worship him exclusively. To depart from the LORD and to call on other gods was spiritual adultery. The LORD revealed himself to be a 'jealous God' (Exod. 20:5; 34:14; Deut. 4:24; 32:21; Josh. 24:19). He was the 'Husband' of his people (Isa. 54:5) to whom he was 'betrothed' (Hosea 2:19).

Idolatry and adultery are alike condemned by the law of God (Exod. 20:3, 14). When the people of Israel worshipped Baal, they were joining themselves to Baal, entering into union with him. And the God who is a Jealous Husband cannot tolerate unfaithfulness on the part of his bride.

The wages of idolatry is captivity.

Now we can understand why God had to bring the

Chapter 14

judgement of captivity on the people of Jerusalem in the days of Jeremiah. They persisted in turning away from the Lord and turning instead to other gods, Baal foremost among them. They had chosen as their 'master', not the Lord their husband; not the Creator God who made the heaven and earth and everything in them, who supplied sunshine, rain, food in season, children, and every other blessing under heaven; not the faithful covenant God who had delivered them from the land of Egypt, from the house of slavery and settled them in their own land as his inheritance. They preferred to run after the false, savage, amoral Baal, with all the abominable practices associated with his worship. Jeremiah compared them to 'a restless young camel running here and there, a wild donkey used to the wilderness, in her heat sniffing the wind! Who can restrain her lust?' (Jer. 2:23–24).

They preferred Baal to the Lord. No matter that the Lord had decisively settled the matter in the days of Elijah (1 Kings 18:36–40). 'My people are bent on turning away from me,' the Lord said through Hosea, a century after Elijah (Hosea 11:7). That was spoken of the Northern Kingdom of Israel. Exactly the same could be said of the people of Judah over a hundred years later. 'Why then has this people turned away in perpetual backsliding? They hold fast to deceit; they refuse to return' (Jer. 8:5).

And so, they went into captivity. *The Lord's judgement in sending his people to Babylon was the physical manifestation of the spiritual captivity which they had already chosen for themselves by departing from him.* Just as 'the wages of sin is death' (Rom. 6:23), so the wages of idolatry is captivity. But this was true not only in Old Testament times. It was still true when the New Testament was being written, and it remains true today.

Invisible captors are still captors.

We are far more sophisticated today, are we not? Baal disappears from the pages of the Bible after the time of the exile; the people of Israel were never drawn back to such blatantly pagan idolatry once they had returned from Babylon. And after all, Baal never even existed, did he? Neither did Asherah, or Chemosh, or Molech; neither did Horus, or Ra, or Osiris; neither did Zeus, or Aphrodite, or Poseidon; neither did Thor, or Woden, or any other pagan deity we might care to mention. The apostle Paul sounds just like most western Christians today when he avows that '"an idol has no real existence," and that "there is no God but one"' (1 Cor. 8:4).

But the spiritual deception of idolatry, resulting in spiritual captivity, does not need to latch onto an idol of wood or stone. The vast majority of ancient civilizations certainly had such visible, tangible deities. But it was not the images and statues themselves which wielded such tyranny over the individuals who worshipped them. It was the *spiritual deception associated with the images*, the

Chapter 14

narratives, ideas and yes, that word again, *'worldviews'*, which controlled and enslaved these people.

When we come to the New Testament, we notice that visible and physical idols of wood and stone are not quite as prevalent as they were in the Old Testament. In Athens, certainly, the apostle Paul's 'spirit was provoked within him as he saw that the city was full of idols' (Acts 17:16). But even there, the object which grabbed his attention was an altar dedicated to 'the unknown God' (17:23) and his confrontation at the Areopagus was with the Epicurean and Stoic philosophers, who seem to represent a step forward in sophistication when compared with Baal-worshippers.

Yet, people can be held in thrall by an invisible, seemingly abstract system of philosophy just as much as they can by a pantheon of deities who are represented by images. Invisible captors are still captors; indeed, in spiritual and moral terms, the only true captors are invisible captors. We do not wrestle against flesh and blood—we might add, neither do we wrestle against wood and stone—'but against the rulers, against the authorities, against the cosmic powers over this present darkness, against the spiritual forces of evil in the heavenly places' (Eph. 6:12).

The New Testament contains many examples of such invisible spiritual captivity. Paul warns Timothy about false teachers 'who forbid marriage and require abstinence from foods that God created to be received with thanksgiving by those who believe and know the truth' (1 Tim. 4:3). But what lies behind these false teachers? They are those who have departed from the faith 'by devoting themselves to deceitful spirits and teachings of demons' (4:1). This does not necessarily imply that these individuals are demon-possessed; but the whole system of doctrine which holds people captive belongs to the invisible, spiritual realm.

Many more New Testament cases could be cited. The Judaizers in Galatia had 'bewitched' the believers there and caused them to submit to 'a yoke of slavery'—a situation which greatly disturbed and perplexed Paul (Gal. 3:1; 5:1). The apostle Peter devotes an entire chapter to the 'false teachers among you, who will secretly bring in destructive heresies' (2 Peter 2:1). The apostle John warns his readers, 'do not believe every spirit, but test the spirits to see whether they are from God, for many false prophets have gone out into the world' (1 John 4:1). Balaam, who sought to curse the people of Israel while they were in the wilderness, may have been dead for many centuries, but the cult of Balaam still held sway in Pergamum (Rev. 2:14), as elsewhere (2 Peter 2:15; Jude 11). In none of these cases are we led to believe that images or statues of pretended deities featured prominently, if indeed they featured at all.

Chapter 14

Where there are idols there are captives.

A very prominent example can be seen in Paul's Letter to the Colossians. One of the key texts in that short letter is Paul's warning in 2:8:

> See to it that no one takes you captive by philosophy and empty deceit, according to human tradition, according to the elemental spirits of the world, and not according to Christ.

Much ink has been spilt on the nature of the 'Colossian heresy' which Paul is combating. Was it an early form of Gnosticism, or a speculative offshoot within Judaism? Did it owe more to the influence of Pythagoras, or of Plato? Was it an astral religion, making much of angelic hierarchies? Colossians 2:18 certainly seems to point in that direction. Was it so-called *merkabah* mysticism, or 'chariot' mysticism, which sprung from a somewhat spiritually intoxicated reading of Ezekiel 1:15–26? Or was it a syncretistic amalgam of all the above?[3]

This is not the place to go into detail, fascinating and illuminating though such an exercise might be. The main point is that the Colossians were in danger of being taken 'captive' by systems of thought which were contrary to what they had received from Christ—indeed contrary to Christ himself who was their life (Col. 3:4). The Greek verb translated as, 'takes (you) captive', *sulagōgeō*, has the sense of someone or something being carried away as a captive, or as booty or spoil. The Colossians would undoubtedly be the losers if they embraced the doctrine of the heretics, however appealing it might be to their intellectual or cultural appetites.

In summary, these were worldview issues, matters of how life, the universe and the whole of reality were to be understood. For the apostle Paul, Jesus Christ was the key to understanding and interpreting everything; no letter in the New Testament has a more exalted Christology or more frequent usage of Paul's 'in Christ' motif than Colossians. That is why, having issued this warning in 2:8, Paul goes on to tell the Colossians, in the following two verses, that 'in [Christ] the whole fullness of deity dwells bodily, and you have been filled in him, who is the head of all rule and authority.'

Idols will always hold people captive, whether or not they can be depicted in paintings, sculptures or any other visual form. One of the most striking verses in the Bible is the final verse of John's First Letter: 'Little children, keep yourselves from idols' (1 John 5:21). It all seems rather abrupt and unexpected; where have been the Baals, Asherahs and all the rest in this Letter? The answer is that anything and anyone other than the Lord Jesus Christ, whether visible or invisible; whether primitive or sophisticated; ancient, medieval or modern; or postmodern, and all the rest—anything which commands ultimate respect, fear, commitment and allegiance from

Chapter 14

any soul—is an idol. Jesus Christ alone, says John 'is the true God and eternal life' (1 John 5:20)—'[t]hat which was from the beginning, which we have heard, which we have seen with our eyes, which we looked upon and have touched with our hands' (1 John 1:1).

This same Lord Jesus Christ stood up in the synagogue in Nazareth one Sabbath morning and announced, in fulfilment of Isaiah's prophecy (Isa. 61:1), that he had come 'to proclaim liberty to the captives' (Luke 4:18). I began this chapter wondering where we may locate the captives. But as we will see shortly, the captives are far more plentiful than we might imagine.

15 A CAPTIVE AUDIENCE

Liberty is one of the most precious gifts which heaven has bestowed on man; with it we cannot compare the treasures which the earth contains or the sea conceals; for liberty, as for honour, we can and ought to risk our lives; and, on for the other hand, captivity is the greatest evil that can befall man.[1]

Miguel de Cervantes

Revolutionaries in America and France at the end of the eighteenth century proclaimed it, writing it into their constitutions and anthems, erecting monuments to it; in the 1960s Che Guevara became an iconic pin-up celebrating it; twenty years later George Michael and Freddie Mercury sang about it; and around the same time the Richard Attenborough film, *Cry Freedom*, following the life of Steve Biko in apartheid-era South Africa, won many prestigious awards. Freedom: is it a good thing? One hundred percent! Like the proverbial motherhood and apple-pie, you criticize freedom at your peril.

Or at least you used to. There are signs today that freedom is not valued quite as highly as it once was. Just how free are we today—I mean in the Western World where political democracy still reigns supreme, at least

Chapter 15

notionally? The United States National Anthem, *The Star-Spangled Banner*, concludes by describing America as 'the land of the free' and 'the home of the brave'. How accurate are these descriptions, not only in America but in other western countries? The even bigger question is this: how free are *Christians* in these societies?

In order to answer these questions, we first need to understand what freedom really is, and then to discern whether people who boast in their freedom are, in fact, truly free.

God is free, God defines free.

Is freedom a good thing? The answer to this question must be a full-throated affirmative, for this reason only: that *God himself is free*, and that freedom is defined by his own nature and character, as are goodness, justice, wisdom, power, knowledge and all his other attributes. In God alone there is infinite freedom, just as in him alone there is infinite love and infinite holiness.

Passages in the Bible which describe God's freedom are far too numerous to list, but a wealth of them can be found in Isaiah 40–49, where the sovereign freedom of the Lord stands out in stark contrast to enslaving and enslaved idols. 'Whom did he consult, and who made him understand? Who taught him the path of justice, and taught him knowledge, and showed him the way of understanding?' (Isa. 40:14); 'I am the Lord, and there is no other. I form light and create darkness; I make well-being and create calamity; I am the LORD, who does all these things' (Isa. 45:6, 7); 'I am God, and there is no other; I am God, and there is none like me, declaring the end from the beginning and from ancient times things not yet done, saying, "My counsel shall stand, and I will accomplish all my purpose"' (Isa. 46:9, 10).

God is entirely free in that there is no one and nothing that can constrain his power or his determination to do whatever he pleases. There is no impersonal, exterior set of 'rules' that God is obliged to follow, because he himself is the absolute, ultimate Lawgiver and Rule maker. 'Who has known the mind of the Lord, or who has been his counsellor?' (Rom. 11:34) The only 'constraint' which God places on himself, if we can use such language when applied to God, is set by his own determination always to act according to his own justice, wisdom, power and other attributes already referred to above. God answers to no one but himself; this is the very meaning and the highest possible definition of freedom.

In his perfect freedom, God determined to create other beings for the demonstration of his own character and glory.[2] And just as God knows perfect joy and freedom in all that he is, as God, so it is that every creature made by God knows perfect joy and freedom in all that *God* is and has done. Man is a creature, the highest and noblest of creatures, uniquely made in the image of God; but as

CHAPTER 15

a creature, his freedom is necessarily found in knowing, loving and obeying the God who defines freedom.[3]

The first deception and temptation—'you will be like God' (Gen. 3:5)—latched onto precisely this point; it was the suggestion that man could be autonomous and detached, an independent, self-sufficient being. It implied that God's commandments were not binding; rather that man was at liberty to follow or not to follow, to obey or not to obey. That way, said the serpent, was to become like God.

But man, to be truly free and happy, must be bound by God's law *just as God himself is bound by God's law*. The lie that our first parents believed was that freedom and joy could be found by casting off God's restraints. Only when the rule book is torn up, only where there are no rules, can genuine freedom be attained. That deception took hold in the Garden of Eden and it has never relinquished its grip on sinful hearts.

The true, biblical corrective to this seems a paradox to us: that true freedom only comes when we obey God. The apostle Paul gloried in his freedom—'Am I not free? Am I not an apostle?' (1 Cor. 9:1)—and sought the freedom of all God's people: 'For freedom Christ has set us free' (Gal. 5:1). And yet the same apostle introduced himself to the church in Rome as 'a servant of Christ Jesus' (Rom. 1:1); the word he used could equally be translated 'bondservant' or even 'slave'. Jesus Christ is the only perfect Master, which means that to follow and obey him wholeheartedly is the only perfect freedom known to man.

It may seem a paradox, but a little thought demonstrates that it is true to life.

Sixteen queens on the board—everyone's a winner!

For many years I have sought to master the game of chess, with somewhat disappointing results. But the more I attempt to play, the more drawn into it I am. Chess is a deeply fascinating game with very clear and unbreakable rules. Each piece on the board is only allowed to make certain, carefully prescribed moves. At the risk of stating the obvious, it is not possible to compete in a game of chess, and develop your skill, unless you abide by these strict rules.

Supposing I were to say, 'Well, I'm tired of losing so often. I'll forget the rules everyone else plays by; I'll make up my own instead.' And I decide that whenever I play chess, all the pieces will be able to move just like the queen: that is, any number of squares in any direction. In no time at all, I become a Grand Master, able to wipe every opponent, virtual or human, off the board in a half-a-dozen moves.

But if I decide to do this, why should not others? Suppose that every other player decided to adopt the rules I operate by, or indeed to make them even more 'liberal'. Suppose, in fact, that I and my opponent operate by our

Chapter 15

very own rules, choosing them with the much-vaunted 'freedom' which we enjoy. The game of chess would become an absurdity. It would lose all value and appeal. In fact, it would entirely cease to be chess.

True freedom only exists where there is a framework of laws or rules, set in place by a wise, intelligent and authoritative being, which are understood to be in operation. Take these laws away and the result is destructive anarchy. An even more obvious example is driving a car: cars are meant to keep to speed limits, to stay in lane—indeed, to drive on roads rather than pavements or over fields. What kind of 'freedom' would it be if I could career off the road in any direction I wanted, as fast as I liked?

This is true in the whole of life. For freedom must not be the ultimate goal in itself; our chief end is to know, love and glorify God, to find all our joy in following him, and only as we do that will we discover that the very best freedom comes as a kind of by-product; that while we were pursuing, not freedom for its own sake, but God for *his* own sake, a better freedom that we ever imagined was thrown into the bargain![4]

We are most free, therefore, when we give God his proper due, recognizing him as our ultimate Lord and Lawgiver. This freedom is not the unbridled licence, in the words of Village People's *YMCA*, to 'do whatever you feel'—but the ability to do what we *should*, as responsible creatures accountable to God.

But there's the rub. The vocabulary of 'should' and 'ought', along with the language of 'duty', 'obligation', 'obedience' and 'submission' kicks against the flawed, degenerate notions of 'freedom' to which our decadent culture is wedded. These categories are viewed as inimical to the freedom that we crave. And this attitude is not some 'new kid on the block' which first showed up in the permissive 1960s, or even the progeny of the French philosopher René Descartes (1596–1650) who said, 'I think therefore I am', and used his self-existence as the foundation of his whole intellectual system.[5] It is as old as sin itself.

A network of obligations

Every human being stands in a relationship to God characterized by dependence and by obligation. We owe our life and existence to God as Creator; we also owe the allegiance of our souls to God as Lawgiver. Much as contemporary culture may chafe at the language of 'obligation' and 'submission', we must insist on nothing less.

But it does not end there. God has not created each human being as if they were individualized atoms—even atoms join other atoms to form molecules of varying complexity! At the most basic level, every person needs

Chapter 15

fellow persons in order to thrive. God's observation that it was not good for the man to be alone (Gen. 2:18) introduces the ordinance of marriage, though it points to an even more essential need than marriage: the need for relationship.

Our Creator God has set in place this fundamental principle of our existence: he has established distinct human relational structures for the organization and proper, healthy functioning of human beings. People are most free, not when they cut themselves loose from these structures, but when they operate within them in accordance with what God commands. And these structures have, embedded within them, levels of obligation which God tells us are good. It is therefore a fallacy to suggest that we owe no obligation to anyone other than God.

This is of the very essence of the fifth commandment, which codifies this principle: 'Honour your father and your mother, as the LORD your God commanded you, that your days may be long, and that it may go well with you in the land that the LORD your God is giving you' (Deut. 5:16).[6] What we need to observe in relation to this commandment, as with all the others, is that its application extends well beyond obedience to parents, though it must start there, in the so-called nuclear family. *The Westminster Shorter Catechism* explains the whole thrust of this commandment:

> The fifth commandment requireth the preserving the honour, and performing the duties, belonging to everyone in their several places and relations, as superiors, inferiors, or equals.[7]

If the language of 'obligation', 'submission' and 'duties' (as here) is out of favour today, much more so the reference to 'superiors' and 'inferiors'—though certainly not 'equals'! Are we not all equal in any case? This is where we need to be clear. Every human being, all of them made in God's image, regardless of any of their personal characteristics or circumstances, are of course 'equal' in value and dignity before God. But this commandment is not addressing that question. It is dealing with people 'in their several places and relations', and in this regard, there is *not* equality. A parent is entitled to require, even demand, that a child behave appropriately. It does not work the other way round.

It begins with the family, though it extends further. The requirement for children to honour their parents is underlined not only in the Old Testament, but in the New (Eph. 6:1; Col. 3:20); and indeed, there are duties laid down for parents as well as children (2 Cor. 12:14; Eph. 6:4). This is a divine commandment, something which God insists on. For children to say to their parents, 'respect must be earned', as a means of side-stepping the honour due to parents, is a wilful act of rebellion.

Chapter 15

But there are other structures which God has established, and 'the preserving the honour, and performing the duties' which pertain to these should be seen as an extrapolation from the biological family and the requirements of the fifth commandment. In the church, of course, honour is due to those who lead (1 Tim. 5:17; Heb. 13:7, 17). The same is true in relation to civil government (Rom. 13:1-7; 1 Peter 2:13-17). Indeed, Peter speaks of being 'subject for the Lord's sake to every human institution' (1 Peter 2:13), and he goes on to apply this to servants and masters—in our day, employees and employers as well as pupils and teachers. A schoolteacher, for example, has traditionally been regarded as *in loco parentis*—in the place of a parent—and should therefore be entitled to the respect and honour due to a parent; and it needs to be added that their authority is derived from the authority of the parent, which is itself conferred by God.

The fifth commandment stands at the head of the second table of the Ten Commandments—those six which are encapsulated in the second great commandment of Jesus: 'You shall love your neighbour as yourself' (Mark 12:31, quoted from Lev. 19:18). It is a striking observation that this specific command, which deals with honour, duty and obligation, occupies this exalted place. The true exercise of love, indeed the free and fullest exercise of love, can only take place when these structures of relationship and obligation are recognized; just as a true and satisfactory game of chess, or tennis, or anything else, can only happen when the rules are observed.

What is more, these networks of obligation owe their existence to God himself, the source of all rule and authority, and preceding the second great commandment is the first and the greatest: 'You shall love the Lord your God with all your heart and with all your soul and with all your mind and with all your strength' (Mark 12:30). God is honoured when we honour every authority structure that he has set in place.

A society of slaves

The flip side is that where God himself is not worshipped, feared, loved and obeyed as he should be, then the entire network of interpersonal obligations that he has set in place are disregarded and dishonoured. When people break loose of God's 'restrictive' commands, do they at last become free? Not at all; once again this was the first lie of the devil. Instead, what happens is that alternative, unworthy, obligations take the place of the ones which God has established, and these ultimately prove destructive and enslaving.

To love and obey God, we have said, is to know perfect freedom; but to love and obey any master other than God is to submit to tyranny and slavery. This was the confession of God's people during Isaiah's time: 'O LORD our God, *other lords besides you have ruled over us*, but your name

Chapter 15

alone we bring to remembrance' (Isa. 26:13). These 'other lords' included the gods of the nations that Israel had dispossessed, but never fully driven out—the Baals and Asherahs we thought about in the last chapter. They also included the Egyptians, the Assyrians, the Babylonians and other cruel physical captors. They brought slavery and misery rather than joy and true freedom.

Above all, they resulted in fear, but not the fear of the LORD, which alone is 'clean, enduring forever' (Ps. 19:9). The fear of the LORD results in knowledge, wisdom, confidence, the prolongation of life and countless other blessings (Ps. 111:10; Prov. 1:7; 9:10; 10:27; 14:26–27; 19:23), but the fear of other 'lords'—when they function in human minds as ultimate lords—leads to the very opposite of these blessings. They confine, they stunt, they ensnare, they restrict and inhibit.

And I am talking now about believers, about Christians. It is no surprise when unbelievers kowtow to a being other than the God of the Bible. But my present concern is with professing worshippers of God, who are found giving respect, honour and allegiance to some 'authority' other than God, when God alone demands that place in their hearts. This was the essence of the problem with the Galatians and, in that letter, Paul courageously calls out his fellow-apostle Peter for an act of spiritual cowardice, in drawing away from eating with Gentile Christians when men from Jerusalem arrived; Paul says very plainly that

Peter was guilty of '*fearing* the circumcision party' (Gal. 2:12). This same spirit of fear had infected Barnabas and indeed the whole church, resulting in the most strenuous, stringent epistle that Paul ever wrote. He must remind the Galatians: 'For freedom Christ has set us free; stand firm therefore, and do not submit again to a yoke of slavery' (Gal. 5:1). The 'circumcision party' in Galatia were calling the shots to such an extent that the whole church were in danger of falling away from the gospel of Jesus Christ crucified, and thus living far beneath their spiritual privileges.

This is the spirit of Pharisaism. It has all the outward trappings of biblical religion and worship, but its motivating principle is not the fear of God, but the fear of man. The Lord Jesus warned his disciples:

> Beware of the scribes, who like to walk around in long robes and like greetings in the market-places and have the best seats in the synagogues and the places of honour at feasts, who devour widows' houses and for a pretence make long prayers. They will receive the greater condemnation.
>
> (Mark 12:38-40)

The entire way of life of the scribes and Pharisees consisted in their desire to be seen, noticed and applauded by other human beings. Like whitewashed tombs, there was an impressiveness on the outside which belied

Chapter 15

the fact that on the inside these men were 'full of dead people's bones and all uncleanness' (Matt. 23:27).

What is even more terrible is that Pharisaism was infectious; their fear of man generated the same kind of fear in those who looked to the Pharisees as an example. John tells us this plainly in his Gospel, right at the end of the public ministry of Jesus:

> Nevertheless, many even of the authorities believed in him, but for fear of the Pharisees they did not confess it, so that they would not be put out of the synagogue; for they loved the glory that comes from man more than the glory that comes from God.
> (John 12:42–43)

The people of Israel, who boasted in their freedom, were in fact a society of slaves, a thought that horrified them. Only by abiding in the Word of Christ would they have become truly free (see John 8:32–33). But their overriding fear of man kept them in chains, and we need to admit quite frankly that the same thing is still happening two thousand years later.

'Whatever you think you need, you come to fear.'

To be 'put out of the synagogue' in first-century Israel was a scandalous disgrace. It was to lose all social standing and respect, to be shunned by the people who had previously received and embraced you. Two millennia on, the apparatus might have changed but the essential spirit of the fear of man is still alive and kicking. Edward Welch gets to the heart of the matter in his very aptly titled book, *When People are Big and God is Small*:

> We've seen that whatever you think you need you come to fear. If you 'need' love (to feel OK about yourself), you will soon be controlled by the one who dispenses love. You are also saying that without that person's love you will be spiritually handicapped, unable to give love to others. With this kind of spiritually crippling logic bearing bad fruit everywhere, it is no wonder that even psychologists are calling for a reformation in our culture's fundamental assumptions.[8]

Welch was writing in 1997, in the early years of the worldwide web, before the advent of smartphones and several years before social networking platforms, such as Facebook and Twitter (renamed 'X'), existed; even longer before social media platforms, such as Instagram, Snapchat and TikTok, burst onto the scene.

What has happened in the intervening years is that *people*, as well as God, have become small: by that, I mean the people who perhaps ought not to be quite as small as others; people that we are bound to by ties of family, work and physical community; the kind of people whose faces we actually see in our homes, streets and workplaces

Chapter 15

from day to day. If it was unhealthy to depend on the love and affirmation of these people back in the late twentieth century, it is far more perverse to calibrate our worth according to the 'likes' and emojis of twenty-first-century social media, or the views broadcast incessantly by round-the-clock news coverage.

It was because the people of Israel began to believe that they really *needed* Baal in order to secure a healthy crop, or plentiful offspring, the longer they settled in Canaan, that they quickly began to *fear* Baal and his various consorts. As we said in the previous chapter, it was not so much the images and depictions of Baal, as the psychological grip that the Baalite worldview had on the Israelite mind.

We need to be able to spot the clear similarities in our own culture. The whole mass of material that pings onto our screens, of whatever size, shouts at us all, 'you *need* me'. Without all this we are led to believe that we are out of step with the world around us: irrelevant, out of touch, effectively put out of the twenty-first-century equivalent of the synagogue. The horrible expression, 'cancel culture', that we hear a good deal about today expresses this perfectly.[9]

We fear people more than we fear God; but unlike the situation even twenty years ago, we are perhaps more likely to fear people we seldom, if ever, meet rather than the people we rub shoulders with day by day. It is a new kind of totalitarianism. It is 'soft' rather than 'hard', virtual rather than physical. It is not expressed by means of chains, prison cells or gulags. But it is real and vicious, nonetheless. Velvet gloves may conceal iron fists.

Capitulation and abdication

Some examples of this 'soft totalitarianism'—and I emphasize once more that I am talking here about Christians—have already been noted in earlier chapters. The way some churches perpetuated a culture of masks, social distancing and inflated fear of the effects of Covid-19, long after any substantial danger had passed and rules relaxed, was symptomatic of a kind of 'groupthink' which was in thrall to the fear of man rather than to the fear of God.

This is not to say that churches should have engaged in civil disobedience or simply disregarded the Covid guidelines. As responsible citizens, Christians must of all people be the most law-abiding. But to *abide* by certain laws does not necessarily imply that those laws must be heartily *approved* as 'A Good Thing'. Christians must be free to discuss their disapproval or approval of the Covid-19 regulations openly, without judgement. The fear of man must not take over and constrain the free speech of an individual soul created in the image of God.

Covid has passed, but the present preoccupation with the environment and net zero certainly has not. As we saw in Chapter 13, Environmentalism is a creed which

Chapter 15

has captured the soul of western culture in such a way that even Christians become nervous about publicly demurring from contemporary orthodoxy.

When Christian people, and in particular those called to leadership, limply capitulate to the pervading cultural consensus of the day, and abdicate the responsible use of their own minds, not giving any thought to what God's Word might say on any given subject, or how a biblical worldview might inform their views, what has happened? They have bartered their supreme and ultimate obligation—to give first place to God and his commandments, to what he has established—for a decidedly inferior and precarious one, which is to pay greater heed to a worldview that is built not on the rock but on shifting sands. And a building that collapses all around you can very quickly become a prison. In Romans 1:22, Paul traces the descent of human thinking: 'Claiming to be wise, they became fools'. We might say today, 'Claiming to be free, they became slaves'.

Christians must not be slaves; they are free and must live as free people. This means, first of all, understanding and appreciating the God-given freedom which is their birthright, as sons of the living God.

16 THE GROWNUPS IN THE ROOM

Bring into captivity every thought to the obedience of Christ. Take what I cannot give: my heart, body, thoughts, time, abilities, money, health, strength, nights, days, youth, age, and spend them in Thy service, O my crucified Master, Redeemer, God. Oh, let not these be mere words! Whom have I in heaven but Thee and there is none upon earth that I desire in comparison of Thee. My heart is athirst for God.[1]

Elizabeth Prentiss

This book has been motivated by the deep desire and longing that the Church of Jesus Christ would emerge from these times of pestilence, sword, famine and indeed captivity, refined and strengthened; that the *judgements* of God which have recently fallen upon the world, and continue to fall, will be means in God's hands to cause his faithful people to exercise wise and right *judgements* in terms of how they should think, speak and act as this twenty-first century progresses.

In writing this book, I have been moved throughout by a great burden for the needs of younger people, for the Millennials and for Generation Z—although the Millennials are now themselves on the verge of being

Chapter 16

middle-aged! Generations born since around the mid-1980s are facing a complex cultural conundrum which would baffle, and indeed *does* baffle, their parents and grandparents. This book has made no attempt to analyse how we reached this point; in one sense I am no less baffled by this question than anyone else. But in this chapter, at least, I make a stab at setting out the type of response which is so urgently needed.

A great lesson from history is that when God's people are strong, they will be strong for their own benefit but also for the benefit of many others. When the Spirit of God is powerfully at work among his people, when Christians are captivated by a full-orbed, biblical worldview and vision, they become leaders and pioneers in their day and generation; they are regarded as blessings to the human population, 'having favour with all the people' (Acts 2:47), and this can permeate into the whole spectrum of human life and culture. There have been seasons when this has evidently been the case, especially during the eighteenth and nineteenth centuries in the Western World.

Heads and tails

One of the most stirring books I have ever enjoyed, and one I go back to when my hands hang loose and my knees are feeble, is Sandy Finlayson's book, *Unity and Diversity*—a selection of mini biographies of the leading lights in the Free Church of Scotland, in the years before and after its foundation in the 'Disruption' of 1843. In his concluding chapter, Finlayson comments that:

> ... the founders of the Free Church all believed that the church should reach out to the world. This commitment was evident in the Free Church from its earliest days. Thomas Chalmers sought to bring about a godly commonwealth through his parish model and through his vision that the Free Church should become a truly national church. James Begg and Thomas Guthrie worked hard for improvements in housing and education, recognising that the church should not remain aloof from the problems of the world. Alexander Duff devoted his life to the belief that the chief purpose of the church was missionary work. While these men took different approaches, all of them were animated by a desire to see the 'Great Commission' put into action both at home and abroad.[2]

Visions of 'a godly commonwealth', whichever nation we inhabit, seem about as far off today as Saturn's moons. And talk of 'a national church', certainly in England, where the Church of England is passing through times of tumultuous crisis, appears unrealistic as well as—maybe?—undesirable. But a burden for the overall welfare of our citizens and neighbours, in areas such as housing,

Chapter 16

education and healthcare, is one that strikes a tender chord today.

However, in writing this book I have given expression to this deeply troubling conviction: the professing Christian Church, certainly in the Western World, does not remotely resemble what it was, for example, in Scotland in the early- to mid-nineteenth century. The position appears to have been reversed. I have quoted from Deuteronomy 28 on several occasions and it is time to do so one last time:

> And the LORD will make you the head and not the tail, and you shall only go up and not down, if you obey the commandments of the LORD your God, which I command you today, being careful to do them.
>
> (Deut. 28:13)

This could be seen as an accurate description, not merely of the people of Israel, God's old covenant community, but of the Church of Jesus Christ—his new covenant people—during times of blessing such as those experienced in the immediate aftermath of Pentecost, as well as in times of reformation, awakening and revival which followed in later centuries. When the people of God knew what it was to 'go up and not down', they became the 'head' which lifted the rest of the body—the men, women and children who rubbed shoulders with them, out of ignorance, superstition, poverty, crime and other forms of darkness.

But today we seem to be closer to Deuteronomy 28:43–44:

> The sojourner who is among you shall rise higher and higher above you, and you shall come down lower and lower. He shall lend to you, and you shall not lend to him. He shall be the head, and you shall be the tail.

The 'sojourner who is among you' is, today, the modern equivalent of the worshippers of Baal and Asherah: those who claim to offer freedom, prosperity and progress—'progressive' is the modern label for this whole attitude and mindset—but who, in truth, drag souls backwards into slavery. It is regression rather than true progression; it is languishing in childhood rather than advancing towards maturity; it is to shrink down into the tail rather than to grow up into the head, even Christ (Eph. 4:15).

'I will make boys their princes.'

In Isaiah 3, we read about a society which had become dysfunctional to the point of being infantilized; and this society was none other than the people of God. We read in verses 1 to 5:

> For behold, the Lord GOD of hosts
>   is taking away from Jerusalem and from Judah
> support and supply,
>   all support of bread,

Chapter 16

> and all support of water;
> the mighty man and the soldier,
> > the judge and the prophet,
> > the diviner and the elder,
> the captain of fifty
> > and the man of rank,
> the counsellor and the skilful magician
> > and the expert in charms.
>
> And I will make boys their princes,
> > and infants shall rule over them.
> And the people will oppress one another,
> > every one his fellow
> > and every one his neighbour;
> the youth will be insolent to the elder,
> > and the despised to the honourable.

What was the problem in Jerusalem at the time? It was that the LORD, in his judgement, had decided to remove the leading men responsible for the exercise of defence and justice in the city—the mighty men, the soldiers, the judges, the men of rank. They had all been pulled out, one by one. The result was that it was boys, rather than men, who became the leaders and rulers in Jerusalem. We should not take this too literally. It is not that Jerusalem became the filmset for *Bugsy Malone,* in which every actor is played by a child. It means instead that God gave his people rulers who were *like* children. They lacked the wisdom, knowledge, experience, discretion and self-control which belongs to adults; the noble and honourable office of ruler fell to those who had no conception of the dignity of government. There was no lack of politicians, but genuine *statesmen* had disappeared.

A society led by childish adults is one which will pursue short-term gain and ignore long-term planning. It will change course frequently, with no fixed and settled purpose other than favouring the interests of those who are shouting the loudest. It will neglect what is of pressing importance in favour of pursuing its own amusements and pleasures. It is a society which will fail to learn any lessons from history because it will *have* no interest in history. Within such a society, individuals will be quick to take offence and to exact revenge. They will abdicate mature responsibility and be very ready to 'pass the buck'. Such a society will be characterised by envy and scheming, will splinter and polarise very easily and will inevitably spiral down into corruption and even anarchy.

I fear that we are some way down that spiral today; but there is one more feature of childishness which we need to appreciate. It is to be enthralled with the world's toys and gadgets, and even become expert in using and exploiting them, but all the time failing to appreciate how they should be used prudently and responsibly, to the greatest benefit of those who stand to profit by them.

CHAPTER 16

Let the grownups help.
I have entitled this chapter, *The Grownups in the Room*. It is a form of words which has begun to feature increasingly in public discourse. But what message does it communicate, indeed where does it come from?

The expression 'the grownups in the room' is a metaphorical phrase used to describe the individuals who are responsible, mature, and capable of making rational decisions in a given situation. The term is often used in political contexts to refer to the individuals who have the necessary experience and knowledge to make informed decisions that are in the best interest of the public.

The phrase gained popularity during the 2008 financial crisis, when a group of high-ranking officials in the United States government were referred to as 'the grownups in the room' for their role in crafting a bailout plan to stabilize the economy. The term was used to describe the officials who had the expertise and experience necessary to navigate the complex financial landscape and make the tough decisions required to stabilize the economy.

The expression has since been used in a variety of contexts, from discussions about international diplomacy to debates about climate change. In each case, the term refers to the individuals who have the knowledge, experience, and maturity required to navigate complex situations and make informed decisions that benefit society as a whole.

However, the use of the expression, 'the grownups in the room', can also be seen as problematic, as it can be interpreted as dismissive of the voices and perspectives of those who may not be considered 'grownups'. It can also perpetuate a narrow and elitist view of leadership, suggesting that only those with specific qualifications or experiences are capable of making important decisions.

In conclusion, while the expression, 'the grownups in the room', has become a commonly used metaphor in political discourse, it is important to recognize its limitations and potentially negative implications. It is crucial to value and consider the diverse perspectives and experiences of all individuals, rather than solely relying on a select group of 'grownups' to make decisions that impact society as a whole.

What do 'the grownups in the room' do? They make use of all available resources in arriving at their solutions, but at the same time they require a level of knowledge, experience and maturity so that their solutions are formed by wisdom and discernment. They exercise responsible leadership—we might say stewardship—over all the means at their disposal.

Dominion with discernment

I now have an important confession to make. The five

Chapter 16

paragraphs preceding the last one; that is, from the paragraph beginning, 'The expression "the grownups in the room" ...', up to the one ending, '... decisions that impact society as a whole', are not my own original words. They were generated by ChatGPT, the free online Artificial Intelligence (AI) tool which was released in November 2022 and since then has taken the world by storm. I simply typed in the instruction, 'write me an essay about the expression "the grownups in the room"', and out popped these five paragraphs. Did you notice anything different about them?[3]

The rise of AI, perhaps with ChatGPT as its current Exhibit A, is causing a huge amount of alarm. There is good reason for this alarm. If it is employed unthinkingly, in such a way that all human judgement and discernment is bypassed, or even if skills which are foundational to healthy human development are neglected, there must be grave cause for concern. To some extent this has already been happening for a generation, since the advent of spell-checkers and automatic text correction and prediction. I no longer need to learn to spell words accurately, because my computer will correct me without so much as a sideways glance, let alone the threat of a breaktime detention.

The correct spelling of words is, perhaps, a human skill which needs to be preserved, especially when I misspell a word as a result of ignorance rather than haste. But AI is

The Grownups in the Room

much older than we might think. If I am attempting a very complicated mathematical calculation, I will save huge amounts of time, and in all probability several errors in mental arithmetic, if I employ a device like a spreadsheet. But before spreadsheets there were pocket calculators; before calculators there were slide-rules; before slide-rules there were abacuses; and before abacuses there was something even older. Search engines are themselves forms of AI, of course. They sift through all the material on the web and display, by means of astonishingly complex algorithms, a number of results in response to a query, which is often a single word. They spare us the labour of wading through several hefty tomes in the reference section of a library, as was necessary before the early- to mid-1990s. ChatGPT, of course, goes further than a search engine by organizing the search results into a ready-to-use form, like an essay, or a letter, or an invitation.

But perhaps the question we should be asking at this point is this: *what is a grownup attitude towards AI?* And the answer must be that we should neither be mastered by it, nor should we utterly neglect it. Instead, if we are to function as mature, responsible adults, we should always ensure that we exercise control and stewardship over AI, as we must over every entity in the created realm. We need to ensure, for example, that AI's capacities do not so far exceed the capability and comprehension of human

Chapter 16

beings that, when the AI system breaks down, we are powerless even to pick up the pieces.

From the very beginning, human beings have been called to exercise kingly dominion over the creation, not cower under its supposed mastery over us. This is the best kind of freedom. A good example can be seen in a recent edition of the Wycliffe Bible Translators' magazine. In a discussion of the modern practicalities of Bible translation, the following is stated:

> Artificial intelligence (AI) tools such as ChatGPT have recently made headlines. And technology development teams are at the forefront in using cutting-edge AI to help local Bible translators produce high-quality translations quicker than ever before.[4]

We must praise and thank the God who gives human beings the skills to develop such sophisticated tools. But AI, like all human tools, must be exercised with responsible understanding and the use of wisdom. It would be quite wrong to simply allow a computer to churn out a Bible translation and send it straight into print without being subjected to the discernment of the eyes and minds of actual *people* with knowledge of languages, theology, people-groups, and cultures, and above all knowledge of God.

This is the most important caution about ChatGPT

and other similar forms of AI: what they produce can only be derived from the database of human knowledge and skill which they sample. And while a great deal of that knowledge and skill may be greatly influenced by Christian thinking, it is not generated by the mind of a responsible, let alone pastorally wise being, or beings, or Being.

A slavish, co-dependent kind of reliance on AI, or any created entities for that matter, is not only the path to what is rightly termed technocracy—'The Computer Says No'— it takes us further along the road to the infantilization of society.

Character and personality

What is childishness or immaturity in the sense I am describing? It has little to do with chronological age, or physical stature. You can find strikingly mature children and teenagers (nothing is more satisfying to pastors!) and equally you can come across depressingly immature people in their eighties (what can be more dispiriting?). Immaturity is stunted development of *character*; and there is nothing more urgent in today's Church, and indeed in the whole world, than the formation of character.

But the very meaning of 'character' needs to be carefully explained. Today the terms, 'character' and 'personality', tend to be used interchangeably. We might say that someone is a 'strong character', or perhaps we say that

Chapter 16

he is a 'strong personality', and we mean much the same thing. We do, however, need to distinguish character from personality, and although there is some overlap between them, they are certainly not identical.

By 'personality' I mean someone's basic temperament—the way he is by nature, through a combination of genetics and life-experience. Some people are chatty, others are quiet; some are ambitious, others are more resigned; some are sporty, others are sedentary; some are creative, others are contemplative; some laugh more than they cry, others cry more than they laugh, still others neither laugh nor cry! Some are more alert in the morning, whereas others come alive in the evening.

But 'character' has a clear moral, ethical dimension; it is about what is morally right and good in the sight of God. In 2 Peter 1:5-7, there is a list of eight qualities of Christian character: faith, virtue, knowledge, self-control, steadfastness, godliness, brotherly affection and love.[5] Peter exhorts his readers, telling them that 'if these qualities are yours and are increasing, they keep you from being ineffective or unfruitful in the knowledge of our Lord Jesus Christ' (v. 8). The point is that the Bible is very concerned about the lifelong development and maturing of *character*, regardless of someone's personality.

We can take the apostles, Peter and Paul, as good examples—they had entirely different personalities and temperaments; they also had very different natural gifts and abilities. But both, like every single Christian, were called to develop and mature the same Christian character which we see here. Whereas Peter listed these eight qualities, Paul supplied nine 'fruits of the Spirit' in Galatians 5:22–23: love, joy, peace, patience, kindness, goodness, faithfulness, gentleness, and self-control. Peter's list of eight and Paul's list of nine should be seen as equally descriptive of Christian character.

A mature Christian, then, is someone in whom Christian character has developed and is continuing to develop. And your personality or mine should never be an excuse for us not pursuing these qualities, or not seeking to grow. It is undoubtedly true that some personality traits might make it more challenging for some people to grow in certain respects. For example, a naturally introverted person might find it difficult to pursue the 'brotherly affection' we are called to; they may need to work harder at expressing love within the Church. Or a naturally extrovert person might struggle to exercise self-control in their speech; they are outspoken and might be in danger of offending people.

But the key point is that personality should never override character. If a believer says, 'I'm not a morning person; I get very stressed and impatient in the morning,' they need to remember that they are called to self-control and steadfastness every hour of every day. You sometimes hear people say, 'I don't do mornings.' All right ... maybe,

Chapter 16

just about! But a Christian can never say, 'I don't do self-control'!

Character nice, competence profitable?

David Wells' books, courageously and even prophetically written, have exerted a considerable influence on many thoughtful Christians for a long time. In one of his more recent publications, *The Courage To Be Protestant*, Wells defines character as being 'about the way this moral world becomes embedded in our nature'. He goes on to ground this claim in history; because wherever there is mature character there will be an inevitable and ardent interest in history:

> In the nineteenth century, letters of recommendation were typically character references and were carried around by the recipients and read with satisfaction. Letters of this kind today, especially if they make unhappy observations on the person's character, might invite a lawsuit. Today, though, we are less interested in a potential employee's character than we are in his or her competence. In a complex, highly competitive, technological, bottom-line-driven world, competence trumps character. Character is nice but competence is profitable. That, at least, is what we think.[6]

Wells is describing an increasingly technocratic

society, one in which the essential personhood of human beings is being squashed into a machine-shaped mould. People become just so many tools along a conveyor-belt of productivity. Psalm 115:8 describes how the makers and worshippers of dumb and lifeless idols become like them, and the same phenomenon is happening today; in a very real sense we become what we worship. The latest generation of smartphones, whatever stage of advancement they have reached by the time you read this, are gadgets of indescribably complex sophistication, able to deliver an almost infinite range of satisfying facts, commodities and outcomes. But they have no soul, no guiding moral compass, and those who rely on them become gradually like them—people with an astonishing array of skills, perhaps, but increasingly devoid of character.

The development of character is not automatic; it necessitates long years of building, testing and refining, and the process of refinement can be painful. But with mature character comes a robustness in the way in which we view life and all its challenges, from pestilence to sword to famine to captivity. It means taking a long-term view, exercising patience, thinking forward to the world which our children, grandchildren and more distant descendants will inherit. Like Jeremiah as he wrote to the exiles in Babylon, we are to think in terms of seventy

Chapter 16

years, at least, seeking the welfare of the present city into which we have been exiled (Jer. 29:7).

And it is God who builds character. I want to finish this chapter by returning to the figure of Joseph in the Book of Genesis, whom we looked at briefly in Chapter 12. A study of the formation of Joseph's mature character is deeply instructive for Christians today.

Joseph: an inspiring character study

We should go right back to the day when Joseph was cruelly sold into slavery by his brothers. Picture the scene if you can: a seventeen-year-old boy being frog-marched through the baking Sinai desert in chains behind a string of other slaves—no doubt treated roughly and barbarically—then brought to an Egyptian slave-market and being paraded in front of potential bidders, before being snaffled up by Potiphar, Pharaoh's captain of the guard (Gen. 37:36). Everything Joseph experienced would have been strange, alien, frightening. He did not know these people, he did not know their customs, he did not know their language.

He was at rock-bottom; he was at ground-zero. He might have given up in despair. But when we meet Joseph again in Genesis 39, we see that the goodness and power of God were at work in him and through him. 'The LORD was with Joseph, and he became a successful man, and he was in the house of his Egyptian master' (Gen. 39:2).

This is what happened, but this verse compresses Joseph's experience of several months and perhaps even years into a single sentence. We should not think that Joseph's emotions fled from him when he came to Egypt, so that he functioned robotically. We know Joseph far too well from the rest of Genesis to imagine that happening; he was a man of profound sentiment and passion. His agony would have been physical, emotional and indeed spiritual; we can only guess how deep he sank.

And yet, what we see here is an outstanding example of godly service, which is synonymous with godly character. Joseph became an exemplary, living embodiment of the devoted servant whom Paul describes in Ephesians 6:5–7:

> Bondservants, obey your earthly masters with fear and trembling, with a sincere heart, as you would Christ, not by the way of eye-service, as people-pleasers, but as bondservants of Christ, doing the will of God from the heart, rendering service with a good will as to the Lord and not to man.

Joseph, whatever wicked injustice and cruelty he had undoubtedly suffered, did not let this injustice affect the quality and above all the attitude of his godly service. 'The LORD was with Joseph'. What this means above all is that the LORD was with Joseph in his heart and soul, his spirit, his godly resolve and determination. If he ever stopped to think to himself, 'How unjust, how unfair, poor me!', he

Chapter 16

quickly moved on and said, 'I am serving the Lord, my God, while I serve Potiphar, my master.' Perhaps he began by sweeping the floor, or scrubbing the pots, or mucking out the stables. It did not matter; he knew he was serving the Lord, however humble and menial his tasks.

The Bible here speaks very directly to the most common, earthly, mundane issues that we all face. We all have to work, to serve, to do something: in the office, in the shop, on the street, in the hospital, in the school and university, and at home. Both in the Genesis narrative and in the Pauline instructions, we have a *locus classicus* of a godly work ethic. And there is nothing more necessary, especially in times which are so desperate and critical as they are today—thinking both economically and spiritually—than that God's people should serve with such a work ethic.

Why does Paul instruct believers to obey their masters with 'fear and trembling'? It is not that we should fear our earthly masters, or employers. It is that we should fear *God*. The attitude we have must be this: 'Whatever I do, wherever I do it, no matter how high or low my position, if I am a Christian, I will do everything in the full awareness that I am the servant of Christ, and people around me will know that. What I fear is bringing shame and dishonour on the name of Christ through poor, shoddy, inattentive, half-hearted, reluctant work.' The Christian employee or the Christian student should say every day, 'I will give of my best for my Lord and Master, because my colleagues/ teachers know I am a Christian, and I live to honour the name of Christ.'

Worldly success and godly success

What is 'success' in God's eyes? It is here, as much as anywhere else, that we are in danger of falling into worldly thinking. What does 'a successful man' look like? We might instantly reply that you can tell 'a successful man' by the car he drives, by the house he lives in, by the clothes he wears, by the places he goes on holiday. A 'successful man' is someone who, we say today, 'has done well for himself.' We do not know what his salary is, but we suspect it is a very substantial one.

We must not fall prey to such materialistic, worldly, unbiblical thinking. The genuine meaning of 'success' is found in relation to Joseph in Genesis 39:3: 'His master saw that the LORD was with him and that the LORD caused all that he did to succeed in his hands.' The successful person is the one who succeeds in what he does, because God is with him.

Perhaps we can apply this to ourselves by spelling out, in very practical terms, how Joseph may have succeeded in Potiphar's house. We can think of it in terms of eyes and ears, hands and feet, heart and mind.

- Joseph used his *eyes and ears*. He was alert, attentive, observant; from early on he looked around, saw

Chapter 16

how the household functioned, picked things up, found out what needed to be done, worked out how it was done and discovered what pleased his master.
- Joseph used his *hands and feet*. He was responsive, ready, prompt. If a job needed to be done, he got on with it. He did not procrastinate; he did not waste time. He did not put something on the bottom of a pile and hope it would go away. He worked out what needed to be done first and did it there and then.
- And Joseph used his *heart and mind*. He was assiduous, careful, thoughtful. He drilled down to the bottom of the task. He was not happy with a half-baked or bodged-up job. He did not apply sticking plasters. He thought to himself, 'How do I deal with this problem substantially and satisfactorily, not superficially?' and he worked steadfastly towards that goal.

In summary, Joseph was a Three-A Employee who exemplified *alertness*, *alacrity* and *assiduousness*.

This is how Joseph came of age—how he became a grownup. These hard years of training, not only in Potiphar's household but in the even more stringent environment of Pharaoh's prison, were the means by which, from the age of thirty, he was ready to step out from behind the bars—from the jail to the throne room—and begin to execute that great work for which he had been prepared. As he told his brothers, years later, 'It was not you who sent me here, but God. He has made me a father to Pharaoh, and lord of all his house and ruler over all the land of Egypt' (Gen. 45:8).

My prayer is that the Spirit of God which was at work in Joseph might be at work today in a rising generation of Christian men and women who are strengthened, so that what was said of Joseph might be said of them:

> His bow remained unmoved;
>   his arms were made agile
> by the hands of the Mighty One of Jacob.
>
> (Gen. 49:24)

PART SIX:
SUMMING UP

Conclusion: Human Judgement

> *For until men recognize that they owe everything to God, that they are nourished by His fatherly care, that He is the Author of their every good, that they should seek nothing beyond Him—they will never yield Him willing service. Nay, unless they establish their complete happiness in Him, they will never give themselves truly and sincerely to Him.*[1]
>
> John Calvin

This book has only been written because of the successive crises which have dominated the last four years: Covid-19, the war in Ukraine and the Cost-of-Living Crisis. These judgements have come about in the providence of an almighty, wise and good God, 'who works all things according to the counsel of his will' (Eph. 1:11). It is beyond our capability and, even more importantly, beyond all human privilege and prerogative, to pry into 'the secret things' which belong to God alone (Deut. 29:29). It is arrogance on our part to suppose that we can know why these events have happened, and it is equally audacious to imagine that we can ascertain how these crises will unfold in future months and years—or to

Conclusion

go still further and predict the next emergency which is poised to take place.

The final words spoken by Jesus before his ascension began in just this vein: 'It is not for you to know times or seasons that the Father has fixed by his own authority' (Acts 1:7). His disciples were curious about the future of Israel; we may be curious about the future of the nation we belong to, or the future of the whole earth. But Jesus did not disclose a prospective national or cosmic timetable to his disciples. Instead, he assured them that power would be given to them when his Spirit had come upon them and, on account of this, they would be his witnesses to the ends of the earth (Acts 1:8)—witnesses of everything that he had committed to them.

The bold prediction I made in 2008, that Britain would be a 'third world country' fifty years later, is sheer speculation on my part: I am no prophet nor the son of a prophet. That does not lessen the strong impression in my mind that Europe and North America are presently staring into an abyss, that western civilization in the early 2000s is in a parlous condition—in some senses paralleling the state of the Roman Empire in the early 200s. But God has called us, not to predict the future, but to live wise and godly lives in the here and now. Like the men of Issachar, we are to know these times and determine what 'Israel'—the people of God in this fallen world at any time in redemptive history—must do in the

334

present (1 Chron. 12:32). What I seek to do in this first Conclusion is give a few pointers as to how this may be attempted.

On repeated occasions in the preceding pages, I have used the category of 'worldview', and have often prefixed it with qualifiers such as 'biblical' and 'Christian'. To a large extent however—with the partial exception of Chapter 13, which dealt with environmental themes—I have not made any attempt to delineate the essential characteristics of the worldview that I am endeavouring to describe.

In this Conclusion, I seek to make good that deficit, taking as my departure point the nature of divine judgements, especially as they were unfolded in Chapter 3. There, as you may recall, using Thomas Brooks' understanding of the Great Fire of London as an example, I drew a distinction between divine judgements (1) in relation to *the whole world*, and his judgements (2) in relation to *God's people*. We need to probe a little deeper into the relationship between these two categories in order to be latter-day men of Issachar, not only understanding the times but also knowing what to do.

Here is a brief health warning: in the sections which follow, the discussion becomes a little more analytical than it has tended to be in the book so far; but there is nothing like sparing your most vigorous intellectual muscles for the final phase of the race!

Conclusion

Drawing the Venn diagrams

In 1 Timothy 4:10, Paul tells Timothy that Christ is 'the Saviour of all people, especially of those who believe.' We should notice that that this statement expresses both *commonality* and *distinction*. In terms of *commonality*, there is only one Saviour of all people, Jesus Christ. Elsewhere, Paul tells Timothy that Christ is the 'One Mediator between God and men' (1 Tim. 2:5). But the *distinction* is seen in the qualifying expression in 4:10: 'especially of those who believe'. The Greek word which is translated as 'especially', *malista*, could also be rendered as 'chiefly', 'most of all', 'above all'. The sense is that Christ is the Saviour 'of those who believe' in a higher, greater sense than he is Saviour of everyone else.

What exactly is the nature of this distinction? With a background in mathematics, I like to think in terms of Venn Diagrams, which tend to be presented as two intersecting circles. Just how do we draw this Venn Diagram? What do the two circles stand for? Indeed, are there only two circles? What lies within the intersection? Is it an intersection, or is one set the subset of another? Or do the circles exactly coincide? Can anything lie outside *both* circles? From which angle should we view the circles? Are they, in fact, circles, or should they be understood three-dimensionally, as spheres or other shapes? And are they static or dynamic?

The more I reflect on it, the more I feel that Venn Diagrams, of the kind generally used in mathematics, are simply not up to the job. And lest all this seem highly abstract and conceptual—maths may not be at all what you are into!—we should ask similar questions using more concrete terms. What are the most appropriate single-word categories to use to denote (1) 'all people' and (2) 'those who believe', in 1 Timothy 4:10? And how do they relate to one another?

The classic twentieth-century work in this regard is undoubtedly H. Richard Niebuhr's magisterial book, *Christ & Culture*, which was based on lectures given at Austin Presbyterian Theological Seminary in 1949.[2] Niebuhr's historical analysis yielded five models—we might (or might not!) think of them as five different Venn Diagrams—setting out the relationship between Niebuhr's chosen categories of 'Christ' and 'Culture'.[3] They may be summarized as follows:

1. Christ *Against* Culture. This posits a sharp antithesis between Christianity and culture, and is exemplified in the cases of the Early Church Father, Tertullian (AD 160–211) and, intriguingly, the Russian novelist Leo Tolstoy (1828–1910).[4]

2. The Christ *of* Culture. This describes the assimilation of culture into Christianity. Examples given include Clement of Alexandria (AD c.150–c.215), Peter Abelard (c.1079–1142) and Albrecht Ritschl (1822–99).[5]

Conclusion

3. Christ *Above* Culture. This presents an architectonic structure in which culture derives its character from Christianity. While there is a distinction between the two, there is no antithesis, rather complementary harmony. This is essentially the high medieval view, personified by Thomas Aquinas (1225–74).[6]
4. Christ and Culture in *Paradox*. This is a dynamic, oscillatory relationship between Christianity and culture, in contrast to the static position just referred to. It is seen most famously in Martin Luther (1483–1546); Niebuhr also cites Emil Brunner (1889–1966).[7]
5. Christ the *Transformer* of Culture. The essential element here is of conversion through interaction between Christianity and culture. Niebuhr lists several 'giants' of church history under this category: Augustine of Hippo (AD 354–430), John Calvin (1509–64), Jonathan Edwards (1703–58) and Karl Barth (1886–1968) but also devotes significant space to a relatively obscure Anglican clergyman, F. D. Maurice (1805–72).[8]

While representatives of all five models can still be found, it is somewhat rare in circles which could generally be described as 'evangelical'—holding to the authority of God speaking in Scripture—to find the first two positions being consistently held. In terms of (3), there has been a recent surge in what has been called Reformed Thomism.[9] However, the latter two models, *Christ and Culture in Paradox*, and *Christ the Transformer of Culture*, come into closer focus, and now need to be developed and nuanced somewhat.

Two kingdoms?

In more recent decades, the relationship between 'Christ' and 'culture' has become a matter of more intense and voluminous debate and it has become necessary to introduce categories and terminology which build significantly on Niebuhr. These discussions have taken place among Reformed scholars, both historians and theologians.

It is helpful to return to 1 Timothy 4:10 and the apostle Paul's description of Christ as 'the Saviour of all people, especially of those who believe.' Can we clarify how Christ is the 'Saviour' of each of these two groups of people; allowing of course for the fact that the second group is a subset of the first?

Westminster Seminary in Escondido, California, has become associated with the resurgence of what is known as 'Two Kingdoms' theology. Contemporary scholars linked to this teaching include David VanDrunen and Michael Horton, and both build substantially on the earlier work of Meredith G. Kline (1922–2007). Their starting point is that Christ exercises two kingly offices,

CONCLUSION

one in relation to the civil realm and the other in relation to the spiritual realm.[10] In relation to the first, Christ is Creator, Sustainer and Judge; in relation to the second he is Redeemer and Head of the Church.[11]

The distinction between 'two kingdoms', indeed the very nature and existence of 'two kingdoms', has not been understood uniformly throughout history, reflecting something of Niebuhr's fivefold division referred to in the previous section. They are given classic expression in Augustine's magisterial book, *City of God*, in which the divine, eternal and righteous City is set against the temporal, doomed City of Man. For Luther, there is a necessary antagonism between the two kingdoms. Calvin, for his part, sought to establish a greater measure of co-operation between the church and civil government, albeit with varying degrees of success.[12]

Since the beginning of the twentieth century, however, three significant rival schools of thought have flourished, each of which have the tendency of collapsing the 'Two Kingdoms' into one. Michael Beck's close and careful study, *Covenant Lord and Cultic Boundary*, engages with each of these:

1. The view often described variously as *Theonomy* or *Christian Reconstructionism*, which has been associated especially with Rousas J. Rushdoony (1916–2001) and Greg Bahnsen (1948–95). According to this position, not only does the

Moral Law (i.e., the Ten Commandments) in the Pentateuch have perpetually binding authority; but the Civil Law—or at least the principles which it articulates—is to be applied, even enforced, across the state as well as the church, with a view to the Christianization of society. This movement is associated with postmillennialism and has largely been restricted to North America. It is only fair to say that its influence is waning, although it has been argued that it is morphing into something a little different.[13]

2. The *Perspectivalism*, or more specifically, *Triperspectivalism*, championed by John Frame (b. 1939) and Vern Poythress (b. 1946). This is essentially a method of hermeneutics which seeks to mirror the 'perspectives' of the Triune God, with the so-called normative, situational, existential perspectives corresponding to the Father, the Son and the Holy Spirit respectively. One tendency of this approach, as Beck argues pervasively in his book, is to flatten the contours of redemptive history and especially the covenantal structure of the Bible.

3. The Dutch tradition known as *Neo-Calvinism*, represented by Abraham Kuyper (1837–1920) and Herman Dooyeweerd (1894–1977). Kuyper taught and wrote extensively on the theme of

Conclusion

God's sovereignty across the whole created order, including such concepts as 'sphere sovereignty'—that no one area or 'sphere' of life or society, being under God's ultimate sovereign rule, has sovereign authority over another—and also developed the doctrine of common grace. Dooyeweerd advanced the frontiers of Kuyper's thinking, especially in terms of what he labelled 'ground-motives, the fundamental assumptions and commitments about the nature of reality which underpin all thought and expression across world history. In his book, *Roots of Western Culture*, Dooyeweerd summarized the four main ground-motives throughout western history as follows:

i. The 'form-matter' ground-motive of Greek antiquity in alliance with the Roman power motive (imperium).

ii. The Scriptural ground-motive of the Christian religion: creation, fall, and redemption through Jesus Christ in communion with the Holy Spirit.

iii. The Roman Catholic [Thomistic] ground-motive of 'nature-grace', which seeks to combine the two mentioned above.

iv. The modern humanistic ground-motive of 'nature-freedom', in which an attempt is made to bring the three previous motives to a religious synthesis concentrated upon the value of human personality.[14]

It was the second of these ground-motives which Dooyeweerd embraced, of course, and I have already referred to the Creation-Fall-Redemption (and Restoration) in Chapter 13.[15]

Each of these three schools of thought provides us with valuable insights, the first of them (Theonomy) perhaps rather less than the other two. Theonomy, speaking broadly, represents a specific intensification and overapplication of certain aspects of the teaching of Cornelius Van Til (1895–1987), who always spoke with the utmost caution about man's capacity to comprehend the divine.[16]

Common grace and the covenant of grace

We return to the problem of *commonality* and *distinction*. The Two-Kingdoms approach of Kline differs from the various 'One-Kingdom' positions which have just been summarized, and this is not simply a matter of emphasis, but of substance.

Jesus Christ is the one and only Mediator between God and man (1 Tim. 2:5) and can in no sense be divided (1 Cor. 1:13). Moreover, Paul tells us in 2 Corinthians 5:19 that 'in Christ God was reconciling the world to himself'; note that Paul says, 'the world' and not 'the Church'.

Conclusion

These considerations appear to lend support to a 'One-Kingdom' approach.

But the 'especially' of 1 Timothy 4:10 refuses to budge; there is a stubborn distinction between 'all people' and 'those who believe' in terms of *how Christ is a Saviour to them*. This is where the redemptive-historical approach of Kline, standing on the shoulders of Geerhardus Vos (1862–1949), appears to me persuasive.[17]

Kline's specific contribution is in the area of distinguishing the various covenants of Scripture. It is not necessary at this point to undertake a systematic study of all the biblical covenants. The key distinction to be drawn here is between (1) common grace and the (2) the covenant of grace. Both covenants are of course divinely administered, and both are gracious, coming from God to man in his state of sin and ruin. In relation to both, Christ is the Mediator. But the first of them, made known first to Noah (Gen. 8:21–9:17), has to do with the preservation of the earth and its inhabitants as well as the provision of divinely authorized human government. It is therefore a *civil* administration. The second of them, made known first to Abraham (Gen. 12:1–3; 15:17–21; 17:1–14), has to do with the redemption of God's elect, their salvation from sin, Satan and death by the blood of Christ, and the application of Christ and his benefits to them by the Holy Spirit. Whereas common grace encompasses 'all people', the covenant of grace embraces 'those who believe'. It is consequently a *spiritual* administration. Alternatively, we could say that common grace has the *world* as its object, while the covenant of grace has the *Church* as its object.

Necessarily, there is a measure of simplicity and generalization in the above paragraph; necessarily because, as Van Til understood, all our knowledge of God, and consequently our language about God, is analogical. It cannot exhaustively comprehend all that God is and what he has done. But that does not prevent such statements being true and helpful.

It should be appreciated that the various themes and chapters in this book may pertain in different degrees (1) to civil matters, such as the state or the society; or (2) to spiritual concerns, that is, the Church. For example, Chapter 6, *Life or Liberty?* focused more on the state and less on the Church than did Chapter 7, *Connection and Communion*. But it is not always easy to draw a hard and fast line of division. So much of our activity and engagement takes place both within the civil and spiritual spheres, often simultaneously.

This is where a Kuyperian distinction between (a) the church as an institution and (b) the Church as an organism is extremely helpful.[18] When the Church is gathered for worship, the distinction between the Church and the world should be more emphatically defined; indeed, it is an anticipation of the Day when God will put an eternal separation between those who are his

Conclusion

people and those who are not. But when God's people are rubbing shoulders with the world, as they should be from Monday to Saturday, they are functioning as an organism rather than an institution, acting as salt and light in the world. As an organism, the Church should be a means of preservation in the world, within the realm of common grace. As an institution, however, the Church meets and worships as the blessed recipients of God's covenant of grace; far more than that, they meet in the very presence of the Triune God himself.

The aim in this book, in conclusion, has been to address the Church, in the light of recent and present events, in her calling both *as the church* (the church as an institution) and *within the world* (the Church as an organism). The Church is one; it does not become a different entity when the congregation file out of the building. Nevertheless, there is a *distinction* here, without *division*; it is wrong to think of the Church in either a strictly monistic or dualistic fashion, just as it is erroneous and even heretical to *divide*, rather than to *distinguish*, the office of Christ and the natures of Christ.

One application needs to be spelt out here. It has become fashionable in recent years to collapse any kind of sacred-secular distinction—to imply that, in the world which God has made, everything is sacred and nothing should be thought of as secular. Playing football to God's glory on Saturday is no less 'sacred' and no more 'secular' than listening to a sermon to God's glory on Sunday. The problem with this viewpoint is that God himself has established this distinction in the world; he has differentiated between the *holy* and the *common* (Lev. 10:10; Ezek. 44:23). The application to be drawn here is that there is a holiness about the specific gatherings of the Church on Sundays which is distinct from the various 'common' activities in which the same individuals engage throughout the week.

Engaging heart and mind

What, then, are the specific priorities we need to begin with as we seek to construct a biblical and Christian worldview? It will be appreciated that the challenges we are facing call for clear minds and careful delineation of categories, in the manner just described. We need to be disciplined and judicious in our use of language, exercising self-control in both speech and the written word, drawing boundaries where they need to be drawn and removing them when they have no right to exist.[19] This approach needs to be applied to the various spheres of authority which have been divinely established, as explained in Chapter 15 on the subject of freedom. These begin with God himself and cascade down to Church, state, family and ultimately the individual.

This worldview, however, is more than an intellectual position, or a set of theological propositions, though it must be nothing less than this. Any worldview, if it is to be

Conclusion

considered robust, must be comprehensive in its scope, realistic in its assessment and consistent in its internal logic. But this worldview must engage the heart as well as the mind, and this takes me to another mighty strand of Reformed tradition: the great emphasis on the desires and attitudes of the soul in its love and worship of the Triune God—an emphasis which finds sublime expression in Jonathan Edwards (1703–58) and his book, *Religious Affections*.

Contrasting the position of Edwards with that of his contemporary Charles Chauncy (1705–87), minister of the First Congregational Church in Boston at the time of the Great Awakening in New England, Robin Gray explains that:

> he [Edwards] was a defender of the genuineness at the heart of the Awakening and was unwilling to concede the heart of authentic Christianity to reason and the intellect. Chauncy's famous statement was: 'an *enlightened mind*, not *raised affections* ought always be the guide of those who call themselves men; and this in the affairs of religion, as well as other things.'[20] In stark contrast, Edwards asserted that a truly enlightened mind *resulted* in raised affections, leading to the significantly more famous thesis of his treatise: 'True religion, in great part, consists in holy affections.'[21]

Gray continues:

Contemporary readers can immediately run into trouble here, by substituting 'emotions' for the less familiar term 'affections'. This is a mistake. To begin with, there is no commonly accepted definition of what is meant by the emotions, but such consensus as there is tends to make emotions very much a 'felt' experience, rooting them in the body in a fundamental way. By contrast, Edwards' understanding of the affections situates them in the soul, not the body. More specifically, for Edwards affections are heightened inclinations of the will. The will exists in the soul. Therefore, although affections generally have an effect on the body, they do not reside in the body; a disembodied spirit is just as capable of experiencing affections as an embodied one.[22] The great need of the hour is for men and women and, may it please God, children and teenagers, who are as deeply acquainted with the 'affections' of the soul as the exercises of the intellect. This is nothing other than what has often been called 'Experimental Calvinism'. What exactly am I talking about?

Captured and enthralled

I am talking about a sight of the glory of God, of his perfections and beauties, of Jesus Christ in all his divine and human fullness, which not only satisfies the mind but enraptures the soul. Edwards, like John Calvin (1509–64),

Conclusion

was possessed of a giant intellect; like Calvin, too, he was a man whose soul had been captured and enthralled by the greatness and majesty of the Triune God.

Calvin and Edwards have this in common too: that their mighty influence on both the Church and the world has persisted during the centuries following their lifetime. The men and women who are called to follow in their footsteps in the present generation need, as the primary and essential requirement, what William Cowper (1731–1800) called 'the soul-refreshing view of Jesus and his Word'.[23] We are talking about people who love God, love the Scriptures and are often moved to prayer; people who love the gospel, being persuaded that nothing but 'the power of God for salvation' (Rom. 1:16) can have any lasting effect on a world that is blind, decaying and dead, perishing for lack of the knowledge of God.

It is only such people, who not only know about God, but *know* God and, in knowing God, *love* God, who will possess the wisdom, realism, courage, patience and prayerfulness which are so needed as we navigate the otherwise impossible challenges of the twenty-first-century world. May it please God to raise up and prepare such a generation today, and into the future.

Conclusion: Divine Judgement

> *Then once more you shall see the distinction between the righteous and the wicked, between one who serves God and one who does not serve him.*
>
> Malachi 3:18

This book has given especial attention to very specific, contemporary and prominent events which have been categorized as 'divine judgements'. But a rather important question needs to be asked: what is the biblical warrant for designating Covid, the Russia-Ukraine War and the Cost-of-Living Crisis in this way?

In this second Conclusion I intend to enlarge our horizon, broadening these few, specific examples of judgement—if indeed that is what they are—into a more systematically theological, though concise, treatment of the whole theme of judgement. The substance of this whole book, and its consequent usefulness, must rest upon a secure, biblical-theological framework.

The driving idea in this Conclusion can be stated in this way: *God must, and will, judge all the creatures he has made.* He does so in the universal and eternal demonstration of what the Bible calls his *name*: that is, his divine character, his attributes—supremely his justice and his grace.[1]

Conclusion

Every knee shall bow, every tongue confess.
What is the goal towards which the whole cosmos is heading? It is that everything in creation will glorify God: the eternal, infinite, almighty Triune God. 'Let everything that has breath praise the Lord! Praise the Lord!' (Ps. 150:6). The Psalms end in this climactic fashion because the great purpose of all creation is ultimately *doxological*—that is, taken up with the glory and praise of God. The cosmos, which endures for ever, will be populated with creatures who declare the glory and praise of God.

The apostle Paul describes that great end in Philippians 2:10–11: 'At the name of Jesus every knee should bow, in heaven and on earth and under the earth, and every tongue confess that Jesus Christ is Lord, to the glory of God the Father.' Here Paul is drawing on Isaiah 45:23:

> By myself I have sworn;
>> from my mouth has gone out in righteousness
>> a word that shall not return:
> 'To me every knee shall bow,
>> every tongue shall swear allegiance.

But we should notice that Paul distributes the praise and glory of God, the bowing of the knee and the confessing of the tongue, among three realms: those who are 'in heaven and on earth and under the earth'. This threefold division corresponds to what Geerhardus Vos calls, 'the three spheres of the universe': the angelic realm 'in heaven', the redeemed who are 'on earth', and those men and angels who are eternally condemned, 'under the earth'.[2] The 'wrath of man' will praise God *'under the earth'* (Ps. 76:10); so will the 'great multitude that no one could number', redeemed out of all the nations *'on earth'* (Rev. 7:9); so too will 'innumerable angels in festal gathering' who are *'in heaven'* (Heb. 12:22).

When that goal is reached, God will make unmistakably clear 'the distinction between the righteous and the wicked, between one who serves God and one who does not serve him' (Mal. 3:18). In this present world we do not see that division clearly, but at the day of judgement, often referred to by the Prophets as 'the day of the Lord', it will be manifested unmistakably and fixed eternally.[3]

The Judgement and the judgements

I am speaking here of the final, conclusive, climactic 'day of judgement'. To repeat from an earlier paragraph, *God must, and will, judge all the creatures he has made*. But what about God's judgements in this present world? We need to perceive the relationship between present judgements and the final judgement, and so I return to the working definition of a 'divine judgement' with which I began long ago in the *Introduction*:

> A divine judgement is a providence of God in this world that significantly affects one or many human lives, intended to cause people to acknowledge

Conclusion

God, putting them in mind of the final judgement and their eternal state.

To maximise and develop our full understanding of what present judgement means—of how weighty it is—it needs to be set in the highest, widest, deepest theological framework possible. Consequently, a major part of this Conclusion will be taken up with constructing this framework.

Careful reflection led me to perceive that the best way to handle this theme is to think in terms of *a series of paired distinctions*. That is how my material will be set out in the sections which follow. In each case I will describe the category within which a distinction is being made and also something of the nature of that distinction. The hope is that the reader's appreciation of how, and why, God's judgements are enacted in this world—in anticipation of the Final Judgement yet to come—will consequently be deepened.

Altogether I have identified eighteen 'paired distinctions' and I have chosen to classify them into five unequal groups: *four essential distinctions* (pertaining to what things *are*); *two ethical distinctions* (pertaining to the *moral character* of things); *seven purposive distinctions* (pertaining to *God's purpose*); *four observable distinctions* (pertaining to *human perception*); and *one final, climactic distinction*, which is in a category all of its own.[4]

Essential distinctions

1. GOD AND CREATION.

This distinguishes among **all that there is**.

All that is, was, will, and can ever be, is either God or it is God's creation. God alone exists necessarily and without contingency. He chose to bring the whole of creation into being by his own will and consequently, the entire creation belongs to him. He is therefore the Lord of all creation, having absolute authority over it, including the right to judge what to do with it. As we saw in Chapter 3 of this book, God's right to judge the world is understood by the apostle Paul, and in the Bible more generally, as a first principle. He is the divine potter and everything else is the clay that he has brought into being (Is. 29:16; 64:8; Jer. 18:4–6; Rom. 9:21).

2. CREATION AND PROVIDENCE.

This distinguishes among **all that God does**.

All the works of God can be subdivided into creation and providence.[5] In the act of creation, God brings all his creatures into being from nothing, by the word of his power. In the act of providence, God preserves and governs those creatures, and all their actions.[6] Creation is an initiatory, inaugural work but, following the work of creation, God's providence continues without interruption. Christ himself 'upholds the universe by the word of his power' (Heb. 1:3). It is also useful to speak

Conclusion

of God's *providences* in the plural, by which we mean all the actions of God that come under this category of providence. These will be further subdivided under section 16 and 17 on pages 267–368.

3. Rational creatures and non-rational creatures.

This distinguishes among **all that God has created**.

Within all that God has made—which includes everything that is, was, or shall be, both visible and invisible (Col. 1:16)—we must distinguish between entities which have a *reasonable soul*, and those which do not. This is a somewhat different distinction to that between animate and inanimate creation. The Hebrew word *nefesh*, 'soul', can refer to the living and breathing nature of an animal (Prov. 12:10), but such a 'soul' is not rational or reasonable. Rational creatures are intelligent creatures, with the godlike capacity to communicate, to respond, to love, to obey and to decide; and to do all these things freely and voluntarily. There is in them a higher principle than the mere instinct which animates beasts. These rational creatures are all accountable to God and will therefore face his judgement.

4. Men and angels.

This distinguishes among **all rational creatures**.

Among rational creatures there are only two clear categories, as revealed in Scripture: men and angels. The Bible is a book written for men, not for angels, and it is predominantly about God's dealing with men, not with angels. Angels, of course, play a significant role in the entire divine-human narrative, but they are 'ministering spirits sent out to serve for the sake of those who are to inherit salvation' (Heb. 1:14). Man, however, is the pinnacle of God's created order, made in the image and likeness of God, with dominion over the creatures (Gen. 1:26–27); the same is not said of angels. And it is the form of *man* which the Son of God has eternally assumed, not the form of an angel. The world to come will be subjected not to angels, but to man (Heb. 2:5), with Christ as the head.

Ethical distinctions

5. GOOD AND EVIL.

This distinguishes between **the ethical character of all attitudes and actions**.

All the attitudes and actions of rational souls are either good, evil, or a combination of good and evil, with the 'good' being defined wholly in relation to the moral character of God. God alone is good, and God alone *does* good (Ps. 119:68; Mark 10:18). Whatever is pleasing to God is good; whatever is displeasing to him is evil. Goodness is defined in Scripture by obedience to the moral law, summarized in the Ten Commandments (Exod. 20:1–17; Deut. 5:6–21). Evil attitudes and actions can be thought of in terms of sin, disobedience, transgression, iniquity and lawlessness—all of which convey the idea of *wilful rebellion* against God on the part of rational souls.

6. THE RIGHTEOUS AND THE UNRIGHTEOUS.
This distinguishes between **the ethical character of rational souls**.

Not only are attitudes and actions either good or evil, but God also regards the character of rational souls as either good or evil, and these souls are viewed by him as either righteous or unrighteous. There are some (righteous) angels who never rebelled against God, and there are other (unrighteous) angels who did rebel and lost their 'proper dwelling' (Jude 6). The first man, Adam, was created with original righteousness, able to obey God's commands but also with the potential to disobey. Because Adam was not an isolated individual being, but the covenant head of the human race, his disobedience meant that 'his posterity, all mankind, descending from him by ordinary generation, sinned in him, and fell with him, in his first transgression.'[7] In consequence of this, all Adam's offspring —Jesus Christ apart—are counted as guilty sinners, have a nature which is wholly corrupted by sin, and commit actual sins. They are all, in a word, *unrighteous* and, as such, are displeasing to God.

Purposive distinctions

7. JUSTICE AND GRACE.
This distinguishes between **the modes of God's response to sinful creatures**.

God's justice means that he *necessarily* acts in accordance with his own character which, as we have seen in section 5, is perfectly good. Abraham pleaded with God on the basis that 'the Judge of all the earth' must do what is right and just (Gen. 18:25). God's actions towards his creatures are therefore carried out in justice; he is 'the judge of all' (Heb. 12:23), and all must appear before the judgement seat of God (Rom. 14:10) and of Christ (2 Cor. 5:10). But God's grace means that he *freely* chooses to deal with some of his creatures, not in terms of mere justice, but in a demonstration of his love and favour, not treating those creatures as their sins deserve. The Parable of the Labourers in the Vineyard (Matt. 20:1–15) illustrates the tension between justice and grace which 'those hired first' (Matt. 20:10) detected; but in the simplicity of the divine mind there *can* be no tension or contradiction. As we have seen, when God declared his 'name', that is his whole nature and character, to Moses in Exodus 34:6–7, he emphasized both his justice and his grace.[8] In the substitutionary death of Christ for sinners, above all, God is demonstrated to be both 'just' (his justice) and 'the justifier' (his grace) 'of the one who has faith in Jesus' (Rom. 3:26).

8. THE ELECT AND THE NON-ELECT.

This distinguishes between **divinely determined destinies**. God's election is his free, sovereign determination to

Conclusion

bring, irresistibly, certain men and angels to righteousness and everlasting life.[9] As we have seen in section 6 of this chapter, all of Adam's race are unrighteous, so that, if God were to deal with them in mere justice, all would be condemned. The elect are those from Adam's race who the Triune God has graciously determined to save in Christ: chosen by God before the foundation of the world; given to his Son who became incarnate and died and rose again in their place; and in time regenerated by the Holy Spirit; united to Christ; brought to repentance and faith; enabled to persevere throughout this present life; and ultimately taken to eternal glory. The whole 'golden chain' of calling, regeneration, justification, adoption, sanctification, perseverance and glorification pertains to the elect.[10] The non-elect are the rest of mankind, who God has determined to 'pass by', ordaining them 'to dishonour and wrath for their sin, to the praise of his glorious justice'.[11]

9. SAVING GRACE AND COMMON GRACE.

This distinguishes among **modes of grace**.

The final sentence of the preceding paragraph may give the impression that God demonstrates nothing by way of grace towards the non-elect. The vitally important doctrine of common grace proves that this is profoundly untrue. As we saw in the first Conclusion, God is 'the Saviour of all people, *especially* of those who believe' (1 Tim. 4:10). God did not immediately bring death on Adam and Eve after they had sinned (Gen. 3:20-21); neither did he execute the sentence of capital punishment on Cain though he was a murderer, but rather protected him from violent attack (Gen. 4:15). God 'makes his sun rise on the evil and on the good and sends rain on the just and on the unjust' (Matt. 5:45). God gives many remarkable gifts to people who will never acknowledge him as their Lord—gifts which believers, who are the recipients of God's saving grace, should heartily recognize. All of this comes from the grace of the God who is no man's debtor; God is under no obligation to be gracious to all. But God has freely determined that *some*, that is the elect, should be the recipients of saving grace, so that they are counted by God as righteous—not for any righteousness in them, but all from Christ, through grace alone and by faith alone—and ultimately, in glory, to be as perfectly righteous in their natures as Christ himself is.

10. THE PRESENT AGE AND THE AGE TO COME.

This distinguishes between **ages**.

From the Fall of Man, right up to the complex of events which includes the return of Christ, the bodily resurrection of the dead and the day of judgement, we are living in what the New Testament calls the 'present age' (Gal. 1:4; 1 Tim. 6:17; Tit. 2:12). It is an age characterized by man being born in sin, and the present creation being subjected to futility and bound to corruption (Rom. 8:20-21). But it is also the age of *probation*, an age in which God's gracious

Conclusion

providences towards fallen man—both in saving grace and common grace—are made known, in order that men may turn to the God who freely offers salvation to all and commands people everywhere to repent and believe (Acts 17:30). The age to come, referred to by Jesus as 'the resurrection' (Matt. 22:30) and in Hebrews 2:5 as 'the world to come', is the age following the day of judgement. This is the age of *consummation*, when all that is promised by God and hoped for by his elect will be eternally fixed. We can also speak of it as the new creation, or indeed the new Jerusalem, with a new heaven and a new earth (Rev. 21:1-4). That new creation is already breaking into the present creation; that is why there is a tension present in believers' experiences, so that they can speak of 'already-and-not-yet. The present age is a time of walking by faith, not by sight (2 Cor. 5:7)—the felt tension between these two ages explains why Paul can speak of being 'afflicted in every way, but not crushed; perplexed, but not driven to despair; persecuted, but not forsaken; struck down, but not destroyed' (2 Cor. 4:8-9). It is the reality of Christ's bodily resurrection and all that it entails for believers' future hope which enables Paul to add these four 'but nots'.

11. THE OLD COVENANT AND THE NEW COVENANT.
This distinguishes between **historical administrations within this present age**.

The most important point to emphasize here is that there

is one, and only one, covenant of grace by which God binds himself to save his elect, uniting them to Christ and bestowing on them all the benefits that Christ has purchased by his obedience, as set out in section 8 of this chapter. Christ is the one mediator between God and man (1 Tim. 2:5), the only Redeemer of God's elect throughout this present age. But it is right to speak of a distinction between the old covenant and the new covenant. In purely historical terms, the old covenant preceded the death, resurrection and ascension of Christ, whereas the new covenant, though foretold long before Christ (Jer. 31:31), was inaugurated by Christ and explicitly linked to his work—specifically the shedding of his blood (Luke 22:20; 1 Cor. 11:25; Heb. 12:24). However, it should not be overlooked that the old covenant and the new covenant are not distinguished simply by time; they should be understood as two distinct administrations of the one covenant of grace.

12. Israel and the Church.

This distinguishes between **the subjects of God's respective covenantal dealings**.

Under the old covenant, the people of Israel were the recipients of God's gracious, covenantal dealings. Under the new covenant, it is the Church of Jesus Christ, composed of both Jews and Gentiles, whom God addresses as his covenant people. A comparison of Exodus 19:5–6 with 1 Peter 2:9–10 illustrates this point

CONCLUSION

perfectly. It must be emphasized, nevertheless, that the degree of continuity between old covenant Israel and the new covenant Church is complex and remains highly controversial. It is extremely helpful, following Paul in Galatians 4:1-7, to appreciate that old covenant Israel was like a child 'under guardians and managers' for an appointed duration, and to see the new covenant Church as the son of mature years. This enables us to understand the way in which the law and the Spirit operate under the two administrations. The addition of the law under the old covenant was 'because of transgressions', to make sin 'become sinful beyond measure' (Gal. 3:19; Rom. 7:13). Under the new covenant, the law is not annulled—its righteous requirements remain—but the power to live a righteous life is explicitly ascribed to the Spirit (Rom. 8:4). As the people of God who have come of age, the Church has outgrown the physical and territorial restrictions which applied to Israel. Despite all of this, however, we must continue to speak of one covenant people of God spanning the present age, from Genesis 3:15 all the way to the return of Christ.

13. TYPES AND ANTITYPES.
This distinguishes between **data relating to God's respective covenantal dealings**.

Under the old covenant administration there were 'types'—people, places, objects and events—which foreshadowed the 'antitypes', the fulfilments, of the new covenant. The antitypes are to be found in the New Testament record, in Christ himself and his work, in his Church, or indeed in the age yet to come. The Westminster Confession speaks of 'promises, prophecies, sacrifices, circumcision, the paschal lamb, and other types and ordinances delivered to the people of the Jews, all fore-signifying Christ to come.'[12] But as we will be thinking largely about judgement, we should also note that certain dramatic events in the Old Testament, such as the flood in the time of Noah, and the destruction of Sodom and Gomorrah, are specifically highlighted in Scripture as typical examples of what God will do 'to keep the unrighteous under punishment until the day of judgement' (2 Pet. 2:9).

Observable distinctions

14. THE INVISIBLE CHURCH AND THE VISIBLE CHURCH.
This distinguishes between **the elect** and **the non-elect** from a human perspective.

Throughout biblical history, a distinction of this kind has always been maintained. God's covenant of grace, under both the old and the new covenant, has always been outwardly administered among the *visible* church, that is those who are publicly identified as belonging to God's covenant people. But the spiritually salvific operations of God's grace take place in the elect, the Church viewed as *invisible*. This does not imply the existence of two churches; rather, it is the one Church viewed from two

| CONCLUSION

different aspects. Among the people of Israel there were righteous and unrighteous individuals, as conspicuously evidenced by the contrasting characters of the many kings of Israel and Judah. Among the twelve disciples, one of them was a traitor, even a devil (John 6:70–71). We need to acknowledge the difficulty in ascertaining whether certain people belong to the elect; even the reference to Judas Iscariot's 'own place' (Acts 1:25) is not explicitly conclusive. But we do know that the elect are those whose names are written in the Lamb's book of life (Rev. 13:8; 21:27), ultimately known only to God, and that the wheat and the weeds grow side-by-side in the same field (Matt. 13:36–43). Neither in old covenant Israel, nor in the new covenant Church, can we visibly identify a congregation of whom it could be said with any human confidence, 'we know that all these people are elect!'

15. God's secret will and God's revealed will.
This distinguishes between **the modes of disclosure of God's purposes**.

This terminology is lifted straight out of Deuteronomy 29:29: 'The secret things belong to the Lord our God, but the things that are revealed belong to us and to our children forever, that we may do all the words of this law.' To take these in reverse order, the revealed will of God is expressly declared to us in Scripture and, though not all Scriptures are equally plain in their meaning, we must hold to the essential perspicuity, or clarity, of the Word

DIVINE JUDGEMENT

of God. It is the revealed will of God, as the Deuteronomy passage indicates, that people obey his moral law. It was the revealed will of God to send his Son into the world as a sacrifice for sins and to make the gospel of Jesus Christ known among the nations. God has also revealed—and this is the consideration we are especially bearing in mind—that there will be a day when he will judge every soul who has lived. But God has chosen not to disclose everything that he has purposed to bring about; this is his secret will, which no human being or gathering of people can ever fully discover. Indeed, the entire catalogue of what God has secretly decreed to take place, throughout all time and space, is so vast that all the books ever written could not begin to unfold it. However, we can rest in the assurance that God's secret will and God's revealed will are entirely consistent with one another and with his own holy, faithful character.

16. THE ORDINARY AND THE EXTRAORDINARY.
This distinguishes among **the perceived magnitude of God's providences executed during this present age**. There is a measure of subjectivity in this distinction, but it is one which we must all recognize. Everything which God brings about in his created order is a providence, and most of them we would categorize as 'ordinary', in the sense of being commonplace, unremarkable. The rising and setting of the sun, the succession of the seasons, even the ongoing cycle of births of babies and deaths of

Conclusion

the elderly; these are 'ordinary' in the sense that they are wholly predictable. Other providences, like a torrential downpour of rain, an isolated incident of violent crime in a city, or an outbreak of flu in a household, are less predictable but we would still count them as 'ordinary'; they would not make the headlines. But some events are unquestionably 'extraordinary' in the sheer scale of their impact: the Black Death of the fourteenth century, the world wars of the twentieth century, and the Great Tsunami of Boxing Day 2004 would all undoubtedly qualify.[13]

17. THE PRIVATE SPHERE AND THE PUBLIC SPHERE.
This distinguishes among **human experience of God's providences executed during this present age**.

Here, too, there is a considerable degree of subjectivity, though it is beyond denial that we observe this distinction. There are providences experienced only by specific individuals, of which others may know nothing: profound personal struggles, inward trials, powerful temptations. But these wholly personal and private experiences may be far more excruciatingly painful for the individuals concerned than the great public or even global crises which are going on all around them. A bitter bereavement or separation, experienced by a close-knit family, could well have a far deeper effect on their lives than the privations of a war or an economic depression that may be going on all around them.

The final and climactic distinction

Having now described these seventeen distinctions in their four categories, we now come to the final, climactic, distinction which is the central subject of this chapter, if not of the whole book.

18. PRESENT JUDGEMENTS AND THE FINAL JUDGEMENT.
 This distinguishes **between God's providences in the present age and those in the age to come**.

The '*Time*' referred to throughout this book has been, for the most part, this present time—above all the time since 'coronavirus' became a household word in the early part of 2020. The 'judgements' I have referred to in relation to Jeremiah 15:2 and 1 Peter 4:17 belong to the ancient world, and yet they were announced, and took place, during this 'present age', as defined in section 10 of this chapter. But all these judgements are anticipatory of *The Judgement*, the great, final, conclusive, permanent, divine-judicial verdicts and actions of God on the 'day of the LORD'.

It is time to return to the definition of a divine judgement which preceded these eighteen pairings:

> A divine judgement is a providence of God in this world that significantly affects one or many human lives, intended to cause people to acknowledge God, putting them in mind of the final judgement and their eternal state.

Conclusion

Careful consideration of this definition in the light of the eighteen preceding paragraphs should freight it with content, meaning and great solemnity. People who have been involved in serious traffic accidents often testify afterwards that 'time slowed down' and 'my whole life flashed before me'. Perhaps something parallel should happen as we give serious thought to the matter of final judgement: we see that all the above pairings and distinctions must loom large in our present thinking, and the final day of judgement will exhibit them—some undoubtedly more than others—in their true character. Such a thought-process could begin with something along these lines:

On that great and final day, God will be seen as the Judge over all that he has made (1). He will bring devastation upon the present world in a cataclysmic demonstration of his supernatural providence (2). The whole cosmos will be renewed and restored and set free from its present bondage to corruption, and all rational creatures summoned to the great white throne of judgement (3), including both men and angels (4). God's judgement will be according to the moral goodness of his own perfection and his own revealed law (5), and the nations will be separated before him into the sheep and the goats, the righteous and the unrighteous (6). On that day there will be a perfect demonstration of both divine justice, which will shut every mouth that would excuse

Divine Judgement

itself; and divine grace, which will open every mouth in endless praise (7). God will vindicate his elect who have cried to him day and night for justice and will reward the good works which he has ordained them to perform in his name, while punishing the non-elect with unimpeachable justice (8). Great praise will be given to God eternally by the righteous for his saving grace in Christ, while those who refused to repent of their sins will acknowledge the common grace of God's patience and long-suffering (9).

That will be the day that fixes a permanent separation between the present age and the age to come, and between those who are in heaven and those who are in hell (10). Members of both old covenant Israel and the new covenant Church will be judged by the same God, through the same Christ, in all justice and wisdom, by the same law and the same gospel (11, 12). All the significant people, places and events of biblical history (13) will be seen to come to a head on this final day of reckoning, in which the Triune God is given all the glory and is publicly vindicated in terms of his justice and his grace.

On that day, the mystery as to who truly belongs to Christ and who is merely a nominal believer will be cleared up beyond all doubt (14). For the present time, we receive the Bible as God's revealed and infallible will, trusting him that all his actions in the world, and across our lives, are in keeping with his holy, wise and faithful character; but on that final day, God will reveal what has been

Conclusion

hidden, and what has been whispered in private rooms will be shouted from the rooftops (15). While, during this present age, we may distinguish between the ordinary and the extraordinary, and between the private and the public, the final day will assign every former providence of God its appropriate place and perspective—because that day itself will constitute the mightiest display of divine providence that any creature has ever witnessed (16, 17).

Providences—severe and gracious

I come back now to the driving thrust of this Conclusion: *God must, and will, judge all the creatures he has made.* The day of judgement is the climactic, consummating occasion when this judgement will be pronounced. It will be, as I intimate in the previous paragraph, a 'providence' more conclusive, extraordinary, awesome, devastating and wonderful than any of us will ever witness. But all the providences in this present age are anticipatory of that Great Providence, and the more significant those providences are, in God's purposes, the more they partake of the character of divine judgements. They become like flashing signs on a motorway, warning motorists that a perilous pile-up of traffic lies ahead; but they also indicate the slip-roads by which motorists can escape the dangers and head to a place of safety, blessing and eternal glory.

God's judgements may be severe, and they may be gracious; in fact, they are invariably *both* these things.

By these judgements God is hastening the day when his final verdict will be pronounced. He may forcibly put people in mind of himself, his holy character, and their accountability before him. He may graciously direct people's paths to the Church, to the Bible, to the gospel of his Son. He may jolt some unbelievers into a sudden realization of their fragility and mortality, so that they give God serious thought. He may, indeed, use certain events to harden the hearts of other unbelievers as he did with Pharaoh, for the demonstration of his power (Rom. 9:17).[14] By means of 'severe trials' which he brings into the lives of believers, God is disciplining them as sons. The experience of discipline is necessarily painful while it lasts, 'but later it yields the peaceful fruit of righteousness to those who have been trained by it' (Heb. 12:11). The divine purpose behind all these providences will become clear only when the books are opened but, through them all, God is setting the stage for the final day of judgement.

But what are the most significant providences/judgements that God has executed, or is executing, in this present world? I finish the chapter with two that stand out, which demand to be included.

Exhibit A: The wrath of God

Consider the present state of western society in relation to the issues of gender and sexuality. Chapter 10 has addressed these questions to some extent. But a sober

Conclusion

reading of Romans 1:18–32 would abundantly confirm to us that we are presently witnessing a clear demonstration of God's judgement against sin. Paul was writing about the sexually deviant ancient world which he inhabited, in which 'the wrath of God is revealed from heaven against all ungodliness and unrighteousness of men' (1:18). In their refusal to honour God or to give thanks to him, and their determination to exchange his uncreated glory for the images of mere creatures (1:21–23), God 'gave them up to a debased mind to do what ought not to be done' (1:28). In the final verse of the chapter, Paul sums up the case against the 'men' he has been describing all along. 'Though they know God's righteous decree that those who practice such things deserve to die, they not only do them but give approval to those who practise them' (1:32).

It is almost impossible to read this whole section without thinking, 'This is right where we are now.' It is not simply that same-sex marriage has been legalized in so many western countries, and that there are now dozens upon dozens of supposed 'gender identities'. It is not only that the Pride Marches of the twenty-first century demand and insist that everyone 'give approval' to the lifestyle and practices which they represent. It is more: it is that twenty-first century society, increasingly, matches the description which Paul provides in 1:29–31:

> They were filled with all manner of unrighteousness,

evil, covetousness, malice. They are full of envy, murder, strife, deceit, maliciousness. They are gossips, slanderers, haters of God, insolent, haughty, boastful, inventors of evil, disobedient to parents, foolish, faithless, heartless, ruthless.

God's judgements in this present world may not be as discretely observable as a pandemic, a war or an economic downturn. They can take effect gradually, largely imperceptibly, as in the common image of the frog submerged in water which is gradually being heated. But if we are conscientious readers of the Bible as well as careful observers of society, we need to make the link. We must not fail to conclude that present phenomena—the redefinition and recasting of marriage and family; the celebration of confusion in relation to gender and sexuality; the cheapening of human life, especially as witnessed through the appalling number of legalised abortions; the undermining of divinely-established authorities in government, law and order, education and more; in short, the near-wholesale violation of the Fifth Commandment—underscore the reality that 'there is no fear of God before their eyes' (Rom. 3:18). This is a demonstration of the wrath of God, and Christian people need to say so as part of their public witness. In so doing they need to say that it is the God of the Bible who is being

CONCLUSION

disobeyed, and the God of the Bible who will call all people to public account.

But, of course, we do not leave it there.

Exhibit B: The Gospel of Jesus Christ

If, as I have stated in section 2 on page 355, all that God ever does is by way of creation and providence, then it is reasonable to ask: '*What is the greatest work of God in creation, and what is the greatest work of God in providence?*' I suggest that the answer to both these questions is one and the same: the gospel of Jesus Christ.

Jesus Christ himself, the God-man, is the greatest of all God's works of creation. In saying this, of course, I am referring to his incarnation because, as the Son of God, he has been from all eternity. But the words of Gabriel to Mary in Luke 1:35 support the claim I am making: 'And the angel answered her, "The Holy Spirit will come upon you, and the power of the Most High will overshadow you; therefore the child to be born will be called holy—the Son of God."' This description is redolent of Genesis 1:2, where we read that 'earth was without form and void, and darkness was over the face of the deep. And the Spirit of God was hovering over the face of the waters.' In both cases, the Spirit is brooding over a dark, unformed environment with the intention of creating life, human life. But, whereas the pinnacle of the first creation was humanity created in God's image—yet liable to sin and to generate a whole race of sinners—the pinnacle of the second creation, the new creation, is Jesus, 'the image of the invisible God, the firstborn of all creation' (Col. 1:15), to whom all creation belongs and in whom it all holds together.

But not only that, Jesus is 'the head of the body, the church. He is the beginning, the firstborn from the dead, that in everything he might be preeminent. For in him all the fullness of God was pleased to dwell, and through him to reconcile to himself all things, whether on earth or in heaven, making peace by the blood of his cross' (Col. 1:18–20). This leads to the conclusion that *the gospel of Jesus Christ, the gospel of grace, is the greatest of all God's works of providence.*

It cannot be denied that the events of the gospel, the historical birth, life, death, crucifixion, resurrection and ascension of Jesus Christ, and the publication of the gospel—'proclaimed among the nations, believed on in the world' (1 Tim. 3:16)—is the greatest and most significant series of events that this world has ever known.

There are ordinary providences; there are extraordinary providences; there are epoch-forming, earth-shattering providences; but far above them all is this:

- 'The saying is trustworthy and deserving of full acceptance, that Christ Jesus came into the world to save sinners, of whom I am the foremost' (1 Tim. 1:15)

Conclusion

- 'For the Son of Man came to seek and to save the lost' (Luke 19:10)
- 'For our sake he made him to be sin who knew no sin, so that in him we might become the righteousness of God' (2 Cor. 5:21)
- 'In this the love of God was made manifest among us, that God sent his only Son into the world, so that we might live through him. In this is love, not that we have loved God but that he loved us and sent his Son to be the propitiation for our sins' (1 John 4:9–10).

God has done this great work, 'sending his own Son into the world in the likeness of sinful flesh and for sin,' and as a result, God has 'condemned sin in the flesh' (Rom. 8:3) and has purchased for himself a people, a holy and righteous nation, who will be with him and belong to him forever.

Reader, you may be in a happy and comfortable situation right now, free from all traces of pestilence, sword, famine or captivity. Or you may be facing a far harder set of circumstances, whether they belong to this well-rehearsed catalogue of four, or whether they are quite different, altogether unique to your own experience. But whatever your state, this is the great question I leave you with: *Are you ready for the judgement to come?* For 'it is appointed for man to die once, and after that comes judgement' (Heb. 9:27), a judgement you cannot face alone.

King David knew this: 'If you, O Lord, should mark iniquities, O Lord, who could stand?' And immediately he gives the only possible answer: 'But with you there is forgiveness, that you may be feared' (Ps. 130:3–4). The fear of God is the beginning of both wisdom and knowledge (Ps. 111:10; Prov. 1:7; 9:10). Knowing the fear of God, and tasting the love of God, we run into the welcoming arms of Jesus Christ, so that we may dwell in his Father's house, and our Father's house, forever.

Afterword: Israelites, Israelis and Israel

> *There are some, and I am among them, who believe that Paul does teach in this chapter [Romans 11] that before the end there will be large numbers of conversions among the Jews. It will be astonishing and it will rejoice the hearts of the believers then alive. It will be like life from the dead.*
>
> Martyn Lloyd-Jones, from a Friday night lecture at Westminster Chapel, London, 1955.[1]

The terrible events of 7 October 2023 took place after the initial manuscript of this book had been submitted to the publisher. Instantly it was clear, following the Israeli declaration of war on Hamas within a few hours of the slaughter, that the situation in Israel and Gaza was likely to escalate very rapidly indeed. This has proved to be the case, so that to an even greater extent than with the war in Ukraine, it is impossible to predict what the state of affairs will be by the time you are reading these words.

Perhaps it hardly needs stating—but to clear up any confusion I will state it in any case—that for Christians

Afterword

the whole subject of 'Israel' is highly complex and controversial because there is a unique and distinctive *theological* perspective on this issue as well as a *historical* and *political* one. To put it as starkly as possible, the word 'Israel' occurs 2,567 times in my copy of the Bible.[2] In case anyone is wondering, that's 2,567 more than all the biblical references to 'Britain', 'France', 'America', 'Russia' and 'Ukraine' combined.[3]

How should Christians view the ongoing conflicts between Israel and its neighbours? Who or what, for that matter, is 'Israel' in the twenty-first century? And what relevance do all these events have in relation to the whole theme of judgement—God's and ours?

A full answer to all these questions will not be attempted here. For the one thing, the literature on this subject is vast. Moreover, the Israel-Palestine conflict has been simmering, and often raging, throughout the lifetimes of most people who are alive today. It is highly emotive and deeply polarising, with contrasting opinions being held and stated with some force, if not necessarily violence. Many of the controversies surrounding Israel and Palestine overflow into other areas of political and cultural discourse where feelings run high. There is always the danger of approaching the debate in a clumsy manner, in such a way that passions are inflamed and positions become more firmly entrenched.

'All Israel will be saved'?

So, I will immediately 'cut to the chase' and narrow our investigation to one very specific question: *How should Christian people think and pray in relation to the present State of Israel, and Jewish people, in the light of Paul's teaching in Romans 9–11, and in particular the words of Romans 11:26: 'And in this way all Israel will be saved'?* (See Appendix 1 on p. 397.)

What does the apostle Paul mean by 'all Israel'? At the risk of considerable simplification, interpretation can be categorized in these three ways:

- *Interpretation 1:* 'All Israel' denotes a sizeable number, perhaps even the majority, of Jewish people who will believe the gospel and be saved at the end of this present age. A representative sample of those who hold to this view include Charles Hodge, John Murray, Errol Hulse and Cornelis Venema.
- *Interpretation 2:* 'All Israel' denotes the full number of people from all ages, at all times, and across all nations, both Jew and Gentile, who believe the gospel and are saved. Exponents of this view include Augustine of Hippo, John Calvin and O. Palmer Robertson.
- *Interpretation 3:* 'All Israel' denotes the full number of Jewish people from all ages, at all

Afterword

times, who believe the gospel and are saved. This understanding is held by Herman Bavinck, Louis Berkhof, Loraine Boettner, A. A. Hoekema and Martyn Lloyd-Jones.

Readers who want to investigate this question in depth should go ahead and do so with enthusiasm, beginning with the sources I have in Appendix 1 on p. 397. It will not be a waste of anyone's time. My own musings on this subject have taken me on a circuitous journey over the last thirty years, oscillating between Interpretations 1 and 2 for most of the time, but latterly being drawn more decisively in the direction of Interpretation 3. My main reasons for embracing Interpretation 3 are contextual: at the beginning of Romans 9 Paul, having concluded that God's elect people in Christ are eternally saved and secure, comes to the vexed question of his own people, the Israelites. In 9:6 he raises the question of whether 'the word of God has failed', and all that follows is a repudiation of that possibility. In 11:1, he asks more pointedly, 'has God rejected his people?' Paul's answer is his characteristic 'By no means!' Paul himself is an Israelite, in company with Elijah and the seven thousand who did not bow the knee to Baal. In every age there is 'a remnant, chosen by grace' (11:5).[4] The full aggregate of this remnant is the 'all Israel' of 11:26.

The following quotation from Herman Bavinck (1854–1921) summarizes this thinking very satisfactorily:

'All Israel'... in 11:26 is not, therefore, the people of Israel that at the end of time will be converted en masse. Nor is it the church of the Jews and the Gentiles together. But it is the *plērōma* that in the course of centuries will be brought in from Israel. Israel will continue to exist as a people alongside the Gentiles, predicts Paul. It will not expire or disappear from the earth. It will remain to the end of the ages, produce its *plērōma* for the kingdom of God as well as the Gentiles, and keep its special task and place for that kingdom. The church of God will be gathered out of all peoples and nations and tongues. Paul does not calculate how large that *plērōma* from Israel will be. It is very possible that in the last days the number of the elect from Israel will be much greater than it was in Paul's time or later in our time. There is not a single reason for denying this.[5]

Bavinck's last two sentences should, however, be noted. While he rejects what I have called Interpretation 1, he in no way disallows the possibility that in God's purposes there *may* be a considerable turning to the Lord on the part of Jewish people.

The conclusion reached by Martyn Lloyd-Jones (1899–1981) is almost identical:

> And here, I suggest to you, is the key to the solution

Afterword

of this problem as to what 'all Israel' means. Paul has talked about 'the fulness of the Gentiles'. Yes, there is also a 'fulness of the Jews'. All whom God has called among the Gentiles; all whom God has called among the Jews: they will all be saved, the total Israel that God had in His mind from the beginning will all be brought in. There may be very few, perhaps, in certain generations, and large numbers in others, but they will all come in. 'All Israel' must carry that meaning and connotation.[6]

In relation to the future salvation of Jewish people, where Bavinck speaks in terms of possibility, Lloyd-Jones is more personally committed and optimistic:

There are some, and I am among them, who believe that Paul does teach in this chapter that before the end there will be large numbers of conversions among the Jews. It will be astonishing and it will rejoice the hearts of the believers then alive. It will be like life from the dead.[7]

It is instructive at this point to recall the fifteenth 'paired distinction' that was made in the previous chapter: that between God's revealed will and his secret will. The fact that there are at least three interpretations of Romans 11:26—and the more research is undertaken the more it may look more like four, five, six, seven, or even more—should caution us from committing unequivocally to any one interpretation. But, if the most esteemed scholars differ so widely on the interpretation of the *revealed* will of God, how much more carefully we should tread when considering the *secret* will of God!

After all, the apostle Paul himself introduces this teaching as 'a mystery'. Matters of sublime, heavenly glory have been revealed to Paul in connection with God's future purposes, and it is altogether fitting that Paul does not go very much further before breaking into doxology: 'Oh, the depth of the riches and wisdom and knowledge of God! How unsearchable are his judgements and how inscrutable his ways!' (11:33).

Time for favour

It is possible to hold to any of the three interpretations I have listed and still pray and hope fervently for a great turning to the Lord on the part of the Jewish people. John Ross's stirring work, *Time For Favour*, describes the sense of spiritual indebtedness to Israel sensed by Scottish believers in the seventeenth and eighteenth centuries, exemplified by men such as Samuel Rutherford (1600-61) and Thomas Boston (1676-1732):

> Immersed as they were in the Bible, it was inevitable that before long Scottish Christians would come to understand that, under God's blessing, the Jewish people had been the source of its greatest good. Was not the Bible they so cherished, both its Old

Afterword

and New Testaments, written almost entirely by Jewish authors? Did not their Bible-reading teach them that God's covenant with Abraham meant that the human ancestry of the Messiah and Saviour, Jesus Christ, was Jewish? And was it not true that spiritually they too were Abraham's children, at least to the extent that if his blood did not course through their veins then his faith was in their hearts? Were not the first members of the Church, God's international family of faith, all Jews who shared with the Gentiles the riches of the gospel? Being compelled by the evidence to answer all these questions in the affirmative produced in Scottish hearts a profound sense of indebtedness, which first found expression in prayer for the Jews' spiritual restoration.[8]

O. Palmer Robertson represents a very different theological stance to several of the authors I have cited in this chapter: he holds that 'all Israel', in Romans 11:26, is equivalent to 'the Israel of God' in Galatians 6:16, 'the single stock' of both Jews and Gentiles that is one olive tree, made up of branches both natural and ingrafted.[9] But even Robertson makes the following plea:

> For whatever the wisdom of man might dictate, it is the wisdom of God's mystery that Jews will be converted as they are moved to jealousy when they

see the blessings of their God on the Gentiles. At the same time, it is essential that Gentile Christians seek out a binding fellowship with Jewish Christians. For the conversion of Jews will enrich the experience of the gospel by the Gentiles immeasurably.[10]

At the same time—and this is fundamental and must be insisted upon—the way of salvation must be identical for Jews and for Gentiles. Martyn Lloyd-Jones wrote the following:

> But they will not be in a special position, the nation of Israel will not be differentiated from the Gentiles. No, the Jews, though thousands together may believe, will have to come into the kingdom by repentance and faith in the Lord Jesus Christ. They will have to trust to the blood of Christ as I have had to and every other Christian has had to; there is no other way into the kingdom.[11]

All the authors quoted here are united on this point and reject the suggestion that any future blessing on the people of Israel would involve the rebuilding of the temple and the restoration of the priestly and sacrificial system of the old covenant.

What about the land?

It is impossible, however, to dodge the inevitable question:

Afterword

What about the land? Is fervent prayer for the conversion of Jewish people necessarily tied up with the territorial issue? Over half a century ago, in light of the Six-Day War of June 1967 and the Israeli acquisition of East Jerusalem, the late Errol Hulse, having quoted Ezekiel 37:21–28 in full, wrote the following:

> If we are to do justice to this passage we must face up to the implications of a dual and territorial restoration of Israel.[12] Not merely a remnant, but the whole body of people is to enjoy the new covenant. They will dwell in the land that God gave to his servant. The heathen will acknowledge the Lord when he arises to sanctify Israel.[13]

Hulse responds to the argument that 'Israel's restoration [to the land] is wholly dependent upon national repentance' and that 'the present restoration is not a fulfilment of Scripture because it is entirely unspiritual'. He concedes that '[t]his argument certainly carries weight but on the other hand we must believe that God rules the nations and nothing happens by chance'.[14] At one level his last point is unanswerable: who can quibble with the physical reality that the State of Israel, an avowedly Jewish nation, now exists in the land that was promised to Abraham and his offspring?

But I suggest that we need to dig somewhat deeper and consider God's written revelation rather than simply interpret present-day providences. Recall the curses pronounced against Israel's disobedience in Deuteronomy 28, specifically verses 63 to 68. In verse 63, God threatened that Israel would be 'plucked off the land that you are entering to take possession of it'; then, in verse 68, he told them that 'the LORD will bring you back in ships to Egypt, a journey that I promised that you should never make again'. This is the 'captivity' that has already been described in some detail earlier in this book.

What did the people of Israel need to do in order to return from captivity and once again inhabit the land God had promised to them? The roadmap was set out for them in Deuteronomy 30:1–6:

> And when all these things come upon you, the blessing and the curse, which I have set before you, and you call them to mind among all the nations where the LORD your God has driven you, and return to the LORD your God, you and your children, and obey his voice in all that I command you today, with all your heart and with all your soul, then the LORD your God will restore your fortunes and have mercy on you, and he will gather you again from all the peoples where the LORD your God has scattered you. If your outcasts are in the uttermost parts of heaven, from there the LORD your God will gather you, and from there he will take you. And the LORD

Afterword

> your God will bring you into the land that your fathers possessed, that you may possess it. And he will make you more prosperous and numerous than your fathers. And the Lord your God will circumcise your heart and the heart of your offspring, so that you will love the Lord your God with all your heart and with all your soul, that you may live.

The modern Zionist movement, which really began in earnest at the end of the nineteenth century with the 1896 publication of *Der Judenstaat*, 'The Jewish State', by Theodor Herzl (1860–1904), has borne no resemblance whatsoever to the scenario envisaged by the Deuteronomy passage quoted here. The Balfour Declaration of 1917, the establishment of the British Mandate which followed, and the foundation of the State of Israel in 1948; all these were about establishing a homeland for Jewish people in Palestine, many of them secular in outlook, and did not at all partake of the spiritual repentance set out in the Scriptures. All this must be borne in mind as we view the situation of the present-day State of Israel, and the conflicts in which she has been more or less continually engaged throughout her history. What should our response be, bearing in mind all the incendiary complexities which I have barely attempted to describe?

Israel's Messiah: Jesus

We must start by wholeheartedly lamenting the horrors

of war. What has been taking place in both Israel and Gaza is harsh, brutal and terrifying. The televised suffering of women, children, the elderly and those in hospital, *whichever side they are on in this conflict*, is harrowing and heart-breaking. None of us should ever wish for war to continue, intensify or spread. As well as hoping and praying for an end to this conflict, we should seek and support every realistic means of relieving the suffering of those caught up in these terrible events.

But, in this present world, wars will rage, and political neutrality is seldom straightforward or honourable. On 19 October 2023, British Prime Minister Rishi Sunak publicly told Benjamin Netanyahu, his Israeli counterpart, 'I'm proud to stand here with you in Israel's darkest hour; as your friend we will stand with you in solidarity, we will stand with your people *and we also want you to win*.' This represented the view of the UK government and many other western governments. It is a view that many people reading these words will share, though not all.

Nevertheless, what I have sought to demonstrate is that this is a view which ought not to rest on any assumption or preconception of Israel as, in popular parlance, 'God's chosen nation'. Whatever our interpretation of Romans 11:26, or other relevant passages, we should be concerned that international law, where applicable, is followed and that war crimes are avoided by both sides in this conflict. Where abuses and atrocities are committed, *by*

Afterword

either side, they need to be called out for what they are, without partiality. Any idea that there is some kind of historical-theological equivalence between (1) Joshua's army conquering Jericho, and (2) the State of Israel subjugating Gaza, should be viewed with the greatest of suspicion. Remember, from an earlier chapter, how the pre-incarnate Christ, stationed at the gates of Jericho, said to Joshua, 'No; but I am the commander of the army of the Lord' (Josh. 5:14). The God of heaven and earth, though he would become eternally incarnate as a son of Abraham and a son of David, did not come to Joshua as a member of the Israelite Popular Front, still less the Israel Defence Forces.

Profound and perplexing questions, however, are bound to arise in the minds of thoughtful Christians. It might be asked whether impartiality is ultimately possible in relation to the subject of Israel. Should Christians not be unashamedly *pro-Israel*, given the promises which God made to them in the ancient past, and perhaps also holding to Paul's teaching that 'they are beloved for the sake of their forefathers'? (Rom. 11:28). Or alternatively, is it not equally logical, and biblical, to adopt an *anti-Israel* position, given that, as a nation, they rejected Jesus as their Messiah, calling down God's wrath on them as they cried to Pilate, 'His blood be on us and on our children!' (Matt. 27:25). Did not the apostle Paul, surveying the way in which the Jews 'killed both the Lord Jesus and the prophets', acknowledge that 'wrath has come upon them at last'? (1 Thes. 2:15–16).

These are deep questions which reverberate throughout history and they ought to be faced rather than ducked, though we must tread here with exceeding care. We must start by saying that it is God's prerogative to judge; he alone is the one who can say, 'Vengeance is mine' (Deut. 32:35; Rom. 12:19); and we are to heed the words of Paul, in 1 Corinthians 4:5, who said, 'do not pronounce judgement before the time, before the Lord comes, who will bring to light the things now hidden in darkness and will disclose the purposes of the heart. Then each one will receive his commendation from God.' We must remind ourselves once more of the great distinction between 'the secret things' and 'the things that are revealed' in Deuteronomy 29:29.

So, what must Christians do in the meantime? While it is 'the day of salvation' (2 Cor. 6:2), while the gospel of Jesus Christ may still be offered to all people, the church must proclaim Christ as Lord and Saviour freely and widely, to Jew and to Gentile, to every nation under heaven. There is no other name by which all must be saved (Acts 4:12). In terms of their eternal standing before God, the Islamic Hamas terrorist and the rigorously observant Orthodox Jew both occupy the same spot: while they do not bow their knees and their hearts to *Jesus Christ*, the 'light for revelation to the Gentiles, and for glory to

Afterword

your people Israel' (Luke 2:32), they are both in the same terrible predicament, 'having no hope and without God in the world' (Eph. 2:12). And the same is true for anyone and everyone from any background, nation or culture who does not know Jesus Christ.

'He is the true God, and eternal life' (1 John 5:20). Come, Lord Jesus.

APPENDIX 1

For a comprehensive summary of Reformed Christian thinking on this great subject, the following should be consulted:

Bavinck, Herman, *Reformed Dogmatics, Volume IV: Holy Spirit, Church, and New Creation,* (Grand Rapids: Baker Academic, 2008), pp. 664–672.

Berkhof, Louis, *Systematic Theology,* (Edinburgh: Banner of Truth, 1958), pp. 698–700.

Boettner, Loraine, *The Millennium,* (Phillipsburg, NJ: Presbyterian & Reformed, 1984), pp. 310–24.

Calvin, John, *Commentaries on the Epistle of Paul the Apostle to the Romans,* (Grand Rapids: Baker Book House, 1996), pp. 421–443.

Hodge, Charles, *Commentary on the Epistle to the Romans,* (Grand Rapids: Eerdmans, 1960), pp. 360–77.

Hoekema, A. A., *The Bible and the future,* (Exeter: Paternoster Press, 1979), pp. 139–147.

Lloyd-Jones, Martyn, *Great Doctrines Series, Volume Three: The Church and the Last Things,* (London: Hodder & Stoughton, 2002), pp. 100–113.

Appendix 1

Murray, John, *The Epistle to the Romans, Volume Two: Chapters IX-XVI,* (Grand Rapids: Eerdmans, 1965), pp. 75–103.

Palmer Robertson, O., *The Israel of God: yesterday, today and tomorrow,* (Phillipsburg, NJ: Presbyterian & Reformed, 2000), pp. 167–92.

Toon, Peter, [ed.], *Puritans, The Millennium and the Future of Israel: Puritan Eschatology 1600 to 1660,* (Cambridge: James Clark & Co. Ltd, 1970), pp. 115–125.

Venema, Cornelis P., *The Promise of the Future,* (Edinburgh: Banner of Truth, 2000), pp. 127–139.

Other titles by Paul Yeulett

Jesus And His Enemies
Reformation Reboot!

Bibliography

Bavinck, Herman, *Reformed Dogmatics, Volume IV: Holy Spirit, Church, and New Creation*, (Grand Rapids: Baker Academic, 2008).

Beck, Michael, *Covenant Lord and Cultic Boundary: A Dialectic Inquiry Concerning Meredith Kline and the Reformed Two-Kingdom Project*, (Eugene, Oregon: Pickwick, 2023).

Berkhof, Louis, *Systematic Theology*, (Edinburgh: Banner of Truth, 1958).

Boettner, Loraine, *The Millennium*, (Phillipsburg, NJ: Presbyterian & Reformed, 1984).

Boston, Thomas, *Human Nature in Its Fourfold State*, (Edinburgh: Banner of Truth, 1997).

Brooks, Thomas, *Works of Thomas Brooks*, Vol. VI, (Edinburgh: Banner of Truth Trust, 1980).

Bruce, F.F., *The Epistles to the Colossians, to Philemon and to the Ephesians*, (Grand Rapids: Eerdmans, 1984).

Calvin, John, *Commentaries on the Epistle of Paul the Apostle to the Romans*, (Grand Rapids: Baker Book House, 1996).

Bibliography

Calvin, John, *Institutes of the Christian Religion*, 2 Vols, (Philadelphia: Westminster, 1960).

Chauncy, Charles, *Seasonable Thoughts on the State of Religion in New England*, (Boston: Rogers and Fowle, 1734).

Currid, John, *A Study Commentary on Genesis, Volume 1: Genesis 1:1–25:18*, (Darlington: Evangelical Press, 2003).

Dooyeweerd, Herman, *Roots of Western Culture: Pagan, Secular, and Christian Options*, (Thorold, Ontario: Paideia Press, 2012).

Edwards, Jonathan, [ed.] Smith, John E., *The Works of Jonathan Edwards: Volume 2: Religious Affections*, (New Haven, CT: Yale University Press, 2009).

Eveson, Philip, *The Book of Origins: Genesis simply explained*, (Darlington: Evangelical Press, 2001).

Finlayson, Sandy, *Unity and Diversity: The Founders of The Free Church of Scotland*, (Fearn: Christian Focus, 2010).

Friedman, Milton, *There's No Such Thing as a Free Lunch: Essays on Public Policy*, (Chicago: Open Court Publishing Co., 1977).

Fukuyama, Francis, *The End of History and the Last Man*, (London: Penguin Books, 2020).

Bibliography

Gray, John, *Men are from Mars, Women are from Venus*, (New York: HarperCollins, 2002).

Gray, Robin, *Divine Light and Holy Love Genuine Conversion in the Works of Jonathan Edwards*, Affinity Theological Study Conference Papers, (Haywards Heath: Affinity, 2023).

Grudem, Wayne, and Asmus, Barry, *The Poverty of Nations: A Sustainable Solution*, (Wheaton: Crossway, 2013).

Hodge, Charles, *Commentary on the Epistle to the Romans*, (Grand Rapids: Eerdmans, 1960).

Hoekema, A. A., *The Bible and the Future*, (Exeter: Paternoster Press, 1979).

Hulse, Erroll, *The Restoration of Israel*, (Worthing: Henry E. Walter Ltd, 1982).

Kuyper, Abraham, *Rooted & Grounded: The Church as Organism and Institution*, (Acton Institute for the Study of Religion & Liberty, 2013).

Lloyd-Jones, Martyn, *Great Doctrines Series, Volume Three: The Church and the Last Things*, (London: Hodder & Stoughton, 2002).

Marsden, George M., *Jonathan Edwards: A Life*, (New Haven: Yale University Press, 2003).

Bibliography

Murray, John, *The Epistle to the Romans, Volume Two: Chapters IX-XVI*, (Grand Rapids: Eerdmans, 1965).

Niebuhr, H. Richard, *Christ & Culture*, (New York: HarperOne, 2001).

Richards, Jay W., *Money, Greed and God: Why Capitalism is the Solution and Not the Problem*, (New York: HarperOne, 2009).

Roberts, Matthew, *Pride: Identity and the Worship of Self*, (Fearn, Ross-shire: Christian Focus, 2023).

Robertson, O. Palmer, *The Israel of God: yesterday, today and tomorrow*, (Phillipsburg, NJ: Presbyterian & Reformed, 2000).

Shellenberger, Michael, *Apocalypse never: why environmental alarmism hurts us all*, (New York: Harper Collins, 2020).

Toon, Peter [ed.], *Puritans, The Millennium and the Future of Israel: Puritan Eschatology 1600 to 1660*, (Cambridge: James Clark & Co. Ltd, 1970).

VanDrunen, David, *Natural Law and the Two Kingdoms: A Study in the Development of Reformed Social Thought*, (Grand Rapids: Eerdmans, 2009).

Venema, Cornelis P., *The Promise of the Future*, (Edinburgh: Banner of Truth, 2000).

Vos, Geerhardus, *The Pauline Eschatology*, (Phillipsburg, NJ: P&R Publishing, 1979).

Welch, Edward T., *When People are Big and God is Small*, (Phillipsburg: P & R Publishing, 1997).

Wells, David F., *The Courage to be Protestant: Truth-lovers, marketers and emergents in the postmodern world*, (Nottingham: IVP, 2008).

Endnotes

Introduction
1. https://www.goodreads.com/quotes/1046665-frodo-i-wish-the-ring-had-never-come-to-me
2. The first draft of this book was with the publishers before the events of 7 October 2023, when Hamas launched a terrorist attack against Israel, causing the deaths of some 1,400 people, with around 240 more taken hostage, just on the first day alone. The numbers have escalated since. This episode, and the Israel-Gaza war which followed, resulted in the inclusion of the Afterword at the end of this book.

Chapter 1
1. https://www.goodreads.com/quotes/44121-my-theme-is-memory-that-winged-host-that-soared-about
2. Younger music afficionados will rush to remind me that Lana Del Rey incorporated similar lyrics into her 2012 hit 'Video Games'.
3. Estimates of death tolls and of the numbers injured are, necessarily, somewhat speculative. This earthquake was of a similar scale to the 7.8-magnitude quake which struck Turkey and Syria on 6 February 2023, resulting in an estimated 57,658 deaths as of 6 April 2023.
4. The Hillsborough Disaster took place at the FA Cup Semi-Final in Sheffield in April 1989, when 97 Liverpool fans were crushed to death. Aberfan is a village in South Wales where, in October 1966, a huge pile of coal waste slid down the mountain and onto the local primary school, killing 144 people, most of them children. Dunblane is a small city in

Endnotes

central Scotland where, in March 1996, a gunman shot dead 16 pupils and 1 teacher.

5 Throughout this book, I have employed the spelling 'judgement' rather than 'judgment', unless I am quoting from a source which uses the latter spelling. The spelling with an 'e' has tended to gain ground in recent years, certainly in British English, whereas the spelling without the 'e' tends to refer to legal judgments, but the jury is probably still out. Please use your own judg(e)ment.

6 See, for example, Lev. 19:15; Deut. 16:19; Prov. 18:5; Gal. 2:6; James. 2:1.

7 Not that Spurgeon indulged in any slavish admiration of Gladstone. In the *Baptist Quarterly*, Spurgeon is recorded as having written, 'I belong to the party which knows no party. To cheapen beer, to confirm the opium curse, to keep in office the shedders of blood, and to put Papists to the front are things I never expected from Mr. Gladstone; but "cursed be the man that trusteth in man."' He then added, 'Yet I am a Gladstonian despite all this.' H. S. Curr, 'Spurgeon and Gladstone', *Baptist Quarterly* 11.1–2 (January & April 1942), p. 48.

Chapter 2

1 Locke, John, 3.1: Second Treatise on Government, https://human.libretexts.org/Bookshelves/Philosophy/Political_Philosophy_Reader_(Levin_et_al).

2 Apart from 15:2, the other sixteen references in Jeremiah containing 'pestilence', 'sword' and 'famine', not necessarily in that order, are as follows: 14:12; 18:21; 21:7; 21:9; 24:10; 27:8; 27:13; 29:17; 29:18; 32:24; 32:36; 34:17; 38:2; 42:17; 42:22; and 44:13.

3 The history of the latter days of Judah, covering the reigns of

these kings, can be read in 2 Kings 22-25, and 2 Chronicles 34-36.
4 It is true that a somewhat less sordid account is found in 2 Chronicles 33, which includes a description of Manasseh's capture at the hands of the king of Assyria, and his subsequent repentance. But even that stirring and gracious episode did not alter the fundamental character of Manasseh's reign, or God's judgement against Judah for its idolatry.
5 See Psalm 99:6: 'Moses and Aaron were among his priests, Samuel also was among those who called upon his name. They called to the Lord, and he answered them.'
6 E.g., Matt. 5:17; 7:12; 22:40; Luke 24:44; Acts 13:15; Rom. 3:21.

Chapter 3

1 https://www.pepysdiary.com/diary/1666/09/
2 I will, throughout this book, often use the label 'man' to describe human beings; this description does not imply 'man' as male rather than female, but the whole human race.
3 Marsden, George M., *Jonathan Edwards: A Life* (New Haven: Yale University Press, 2003), pp. 196-197.
4 'Murrain': a somewhat archaic synonym for a plague or a blight.
5 "The Finger of God"—Free Presbyterian Church of Scotland (fpchurch.org.uk), April 2001.
6 Brooks, Thomas, *Works of Thomas Brooks*, Vol. VI, (Edinburgh: Banner of Truth Trust, 1980), p. 2.
7 Ibid., p. 22.
8 Ibid., pp. 22-35. Emphasis original. Each of these points made by Brooks is then developed at length; it is a very substantial work, as was common with the leading Puritans.
9 That is, providences that cause God's people to 'smart', to experience a sharp and stinging blow. Brooks was not

thinking of 'smart technology', at least not in the sense that we might today!

10 The Puritans often spoke of 'graces' in the plural, meaning distinct godly characteristics which God graciously cultivates in his own people.

11 *The Works of Thomas Brooks*, pp. 35-50.

12 Lot is a most interesting and, in some respects, a comforting case. Three times, in the passage quoted from 2 Peter, he is referred to as 'righteous', but the details of his life suggest a mixed picture, to put it mildly. He would not be mentioned in the same breath as Joseph, Daniel, Josiah, Job, Jeremiah or even David. Here is an ever-needed reminder that God 'justifies the ungodly' (Rom. 4:5).

13 In Revelation 6:7-8 we read about the opening of the fourth seal and the appearance of the fourth horse, the pale one. We are told that Death and Hades 'were given authority over a quarter of the earth, to kill with sword and with famine and with pestilence and by wild beasts of the earth.' This is the only NT appearance of the sword-famine-pestilence triad, but I would interpret it as applying predominantly to the world in its unbelief, not to believers. As my focus is on what the church should learn from current events, I will not be investigating this passage any further.

Chapter 4

1 Schaeffer, Francis, From private correspondence, Autumn 1951. http://www.churchleadership.org/apps/articles/default.asp?articleid=48195&columnid=4545

2 These verses, in 1 Corinthians 11:30-32, make for stark and sober reading. 'That is why many of you are weak and ill, and some have died. But if we judged ourselves truly, we would not be judged. But when we are judged by the Lord, we are

disciplined so that we may not be condemned along with the world.' Without embarrassment, Paul tells the factious and fractious Corinthian church that God has carried out his judgement against them by removing some through death. The question of whether those who have died were regenerate is not one that we can easily answer. If they were regenerate, they could not be eternally lost. We need to hold in tension (1) the security and the assurance of the believer and (2) the zeal which God has for the purity of his Church, and his determination to sanctify her. We could also do with a higher and holier regard for the Lord's Supper. In how many churches might God be carrying out a similar judgement today?

Chapter 5

1. https://www.reuters.com/article/uk-health-coronavirus-quotes-idUKKBN23Z04M/
2. The words of John Murray here are instructive: 'There are people who think that it is not a mark of Christian grace to show sorrow and tears at the death of our loved ones. They would aver that Christian character will be emotionally unmoved in such situations. Well, such an attitude may be magnificent stoicism but it is not Christianity. When we read Genesis 50:1 with true insight, we shall see that it is in line with the example of our Lord when he wept at the grave of Lazarus … Joseph's conduct now was in complete harmony with that virile integrity and competence of which his whole life is so conspicuous an example'. *Collected Writings of John Murray – Volume One: The Claims of Truth*, (Edinburgh: Banner of Truth, 1976), p. 6.
3. COVID Live – Coronavirus Statistics – Worldometer (worldometers.info). This data is current for 16 September 2023. https://www.worldometers.info/coronavirus/
4. For example, on 5 May 2022, the BBC reported as follows.

Endnotes

'More than 4.7 million people in India—nearly 10 times higher than official records suggest—are thought to have died because of Covid-19, according to a new World Health Organization (WHO) report. India's government has rejected the figure, saying the methodology is flawed. Will we ever know how many Indians died in the pandemic?' (Why India's real Covid toll may never be known—BBC News).

5 Covid: World's true pandemic death toll nearly 15 million, says WHO-BBC News https://www.bbc.com/news/health-61327778

6 It was thus named because Spain, as a neutral country in World War One, was able to report the disease without the restrictions which applied in belligerent countries.

7 Covid-19 and the deaths of care home residents | The Nuffield Trust https://www.nuffieldtrust.org.uk/news-item/covid-19-and-the-deaths-of-care-home-residents

8 As the first draft of this chapter was being written, the news was full of reports from Uvalde, Texas, where nineteen children and two adults were gunned down at Robb Elementary School on 24 May 2022. This came just ten days after a massacre in Buffalo, New York, where ten people were shot and killed in a grocery store. In both cases the gunman was just eighteen years of age.

Chapter 6

1 https://drhyman.com/blog/2012/01/31/how-social-networks-control-your-health/

2 It was, in fact, reported in *The Guardian*. 'Mexico braced for an unprecedented nationwide lockdown after the government ordered most of the economy to shut and for people to stay indoors for five days. The nation of 111 million people will grind to a halt tomorrow until 5 May in an effort to stifle the spread of swine flu which is on the brink of

ENDNOTES

becoming a global pandemic.' Swine flu: Mexico braces for unprecedented lockdown | Swine flu | *The Guardian*, 30 April 2009. https://www.theguardian.com/world/2009/apr/30/swine-flu-mexico-government-lockdown

3   Coronavirus: Half of humanity now on lockdown as 90 countries call for confinement | *Euronews*, 3 April 2020.
4   New hard-hitting national TV ad urges the nation to stay at home – GOV.UK (www.gov.uk), 22 January 2021.
5   I have borrowed this subheading from the lyrics of the Marsh family's tragi-comic parody of the song 'One Day More' from the musical *Les Misérables*. Family's brilliant lockdown adaptation of Les Mis' 'One Day More' will put a smile on your face | *The Sun*, 31 March 2020. https://www.thesun.co.uk/fabulous/11294220/family-les-miserable-coronavirus-cover/
6   *Joe Wicks: Facing My Childhood* – all about Joe's documentary | What to Watch https://www.whattowatch.com/watching-guides/joe-wicks-facing-my-childhood-air-date-trailer-frank-interview-and-all-about-the-new-documentary
7   Covid-19: Pandemic has disproportionately harmed children's mental health, report finds | *The BMJ*, 18 February 2022. https://www.bmj.com/content/376/bmj.o430
8   'What Is Scientism?' | *Crossway Articles*, 24 September 2018. https://www.crossway.org/articles/what-is-scientism/
9   'For he is your life and length of days' (Deut. 30:20).

Chapter 7

1   https://www.azquotes.com/quote/1557760
2   See John 4:24 – 'God is spirit, and those who worship him must worship in spirit and truth.' Note also the Answer to Question 4, 'What is God?', in the *Westminster Shorter Catechism*: 'God is a spirit, infinite, eternal, and unchangeable, in his being, wisdom, power, holiness, justice, goodness, and truth.' https://

Endnotes

www.apuritansmind.com/westminster-standards/shorter-catechism/

3 This is the so-called bipartite view of human nature, as against the tripartite understanding which regards man as being composed of body, soul and *spirit*. The tripartite view may seem to be supported by 1 Thess. 5:23: 'May your whole spirit and soul and body be kept blameless at the coming of our Lord Jesus Christ', as well as Heb. 4:12 which speaks of 'the division of soul and of spirit'; but the arguments on the basis of these texts is not compelling. I am not contending strenuously for the bipartite interpretation, but it is my preferred option as well as the majority view among theologians from the Early Church right through to the Reformation. It seems to do justice to the narrative of the creation of man in Gen. 2:7: 'The LORD God formed the man of dust from the ground and breathed into his nostrils the breath of life, and the man became a living creature.' The body of the man existed before the breath or the spirit (Hebrew *ruach*) of God was breathed into him.

4 'Gnosticism'|*Theopedia* https://www.theopedia.com/gnosticism

5 Peter writes to the same effect: 'Though you have not seen him, you love him. Though you do not now see him, you believe in him and rejoice with joy that is inexpressible and filled with glory, obtaining the outcome of your faith, the salvation of your souls' (1 Peter 1:8–9).

6 I am aware that there is, and has been, considerable diversity of practice in this regard. Prior to Covid, some pastors would take the bread and wine to elderly 'shut-ins' and celebrate communion with them in their homes. Other churches do not follow their practice. In allowing for a certain, reasonable flexibility, we must insist that the 'norm' for the Church is for the Lord's Supper to be administered 'when you come

together' (1 Cor. 11:20, 33, 34). The 'you' is important as well; it is the *Church* and not any other gathering of believers, such as a university Christian Union.
7 There are occasions, perhaps relatively infrequent ones, when a preacher may ask the congregation for verbal responses when he suspects that some are falling asleep (like Eutychus), or simply to check that they are keeping up. In my experience, this generally works best at the beginning of a sermon.
8 The extent of these restrictions varied across the constituent parts of the United Kingdom. On 24 March 2021, Judge Lord Braid ruled that the Scottish Government had acted unlawfully in criminalizing gathering for public worship, as such restrictions 'disproportionately interfered with the freedom of religion secured in the European Convention on Human Rights (EHRC)'. Closure of Scottish churches during pandemic ruled illegal by judicial review – *Daily Record*, 24 March 2021.
9 The Greek of Romans 13:1 addresses, literally, 'every soul', *pasa psyche*, implying individual living, breathing souls going about their everyday, civic duties and activities; not their ecclesiastical ones.

Chapter 8
1 From a speech at Chautauqua, NY, 14 August 1936. https://
2 Fukuyama, Francis, *The End of History and the Last Man*, (London: Penguin Books, 2020), pp. 211–12. www.oxfordreference.com
3 A memorable phrase near the climax of Churchill's famous 'Their Finest Hour' speech, 18 June 1940, *Their Finest Hour* – International Churchill Society (winstonchurchill.org)
4 'Recessional by Rudyard Kipling'. *Poetry Foundation*. https:// www.poetryfoundation.org/poems/46780/recessional. The refrain, 'Lest we forget', is an allusion to Deuteronomy 6:12 – 'Then take care *lest* you *forget* the LORD, who brought you

Endnotes

out of the land of Egypt, out of the house of slavery.' It was because the people of Israel *did* forget the Lord, and turned to other gods, that disaster came upon them, most notably in the time of Jeremiah.

5   The Russian assaults on both Mariupol, in the spring of 2022, and on Bakhmut, in the spring of 2023, were devastating and costly—to both sides. But Mariupol's fate seemed more alarming and terrible to many looking in from the outside; inevitably by the time of Bakhmut's demise a certain war-weariness had set in.

6   The Hebrew verb 'to rule' is *mashal*.

7   I will come to a further discussion about the roles of men and husbands in Chapter 10.

8   In this I am indebted to the expert opinion of John Currid, who comments on this verse: 'It is customary to understand the woman's longing for her husband to be one of sexual desire, or at least, one of great affection. But that is probably incorrect. The proper signification comes from comparing this verse with Genesis 4:7, which uses both verbs, to 'long' and to 'rule', from 3:16. Also, the proximity of the two verses is weighty.' Currid, John, *A Study Commentary on Genesis, Volume 1: Genesis 1:1–25:18*, (Darlington: Evangelical Press, 2003), p. 133.

9   One thinks here of Proverbs 16:32: 'Whoever is slow to anger is better than the mighty, and he who rules his spirit than he who takes a city.'

10 Thomas Aquinas' famous 'Just War Theory', from his *Summa Theologiae* II–II, q. 40, can be summarized as follows:

- War is justified (nation A wars justly against nation B) on the following conditions:
    - A. It is called by a sovereign authority.
    - B. It has a just cause.
    - C. The combatants have morally right intentions.

D. Qualifying Conditions:
   - » Cannot intend intrinsically evil actions.
   - » A good action, or at least a morally neutral action, will have two effects: a good intended, and an evil, not intended, but tolerated.
   - » Proportionality: the good to be achieved outweighs the evil of war.

   From *Just War–Thomistic Philosophy* page (aquinasonline.com/just-war/)

11 One suggestion, difficult to verify, is that the English Reformer, John Bradford (1510–1555) used these words about himself when he saw criminals being led to their execution; Bradford himself was burned at the stake, not of course, as a criminal, but as a martyr and a hero.

Chapter 9

1 https://www.powerquotations.com/quote/patriotism-is-a-lively-sense

2 The attack on the World Trade Center in New York and the Pentagon on 11 September 2001 where 2977 people lost their lives, not including the terrorists themselves.

3 If we glance back to Chapter 10, it seems likely that Nimrod, son of Cush, son of Ham, was a prime mover in this act of rebellion. He is styled, 'a mighty hunter before the Lord' (Gen. 10:9); Currid believes this description could well convey 'a hostile sense, on the lines of "openly before Yahweh"; in other words, Nimrod is flaunting his human prowess. The name, 'Nimrod', may add weight to [this] interpretation because it probably means, 'Let us rebel!'" Currid, John, *A Study Commentary on Genesis, Volume 1: Genesis 1:1–25:18*, p. 233.

Endnotes

4 Eveson, Philip, *The Book of Origins: Genesis simply explained*, (Darlington: Evangelical Press, 2001), p. 226.

5 On my music streaming playlist, I enjoy various national anthems including the rabidly anti-English 'Flower of Scotland' as well as 'Soyuz Nerushimy', the old Soviet anthem, and also 'Dear Old Skibbereen', an Irish folk song lamenting the brutality of English landlords following the potato famine of the 1840s. I may not sympathize with all the political persuasions underlying these songs, but I can sense and appreciate the passion they convey. I trust this keeps me from being a nationalist.

6 As this book was going to press in December 2023, the British Government was convulsed by the question of illegal immigration and the possibility of sending migrants to Rwanda to be processed.

7 Former US National Security Advisor, John Bolton, wrote in the *Daily Telegraph* on 15 June 2022: 'American and British constitutional law is well-settled that treaties can be modified or vitiated by subsequent legislation; no legislature can control the acts of its successors. Ultimately, the only legitimacy for governmental acts is the consent of the governed, which is why reversing prior legislative action is easily understood. Treaties or other international accords stand in no better place than domestic legislation.' Joe Biden's clueless support for Ireland weakens the West (telegraph.co.uk)

Chapter 10

1 https://gracequotes.org/topic/men-masculinity/

2 Just five days after the invasion, NPR (National Public Radio) reported the following statement from Putin: "'The purpose of this operation is to protect people who for eight years now have been facing humiliation and genocide perpetrated by

ENDNOTES

the Kyiv regime," he said, according to an English translation from the Russian Mission in Geneva. "To this end, we will seek to demilitarize and denazify Ukraine, as well as bring to trial those who perpetrated numerous bloody crimes against civilians, including against citizens of the Russian Federation."' Rachel Treisman, How Putin's 'denazification' claim distorts history, according to scholars : NPR, 1 March 2022.

3 Nor, for the matter, is God an Israeli; I will return to this point in the Afterword which concludes this book.

4 'Putin's Anti-Gay War on Ukraine'—*Boston Review*, 14 March 2022. Readers may want to take time to read the whole article, which is a very revealing exposé of the convictions and aims of the pro-LGBTQ etc. lobby.

5 Idem.

6 "'I'm Not Reviewing A Film By A Bigot": Film Critics Won't Even Watch Matt Walsh's "What Is A Woman?"' *The Daily Wire*, 4 June 2022.

7 The response of Dr Patrick Grzanka, Professor of Women, Gender, and Sexuality Studies at the University of Tennessee. https://www.youtube.com/watch?v=HXVJvsZRbBs

8 Gen. 2:23: 'She shall be called Woman, because she was taken out of Man.' The Hebrew for man is *'ish*, and for woman *'ishshah*.

9 Roberts, Matthew, *Pride: Identity and the Worship of Self*, (Fearn, Ross-shire: Christian Focus, 2023), p. 94.

10 Gray, John, *Men are from Mars, Women are from Venus*, (New York: HarperCollins, 2002).

11 In saying this, I do of course acknowledge that in a fallen world some babies are born with an intersex condition, but the proportion, it should be stated, is very small, probably in the region of 0.02% to 0.05%. See Selma Feldman Witchel, 'Disorders of sex development'—PMC (nih.gov). https://www.ncbi.nlm.nih.gov/pmc/articles/PMC5866176/

Endnotes

12 I am fully aware that there are task-oriented women just as there are people-oriented men, for example. I am talking here about traits which become more evident with groups of men and groups of women.

13 I quite deliberately emphasize the words *front-line* and *predominantly*. To disregard or disparage the part played by women in armed conflicts across the globe for more than a century would be a gross oversight. To bring this right up to date, it is worth reporting that a high proportion of those serving in the Ukrainian army are women. 'According to Ukraine's Ministry of Defense, female soldiers and officers make up about 15% of Ukrainian army combat forces. Since 2014, more than 30,000 Ukrainian women have become combat veterans. Those numbers have shot up (sic.) since the Russian invasion'. Female Soldiers Fight for Ukraine, Equality With Male Peers (voanews.com), 28 April 2022. https://www.voanews.com/a/female-soldiers-fight-for-ukraine-equality-with-male-peers/6548728.html

14 For those people who don't live anywhere near teenagers, these are video games.

15 I use this description of Christ from the English translation of Luther's hymn, 'Ein feste Burg ist unser Gott'—'A safe stronghold our God is still', A Safe Stronghold | Hymnary.org. https://hymnary.org/text/a_safe_stronghold_our_god_is_still

Chapter 11

1 https://www.goodreads.com/quotes/911106-keep-climbing-he-told-himself-cheeseburgers-his-stomach-replied-shut

2 From their website, *Barnabas Fund: Hope and Aid for the Persecuted Church*, 30 June 2022. https://www.barnabasaid.org/za/

3 'Unprecedented drought brings threat of starvation to

millions in Ethiopia, Kenya, and Somalia' (Issue Date: 9 June 2022) – Ethiopia | ReliefWeb

4 Leiva, Marina, 'Which countries are most exposed to interruption in Ukraine food exports?' Investment Monitor, 2 March 2022. According to this data, $119.1m worth of grain was exported from Ukraine to Lebanon in 2019, out of a total of $148.49m; that is more than four-fifths. https://www.investmentmonitor.ai/special-focus/ukraine-crisis/countries-exposed-ukrainian-food-exports/

5 See *Westminster Confession of Faith*, V.2: 'Although in relation to the foreknowledge and decree of God, the first cause, all things come to pass immutably and infallibly, *yet by the same providence he ordereth them to fall out, according to the nature of second causes, either necessarily, freely, or contingently.*' https://www.reformation21.org/confession/2013/02/

6 The comparison is not exact, but there is significant overlap. Both gender identities and eating disorders can be linked to some type of dysphoria and reflect the growing fixation and unease with self-image, and the quest for identity in a despairing, lonely, fractured society. chapters 52–53.php

7 The Authorised King James Version translates 'rabble' as 'mixt multitude', implying that these were the same 'mixed multitude who left Egypt with the Israelites' (Exod. 12:38), though different Hebrew terms are used.

Chapter 12

1 https://www.brainyquote.com/quotes/edmund_burke_136336

2 Grudem, Wayne, and Asmus, Barry, *The Poverty of Nations: A Sustainable Solution*, (Wheaton: Crossway, 2013), p. 30. Here is a resource that is wonderfully lucid and well-structured,

Endnotes

precisely the kind of guide to the subject that I searched for in vain in the past.

3 Richards, Jay W., Money, *Greed and God: Why Capitalism is the Solution and Not the Problem*, (New York: HarperOne, 2009), pp. 222–23.
4 The word 'weal' has an additional, very different meaning: a raised sore in the skin, often as a result of a physical blow.
5 *Westminster Confession of Faith*, Chapter 2, Paragraph 2. https://www.reformation21.org/confession/2013/01/chapter-22.php
6 Lakewood Church, https://www.lakewoodchurch.com/. Accessed 19 July 2022
7 Daly, Janet, The anti-growth lobby sees humanity as a threat to survival (telegraph.co.uk), 28 May 2022. https://www.telegraph.co.uk/news/2022/05/28/anti-growth-lobby-sees-humanity-threat-survival/
8 Grudem, Wayne, and Asmus, Barry, *The Poverty of Nations: A Sustainable Solution*, p. 126.
9 'Basic income for care leavers in Wales', pilot announced | GOV.WALES, 15 February 2022. https://www.gov.wales/basic-income-care-leavers-wales-pilot-announced
10 'Public spending during the Covid-19 pandemic'—House of Commons Library (parliament.uk), 29 March 2022 https://commonslibrary.parliament.uk/research-briefings/cbp-9309/
11 The title of a book by Milton Friedman: *There's No Such Thing as a Free Lunch: Essays on Public Policy*, (Chicago: Open Court Publishing Co., 1977). Friedman won the Nobel Prize for Economics in 1976.

Chapter 13

1 https://www.theguardian.com/tv-and-radio/2019/jan/21/david-attenborough-tells-davos-the-garden-of-eden-is-no-more

Endnotes

2. UK climate extremes – Met Office https://www.metoffice.gov.uk/research/climate/maps-and-data/uk-climate-extremes
3. In citing such scientific and historical data, I am indebted to the work of Creation Ministries International and in particularly their regularly-updated book, *Anthropogenic Global Warming (AGW) – a biblical and scientific approach to climate change*, by Don Batten. This is a serious work of scholarly robustness as well as a deep and courageous reflection. A biblical and scientific approach to climate change (creation.com), accessed 7 March 2023. https://creation.com/climate-change
4. For a comprehensive coverage of such areas, see *The Late Maunder Minimum (1675-1715) – Climax of the 'Little Ice Age' in Europe* | Request PDF (researchgate.net) by Jürg Luterbacher from the World Meteorological Organization. In addition, my good friend Tom Brand has drawn my attention to the Milankovitch cycles, gradual changes in the earth's axial tilt and orbit which affect the amount of solar radiation the earth receives. The causes of climate change are far more complex and labyrinthine than perhaps any of us realize.
5. Shellenberger, Michael, *Apocalypse never: why environmental alarmism hurts us all*, (New York: Harper Collins, 2020).
6. Ibid., p. xiii.
7. Ibid., p. 10.
8. IPCC – the Intergovernmental Panel on Climate Change.
9. Shellenberger, Michael, *Apocalypse never: why environmental alarmism hurts us all*, p. 12, emphasis mine.
10. Ibid., p. 260.
11. Ibid., p. 263.
12. COP26 stands for the Conference of the Parties and was the 2021 United Nations climate change conference.
13. 'Education Secretary puts climate change at the heart of

education' – GOV.UK (www.gov.uk), 5 November 2021. https://www.gov.uk/government/news/education-secretary-puts-climate-change-at-the-heart-of-education--2

14 It is possible to obtain educational packs from the online resources bank, Twinkl, which 'Support Teaching of Dear Earth', https://www.twinkl.co.uk/resource/lesson-pack-to-support-teaching-of-dear-earth. Better known is the 'Earth Day Song' with Elmo and Friends! from *Sesame Street*. See *Sesame Street: Dear Earth | Earth Day Song with Elmo and Friends! – YouTube*. https://www.youtube.com/watch?v=I43506hErkY

15 On 22 September 2023, Melanie Phillips, in her regular blog, described the response to some policy changes announced that week by UK Prime Minister Rishi Sunak. These 'produced mass hysteria, with cries that what Sunak had announced was "totally evil", "dangerous and desperate", "a betrayal of our planet survival plans" and a "moment of shame"'. These policy changes amounted to adjustments to the Government's timescale in attempting to reach Net Zero, not to the abandonment of that aim; and yet, said Phillips, 'The roof has fallen in on him'.

16 EIS Emergency Communication For Doomsday (eiscouncil.org)

17 'Net zero [simply put] refers to a state in which the greenhouse gases going into the atmosphere are balanced by removal out of the atmosphere.' https://netzeroclimate.org/what-is-net-zero-2/

18 https://www.luther.de/en/worms.html

19 Later in this book, in the 'Conclusion on Human Judgement' pp. 333–350, I will elaborate this point somewhat further by drawing important distinctions between common grace, which applies to the whole world, and God's covenant of grace, which relates to the spiritual salvation of the elect.

20 Boston, Thomas, *Human Nature in Its Fourfold State*,

(Edinburgh: Banner of Truth, 1997). Boston lists these 'States' as (1) The State of Innocence, (2) The State of Nature, (3) The State of Grace and (4) The Eternal State. The book is a true Christian classic and was one of the most widely read Christian books in Scotland, in particular during the two centuries following its publication.

21 This was in 1979 and it was the first time I ever heard the word 'environment' being used in any context, when fears of a new ice age, rather than of global warming, were current.

22 More fully and properly, I might add, God is a 'mighty, wise, artistic Creator and *gracious Sustainer*'. It is essential to see that the promise of Genesis 8:23 was made in the aftermath of the Flood, and to a world where sinfulness still reigned in the inclinations of every human being (Gen. 8:21).

23 The words of this verse, albeit in Latin, were carved over the entrance to the Cavendish Laboratory in Cambridge in 1874. This laboratory was established by James Clerk Maxwell (1831–79), who formulated the classical theory of electromagnetic radiation. A nobler description of true science is impossible to find. The original laboratory no longer stands, but a replacement has been built, and the inscription has now been translated into English—a good thing.

24 For example, Job 19:25; Ps. 19:14; 78:35; Isa. 41:14; 43:14; 44:6; 54:5; Jer. 50:34. Though it is certainly not improper to speak of Christ as the Redeemer of his people (as per the statue on Corcovado Mountain, overlooking Rio de Janeiro), he is not explicitly given this title in the New Testament.

25 Even here, it is right to speak about the future aspect of believers' redemption; for example, Paul speaks about 'the day of redemption' in Ephesians 4:30.

Endnotes

Chapter 14

1 https://www.goodreads.com/quotes/465551-i-was-in-misery-and-misery-is-the-state-of
2 This is the essential background to the message of Hosea, who prophesied in the Northern Kingdom of Israel over a century before Jeremiah but had very much the same burden. Notice especially Hosea 2:16–17: 'And in that day, declares the LORD, you will call me "My Husband," and no longer will you call me "My Baal." For I will remove the names of the Baals from her mouth, and they shall be remembered by name no more.'
3 F. F. Bruce supplies a comprehensive treatment of this 'Colossian heresy' in the NICNT (The New International Commentary on the New Testament) on *The Epistles to the Colossians, to Philemon and to the Ephesians*, (Grand Rapids: Eerdmans, 1984), pp. 17–26.

Chapter 15

1 https://www.blinkist.com/magazine/posts/don-quixote-quotes-inspire-pursuit-dreams
2 Readers who wish to explore this theme further could do no better than consult Jonathan Edwards, *A Dissertation Concerning the End for Which God Created the World*. A free online version is available at *A Dissertation Concerning The End For Which God Created The World* by Jonathan Edwards | Monergism. https://www.monergism.com/dissertation-concerning-end-which-god-created-world-jonathan-edwards
3 This is, of course, the essence of the answer to the first question of the *Westminster Shorter Catechism*: 'Man's chief end is to glorify God, and to enjoy him for ever.' http://proclamationpca.com/blog/2015/1/9/westminster-shorter-catechism-qa-1

4 This is the whole thrust of the precious words of Jesus in Matthew 6:33: 'But seek first the kingdom of God and his righteousness, and all these things will be added to you.'
5 Descartes is reputed to have said on his deathbed, 'So, my soul, it is time to depart.' He seemed to hold prior communion with his soul, with himself, right to the bitter end. If this is the whole story, it is a tragedy. https://en.wikipedia.org/wiki/Cogito,_ergo_sum
6 I have cited the version from Deut. 5:16 rather than from Exod. 20:12 because it is somewhat longer and fuller.
7 *Westminster Shorter Catechism*, Question 64. https://www.apuritansmind.com/westminster-standards/shorter-catechism/
8 Welch, Edward T., *When People are Big and God is Small*, (Phillipsburg: P & R Publishing, 1997), p. 87, emphasis original.
9 'Cancel culture' is the mass withdrawal of support from people, often, though not always, celebrities, who have said and done things that are regarded as socially unacceptable.

Chapter 16

1 Prentiss, Elizabeth, *Stepping Heavenward*. https://www.azquotes.com/quote/804898
2 Finlayson, Sandy, *Unity and Diversity: The Founders of The Free Church of Scotland*, (Fearn: Christian Focus, 2010), p. 290.
3 Reading through these paragraphs, I think that the 'In conclusion' which introduces the final paragraph is a somewhat stylized, clichéd, ChatGPT 'giveaway'.
4 Wycliffe Bible Translators, *Words for Life*, (Oxford: May 2023), p. 14.
5 It is reasonable to comment that of these eight qualities, all of which should be cultivated in every believer over time—

Endnotes

we ought not to think of one-by-one incrementation—the second of them, 'virtue' (Greek: *gretē*), comes rather close to the idea of 'character' that I am seeking to describe.

6 Wells, David F., *The Courage to be Protestant: Truth-lovers, marketers and emergents in the postmodern world*, (Nottingham: IVP, 2008), p. 145.

Conclusion: Human judgement

1 Calvin, John, *Institutes of the Christian Religion*, 2 vols, (Philadelphia: Westminster, 1960), 1.2.1. https://gospelreformation.net/a-reformed-and-confessional-view-of-piety/
2 Niebuhr, H. Richard, *Christ & Culture*, (New York: HarperOne, 2001).
3 We should understand 'Christ' here as shorthand for the whole Christian testimony, or more broadly 'Christianity', however these terms may be interpreted and manifested in various models.
4 Niebuhr, H. Richard, *Christ & Culture*, pp. 45–82.
5 Ibid., pp. 83–115.
6 Ibid., pp. 116–148.
7 Ibid., pp. 149–189.
8 Ibid., pp. 190–229.
9 See for example, Erlandson, Doug, *The Resurrection of Thomism*, https://reformed.org/apologetics/the-resurrection-of-thomism-by-doug-erlandson/
10 It might be more appropriate to speak of Christ's *one office* of king, exercised in relation to distinct spheres. Any tendency to 'divide' or 'separate' Christ and his office(s) runs the risk of repeating the fifth-century heresy of Nestorianism, in which the Two Natures of Christ approximated to a division within the One Person.

11 For further reading in this whole area, consult VanDrunen, David, *Natural Law and the Two Kingdoms: A Study in the Development of Reformed Social Thought*, (Grand Rapids: Eerdmans, 2009), and Beck, Michael, *Covenant Lord and Cultic Boundary: A Dialectic Inquiry Concerning Meredith Kline and the Reformed Two-Kingdom Project*, (Eugene, Oregon: Pickwick, 2023).

12 It must not be overlooked, of course, that up to the time of Calvin and indeed for some generations afterwards, theologians operated within the realm of Christendom and this greatly influenced their thinking and their actions, both in terms of what they could do and what they might have chosen to do.

13 See, for example, Joseph Thigpen's article, 'Reconstruction Theonomy vs. General Equity Theonomy: 9Marks'. https://www.9marks.org/article/reconstruction-theonomy-vs-general-equity-theonomy/

14 Dooyeweerd, Herman, *Roots of Western Culture: Pagan, Secular, and Christian Options*, (Paideia Press, 2012), p. 15. Cited from: DOOYEWEERD: 'The Four "Ground-Motives"—The Cosmic-Root Christian Philosophy of Herman Dooyeweerd (1894–1977)' (wordpress.com)

15 The inclusion of 'Restoration' as a separate category to 'Redemption' in this scheme is significant, as I trust will become clear.

16 Van Til says, 'The question will at once be asked how it is possible that man should say anything at all about a God who is infinite, eternal and unchangeable in all his perfections.' Arne Verster, 'Analogical knowledge of God, and the Clark–Van Til controversy.' https://www.apologeticscentral.org/post/clark-van-til-controversy Van Til's great humility, allied to his knowledge, is exemplary. Many scholars, not only

Endnotes

Bahnsen and Frame but also Kline, have claimed a huge debt to Van Til. The trouble is that they disagree among each other and it seems unlikely that Van Til would agree with all their pronouncements!

17 That is not to say that I am in agreement with Kline, VanDrunen and the so-called 'Escondido Theology' at every point, and would personally distance myself from the 'Reformed Two Kingdoms' label so as to avoid misunderstanding. But that is also not to say that these theologians do not provide valuable insights on the subject under discussion here.

18 See Kuyper, Abraham, *Rooted & Grounded: The Church as Organism and Institution*, (Acton Institute for the Study of Religion & Liberty, 2013).

19 The perverse tendency we witness today is the erasing of hard lines where God himself has established them and where they ought to exist—that is, between the categories of male and female—but the imposition of boundaries where we ought to be breaking them down, i.e., between people on the basis of ethnicity and especially skin colour.

20 Chauncy, Charles, *Seasonable Thoughts on the State of Religion in New England*, (Boston, 1734), p. 327.

21 Edwards, Jonathan, [ed.] Smith, John E., *The Works of Jonathan Edwards: Volume 2: Religious Affections*, (New Haven, CT: Yale University Press, 2009), p. 95.

22 Gray, Robin, *Divine Light and Holy Love Genuine Conversion in the Works of Jonathan Edwards*, Affinity Theological Study Conference Papers, (Haywards Heath: Affinity, 2023), pp. 46–47, emphasis original.

23 From the hymn, 'O for a closer walk with God'.

Conclusion: Divine judgement

1 The classic biblical text in relation to God's name is Exodus

34:6-7: 'The Lord passed before [Moses] and proclaimed, "The Lord, the Lord, a God merciful and gracious, slow to anger, and abounding in steadfast love and faithfulness, keeping steadfast love for thousands, forgiving iniquity and transgression and sin, but who will by no means clear the guilty, visiting the iniquity of the fathers on the children and the children's children, to the third and the fourth generation."'

2 Vos, Geerhardus, *The Pauline Eschatology*, (Phillipsburg, NJ: P&R Publishing, 1979), p. 280.

3 A sample of references from the Prophets to 'the day of the Lord' may include Isa. 13:6, 9; Jer. 46:10; Ezek. 30:3; Joel 1:15; 2:1, 11, 31; Amos 5:18, 20; Zeph. 1:7, 14; Mal. 4:5. The one cited at the end is significant: here God promises to send Elijah before 'the great and awesome day of the Lord comes.' This prophecy was fulfilled in the coming of John the Baptist, according to Christ himself (Mark 9:13). And yet, the coming of Christ himself did not immediately presage 'the day of the Lord' foretold by the prophets. Two thousand and more years of gospel witness throughout the world have intervened, in demonstration of God's grace, both saving grace and common grace – see 'Section 9: Saving Grace and Common Grace' on pp. 360–361.

4 This list is not meant to be exhaustive, nor have I intended to say everything about these categories which could possibly be said. I have included only what is germane to the discussion about divine judgement.

5 The sense of the word 'creation' in this paragraph is somewhat different to that in the previous one. In the first section, 'creation' is an *entity*; in the second section it is an *action*. There is only one creation of the one God, but God's

actions in relation to his creation are rightly divided into creation and providence.

6 See *Westminster Shorter Catechism*, Questions 8 to 11, for an immaculately pithy summary of all this teaching. https://prts.edu/wp-content/uploads/2016/12/Shorter_Catechism.pdf

7 *Westminster Shorter Catechism*, Question 16. http://proclamationpca.com/blog/2015/4/21/westminster-shorter-catechism-qa-16

8 See footnote 1 in this chapter on Exodus 34:6–7, pp. 428–429.

9 The elect angels are those angels who never sinned; there is no gracious election of fallen angels to everlasting life and salvation. This will not be discussed any further, and angels now fade back from the scene.

10 The 'golden chain' is an allusion to the famous 'golden chain' chart produced by William Perkins (1558–1602) which set out the entire electing purpose of God in architectonic, panoramic form, comprising both the elect and the non-elect. See, for example, *The Golden Chain—A Chart* by Dr. William Perkins | Reformed Theology at A Puritan's Mind (apuritansmind.com). https://www.apuritansmind.com/puritan-favorites/william-perkins/the-golden-chain/

11 *Westminster Confession of Faith*, III.7. https://www.apuritansmind.com/westminster-standards/chapter-3/

12 *Westminster Confession of Faith*, VII.5. http://www.covenantofgrace.com/westminster_chapter7.htm

13 We could, of course, go a stage further and discuss supernatural miracles, which are 'extraordinary' to an even greater degree, but are still rightly termed 'providences'.

14 In these two sentences I want to give expression to the reality that an 'unbeliever' is not necessarily one of the 'non-elect'. The elect were all unbelievers before God opened

ENDNOTES

their eyes. We must always hold to the hope that 'God may perhaps grant them repentance leading to a knowledge of the truth' (2 Tim. 2:25).

Afterword: Israelites, Israelis, and Israel

1 Martyn Lloyd-Jones, *Great Doctrines Series, Volume Three: The Church and the Last Things*, (London: Hodder & Stoughton, 2002), p. 113.
2 That is, the English Standard Version (ESV).
3 Mind you, Greece makes five appearances, Italy four, and Spain two.
4 As a snapshot of this 'fullness of Israel', John Ross quotes William Wingate, Minister of the Scottish Mission in Budapest, 1843–51: 'Hebrew Christians are everywhere. Every class of Jewish society contributes these converts—professors in universities, lawyers, medical men, literary men, musicians, artists, merchants, mechanics, poor and rich are quickened by the Spirit of all grace, convinced of their sin and guilt. They are at the feet of Jesus, and enabled to say with every believer, "We have redemption through the atoning blood of Jesus, even the forgiveness of our sins."' John S. Ross, *Time For Favour: Scottish missions to the Jews 1838–1852*, (Stoke-on-Trent: Tentmaker Publications, 2011), p. 272.
5 Herman Bavinck, *Reformed Dogmatics, Volume IV: Holy Spirit, Church, and New Creation*, pp. 670–71. The word *plērōma* is a transliteration from the Greek word in the New Testament, translated 'fullness' (Rom. 11:25).
6 Martyn Lloyd-Jones, *Great Doctrines Series, Volume Three: The Church and the Last Things*, p. 112.
7 Ibid., p. 113.
8 John S. Ross, *Time For Favour: Scottish missions to the Jews*

Endnotes

   1838-1852, pp. 28-29. This book makes for stirring reading indeed.
9. O. Palmer Robertson, *The Israel of God: yesterday, today and tomorrow*, p. 188.
10. Ibid., p. 191.
11. Martyn Lloyd-Jones, *Great Doctrines Series, Volume Three: The Church and the Last Things*, p. 113.
12. It is helpful citing Ezekiel 37:25-26 at this point. 'They shall dwell in the land that I gave to my servant Jacob, where your fathers lived. They and their children and their children's children shall dwell there forever, and David my servant shall be their prince forever. I will make a covenant of peace with them. It shall be an everlasting covenant with them. And I will set them in their land and multiply them, and will set my sanctuary in their midst forevermore.'
13. Hulse, Erroll, *The Restoration of Israel*, (Worthing: Henry E. Walter Ltd, 1982), p. 91.
14. Idem.